# VISUAL QUICKSTART GUIDE

## MICROSOFT WINDOWS

# MOVIE
# MAKER 2

Jan Ozer

 Peachpit Press

Visual QuickStart Guide
## Microsoft Windows Movie Maker 2
Jan Ozer

## Peachpit Press

1249 Eighth Street
Berkeley, CA 94710
510/524-2178
800/283-9444
510/524-2221 (fax)
Find us on the World Wide Web at: http://www.peachpit.com
To report errors, please send a note to errata@peachpit.com
Peachpit Press is a division of Pearson Education

Editor: Jill Marts Lodwig
Copy Editor: Judy Ziajka
Technical Editor: Stephen Nathans
Production Editor: Lupe Edgar
Composition: Owen Wolfson
Cover Design: Peachpit Press
Cover Production: Nathalie Valette
Indexer: Emily Glossbrenner

## Notice of rights

## Notice of liability

## Trademarks

ISBN 0-321-19954-5

9 8 7 6 5 4 3 2

Printed and bound in the United States of America

*For the three girlies in my life:*
*Barb, Whatley, and Rose.*

# Acknowledgments

Thanks to the team who helped pull this book together smoothly at a rapid pace, including Stephen Nathans (technical editor), Judy Ziajka (copy editor), Jill Marts Lodwig (developmental editor), production coordinator Lupe Edgar, and compositor Owen Wolfson. Thank you all for your efforts.

Special thanks to the Microsoft folks, particularly Michael Patten and David Caulton, for answering my frequent and frantic inquiries, and the folks at Pixelan for providing me with software and assistance.

As always, thanks to Pat Tracy for technical and other assistance.

# TABLE OF CONTENTS

# INTRODUCTION

I've worked with a diverse range of video editing programs, some that cost thousands of dollars, and some, like Microsoft's Windows Movie Maker 2, that are free. How does Movie Maker stack up?

Well, when comparing editors, I look at both usability and functionality. The first assesses how quickly and easily a new user can start to use the program effectively. In this regard, Movie Maker rates very high, since most users should be able to quickly get up to speed and start editing, especially (ahem) with a good book to help.

Movie Maker also does well at providing basic levels of functionality, with good capture, trimming, and clip organization features that let you capture video from your camcorder and arrange it into a cohesive movie.

If you're looking for slightly more advanced functionality than what Movie Maker offers, you should still be in luck. As shown in **Table i.1**, Microsoft and several other companies offer a range of products and tools, some free and some available at a nominal cost, to round out Movie Maker's capabilities. Each of these products and tools, plus the URLs for downloading the tools or getting more information, is discussed in some detail in this book (see the corresponding chapter listings in the table). Throw these into the mix, and you have quite a formidable product.

Once you realize how many options you have to bolster Movie Maker's functionality, however, you will probably eventually ask yourself how much money you should invest to enhance a free product. It's a good question, and one that you'll ultimately have to answer yourself.

From my perspective, several enhancements, most notably Pixelan's Color/Tint/Contrast/Blur effects, add so much value that the dollars are well worth spending. Similarly, if your goal is to produce DVDs playable on living room DVD players, Sonic Solutions MyDVD is a relatively inexpensive, but highly capable, program.

That said, even with additional software from Microsoft or third parties, there are some creative options that Movie Maker simply cannot provide. For example, Movie Maker can't overlay a logo or watermark in videos—a very common effect—and its ability to mix multiple tracks of audio is very limited. So if you have your heart set on these effects, you'll have to purchase a completely different editor.

Overall, my approach in this book was to describe Movie Maker's native capabilities and identify other programs, when available, that complement and enhance its operation. I also try to be frank about letting you know when Movie Maker has reached its limits.

**Table i.1**

### Movie Maker Tools and Enhancements

| PRODUCT | PRICE | FUNCTION | CHAPTER |
|---|---|---|---|
| **CONTENT-CREATION TOOLS** | | | |
| Windows Media Player | Free | Rip CD-Audio tracks | Chapter 7 |
| Microsoft Plus! Analog Recorder | $19.95* | Digitize analog audio | Chapter 7 |
| SmartSound Movie Maestro | $49.95 | Create custom background music tracks | Chapter 12 |
| **CONTENT** | | | |
| Windows Movie Maker 2 Winter Fun Pack | Free | Background music, transitions, effects, animations | Chapters 10 and 11 |
| Microsoft Plus! Digital Media Edition | $19.95 | Effects, transitions, tools | Chapters 7, 10, and 11 and Appendix B |
| Microsoft Creativity Fun Pack | Free | Titles, sound effects, music tracks | Chapters 12 and 13 |
| Pixelan SoftFX, PiPFX, CoolFX Transitions | $29 | Transitions, including picture-in-picture transitions | Chapter 10 |
| **EDITING ENHANCEMENTS** | | | |
| Pixelan Color/Tint/Contrast/Blur Effects | $19 | Color correction | Chapter 11 |
| Pixelan Pan/Zoom Effects | $19 | Pan and zoom effects for still images | Chapter 11 |
| Microsoft PhotoStory 2 | $19.95* | Animated slide shows | Appendix B |
| **RENDERING AND POST-PRODUCTION TOOLS** | | | |
| Sonic Solutions MyDVD | $49.99+ | DVD authoring | Appendix A |
| Microsoft Windows File Editor | Free | Trimming and adding markers, text, and URL scripts | Appendix C |
| Microsoft Windows Media Encoder | Free | Screen capture and enhanced encoding capabilities | Appendix C |

*Component of $19.95 Plus! Digital Media Edition*

# How to Use This Book

As a downloadable program, Movie Maker does not ship with a manual, but Microsoft does offer online help and many tutorials, the latter available on the Web (www.microsoft.com/windowsxp/moviemaker/). This book complements these facilities in two ways.

First, like all *Visual QuickStart Guides*, this book is visual and task oriented, describing and showing you how to perform most common production tasks. These descriptions are precise and exhaustive, identifying with screen shots and text the best alternatives for getting the job done.

In addition, having worked with digital video for many years, I know that video editing can be an incredible time sink, probably the most significant reason most folks don't edit their camcorder tapes. So many sections and tips focus on how to work as efficiently as possible.

# What's in the Book?

Although Movie Maker is installed on some computers shipped by Microsoft licensees, the vast majority of readers will obtain the program via download. Chapter 1 discusses how to prepare your computer for Movie Maker by clearing disk space and uninstalling programs to promote smooth and efficient operation.

All good movies, however delivered, must start with an appreciation of how to create movies worth watching. Chapter 2 explores this issue and provides a valuable primer on the proper settings for your video camera and shooting basics. Chapter 3 answers some fundamental questions about analog and digital formats, describes the video editing work flow, and introduces the Movie Maker interface.

I strongly suggest that you at least scan these first three chapters before diving into the operational chapters. They offer lots of valuable information that will help you understand the procedures described throughout the book.

After you've shot your videos, the process of editing and production involves the following four steps:

◆ **Gathering assets:** This is where you capture your video, import still images or grab them from your captured video, and import any background audio files. These activities in covered in Chapters 4, 5, 6, and 7.

◆ **Trimming and organizing:** In most instances, you won't want to include every minute that you shot in your final production; you will want to trim unwanted sections and then place your video clips and still images in the desired order. Chapter 8 describes how to organize your content in Movie Maker's Contents pane, and Chapter 9 takes you to the Storyboard/Timeline window, where you actually sequence and lay out your video, audio, and still images.

*continues on next page*

INTRODUCTION

◆ **Garnishing:** During this stage, you add title tracks, special effects, and transitions between clips. You can also enter a narration or background music track. Chapters 10 through 13 cover these activities.

◆ **Using AutoMovie:** Chapter 14 describes how to use AutoMovie, a feature in Movie Maker that automatically creates music video–like segments for your videos. You can use AutoMovie to create stand-alone movies or integrate AutoMovie-produced movies into longer productions.

◆ **Outputting:** This is where you produce your final output. Chapter 15 describes how to write your video back to tape, and Chapter 16 discusses how to produce digital files for viewing on your computer, sending via e-mail, or posting to a Web site.

Depending on your production goals, you may find the appendixes at the back of the book particularly useful.

Appendix A provides an overview of Sonic Solutions MyDVD, an inexpensive, consumer-oriented DVD authoring program. Appendix B describes how to create movies from still images in Microsoft Photo Story 2, a great option for those with digital cameras. Appendix C describes some advanced editing and encoding functions available using Microsoft's Windows Media Encoder and its associated tools.

## System Requirements

Most products have two sets of requirements: minimum and recommended. Here are Movie Maker's minimum and recommended requirements.

### Minimum system requirements

◆ Microsoft Windows XP Home Edition or Windows XP Professional

◆ 600-MHz processor, such as an Intel Pentium III, Advanced Micro Devices (AMD) Athlon, or equivalent processor

◆ 128 MB of RAM

◆ 2 GB of free hard disk space

◆ An audio capture device (to capture audio from external sources)

◆ A DV or analog video capture device (to capture video from external sources)

◆ An Internet connection (to send movies to the Web or to send movies as e-mail attachments)

◆ CD-Recordable or CD-Rewritable drive for producing CDs.

### Recommended system setup

To optimize Movie Maker performance, Microsoft recommends the following system setup:

◆ 1.5-GHz processor, such as an Intel Pentium 4, AMD Athlon XP 1500+, or equivalent processor

◆ 256 MB of RAM

### Playback requirements

The following software is required to play back a movie:

◆ Microsoft Windows 98 or later or Windows NT 4.0 or later

◆ Software that can play Windows Media Video (WMV) files, such as Microsoft Windows Media Player 6.4 or later (Windows Media Player 9 Series is recommended to optimize movie playback)

**Table i.2**

| Calculating Disk Requirements | | | |
|---|---|---|---|
| ITEM | DURATION | MB/MINUTE | TOTAL |
| Capture footage | 60 minutes | 216 | 12.96 GB |
| Production footage | 30 minutes | 216 | 6.48 GB |
| Narration track | 30 minutes | 10.5 | 315 MB |
| Background audio | 30 minutes | 10.5 | 315 MB |

Total disk space required: 20.07 GB

## Disk requirements

A faster processor and more RAM are certainly better when it comes to video production, but disk space is the factor most likely to cause you trouble. Here's a quick example that illustrates how to estimate how much disk space you'll need for your projects.

Assume that you've shot 60 minutes of video that you want to edit down to a 30-minute production. You plan to include both a narration track and a background audio track and will render the production back to your DV camera. **Table I.2**, which presents a worst-case estimate of required disk space, assumes that you'll be applying edits to every single frame in the production footage. If you edit more sparingly, you'll need less space.

Back in 1994, the required 20 GB would have cost close to $30,000, and your electric bill would have jumped significantly. Today, you can buy a 200-GB drive for well under $200, a great investment if you plan to pursue multiple editing projects.

INTRODUCTION

# Part I:
# Getting Started

# GETTING YOUR PC READY FOR MOVIE MAKER

Installing Movie Maker is a big deal, primarily because it will likely consume many more resources in disk space, processing power, and RAM than any other program you're currently running. If there are any weaknesses in your computer, like old drivers, fragmented disks, or outdated operating system service packs, pushing the computer to the limit of performance, as Movie Maker will do, typically brings them to the fore. For this reason, you should prepare your computer for the occasion before the installation actually takes place.

Imagine how you would prepare if you owned a rental home and were just welcoming a new tenant. You'd scrub the floors extra hard, perhaps throw a new coat of paint on the walls, and clean out the attic and the garage. You'd want the home in prime move-in condition before the moving van arrived, to put your best foot forward, and all that.

Pretty much the same thing applies to installing Movie Maker, metaphorically speaking of course. You definitely want your computer as spiffy as possible before the installation, so that it will progress as smoothly as possible.

If you plan to add RAM or disk capacity, do this first, before installing any updates or Movie Maker. Always install each hardware upgrade one at a time, checking that the system is operating normally before installing the next.

For example, don't open your computer to add RAM and then add a disk drive and a FireWire card (see Chapter 4) just because the system is conveniently open. Add the RAM, boot up your computer, and make sure it's operating properly; then shut down and add the next component. That way, if your computer doesn't boot, you'll know exactly which component is causing the problem.

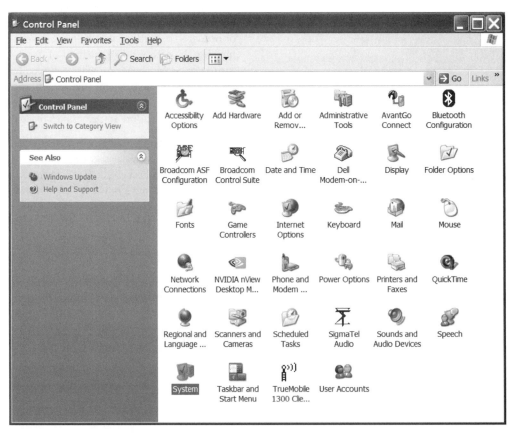

**Figure 1.1** Windows XP's Control Panel, the nerve center of your computer.

**Figure 1.2** Here's where you select your Automatic Updates options. It's a pain seeing the periodic messages from Microsoft regarding updates, but staying current can prevent the agony of a virus attack.

# Downloading the Latest Updates

It's a good idea to address two types of updates before installing Movie Maker.

You need to update your version of XP to the latest Microsoft Windows service pack. Service packs are periodic updates that Microsoft creates to fix bugs, update code, and respond to new hacker attacks. You can do this automatically or manually; we'll cover both options in the following tasks.

You also want to make sure that you're working with the latest drivers, which are bits of software that link hardware devices like sound cards and graphics cards with Windows. You'll find instructions for updating drivers at the end of this section.

### To automatically update Windows XP:

1. Click Start > Settings > Control Panel. The Control Panel opens (**Figure 1.1**).

2. Double-click the System icon. The System Properties window opens.

3. Click the Automatic Updates tab (**Figure 1.2**).

4. Select the Keep My Computer Up to Date box and choose one of the three settings.

5. Click OK to close the System Properties window and click the X in the upper-right corner of the Control Panel to close that window.

*continues on next page*

## ✔ Tips

■ I used to update manually until I got burned by the Sobig virus in front of a class I was teaching. One second I was sailing along; the next my computer started crashing every time I clicked the mouse. When I discovered I could have avoided the problem by automatically updating, I started doing this with all of my XP computers.

■ I generally don't download any updates without first reviewing them (the first setting), but it's your choice. In automatic update mode, Windows will tell you when updates are available and allow you to click over to the Windows Update site and choose the desired downloads. Typically, I choose all security-related downloads and bug fixes.

■ On the Automatic Updates tab of the System Properties window, don't choose to automatically download the Windows updates (Figure 1.2) unless you're on a broadband connection, because some of the updates can be quite large and can tie up your modem connection for long periods of time. You definitely want to pick the ones you want to install.

**Figure 1.3** You also can update Windows manually just before installing Movie Maker. Here's where you start.

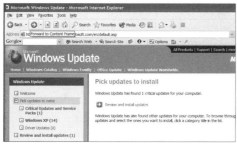

**Figure 1.4** Windows scans your system and identifies all relevant updates.

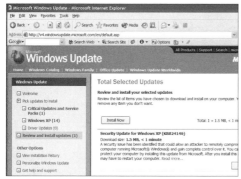

**Figure 1.5** Then you get to choose which updates to install—definitely a recommended procedure before any significant program installation.

## To manually update Windows XP:

1. Log on to the Internet and go to v4.windowsupdate.microsoft.com/en/default.asp.

   The Windows Update page opens (**Figure 1.3**).

2. Click Scan for Updates.

   Windows scans your computer for updates (**Figure 1.4**).

3. Click Review and Install Updates.

   The Web page lists all updates (**Figure 1.5**).

4. Click remove for any updates you don't want to install.

5. Click Install Now to download and install the updates, following all instructions.

## To manually update critical drivers:

1. Log on to the Internet and navigate to the support downloads page for the vendors of your graphics card and sound card. Check the documentation that came with your system to identify these vendors.

2. If you've owned your computer longer than three-to-six months, download and install the latest drivers for each device.

## ✔ Tip

■ If your driver is the most current version, the installation routine should advise you appropriately and terminate the driver installation.

# Uninstalling Unnecessary Programs

Having too many programs performing similar functions on your computer is like having too many cooks in a kitchen; conflict inevitably occurs, and the result is usually not good. For this reason, if you have another video editing program on your system, you should consider uninstalling it

Programs have gotten much more "polite" with each other over the years, especially with Windows XP, so you don't need to delete any programs you still intend to use. However, it's generally a good idea to keep games and other multimedia programs to a minimum on your primary authoring station, as they often tend to conflict with authoring applications. Basically, if you don't need it on your computer, uninstall it, especially if it's multimedia related.

### To uninstall unnecessary programs:

1. Click Start > Settings > Control Panel.
   The Control Panel opens (Figure 1.1).

2. Double-click the Add or Remove Programs icon.
   The Add or Remove Programs window opens (**Figure 1.6**).

3. Select the program you want to uninstall and click Change/Remove.
   Follow the prompts from there, which are different for each program.

4. Repeat Step 3 as necessary.

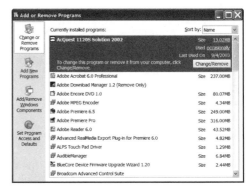

**Figure 1.6** Here's where you remove programs from Windows, saving disk space and getting rid of applications that might conflict with Movie Maker.

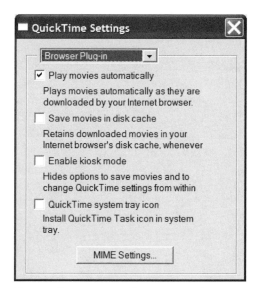

**Figure 1.7** Some programs, like Apple's QuickTime Player, can be removed in the application's Settings or Preferences window.

## Unloading Memory-Resident Programs

Have you ever wondered what all those icons are on the bottom right of your toolbar? They're programs that load into memory each time you boot your computer, primarily because the application developer who wrote the program felt it was appropriate.

Sometimes they do serve a useful purpose, but most of the time they simply steal precious memory, slow down your system, and introduce the potential for unstable operation. Some programs, like QuickTime Player, allow you to go into the preferences settings and disable the memory-resident portion (**Figure 1.7**). Generally, you should run the program, either from the Start menu or by clicking on the icon in the system tray, check its Options or Preferences for references to "loading into memory" or "system tray," and decline the option if you can.

Unfortunately, however, most programs don't provide this option. The best choice then is to use a program called a startup manager, which lets you control which programs load in the background. I use *PC Magazine's* StartupCop Pro for this function (**Figure 1.8**), and I'm generally pretty aggressive, disabling all programs I don't specifically need.

Don't worry; you're not uninstalling the program or disabling it in any true sense. For example, RealNetworks wants to keep some software running in the background, a preference that I permanently disable, yet the RealOne Player software runs fine when I call it up from the Start menu.

Of course, StartupCop Pro also lets you reverse your decision, so if your system starts to get flaky, you can change your mind. Get more information on Startup Cop at www.pcmag.com/article2/0,4149,2173,00.asp. Get the program itself at www.pcmag.com.

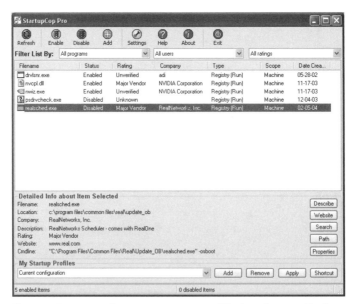

**Figure 1.8** To remove other programs, you can call in the police, specifically StartupCop Pro, which lets you pick and choose which programs automatically load into memory.

**Figure 1.9** Once you have your system in pristine condition, create a restore point that you can return to if your system becomes unstable in the future.

**Figure 1.10** Label your restore point so that you know what point it will take you back to.

# Creating a System Restore Point

Once you have your system totally tuned and optimized—that is, updated and cleared of extraneous applications—and before you install Movie Maker, create a *restore point* with Windows XP's System Restore utility. This feature, new in XP, can restore your computer to its status at an earlier time and date—the restore point—modifying only programs, not documents, e-mail, or Favorites selections. This way, if your computer ever becomes unstable, you'll have a very stable point to return to.

### To create a restore point:

1. Click Start > Programs > Accessories > System Tools > System Restore.
   The System Restore Window opens (**Figure 1.9**).

2. Select Create a Restore Point and click Next.

3. Type a restore point description (**Figure 1.10**) and click Create.
   Windows creates the new restore point.

### ✔ Tips

- To restore your computer to a restore point, open the System Restore window and select Restore My Computer to an Earlier Time; then follow the prompts to select the restore point and restore your computer.

- If you don't have System Restore enabled, a dialog box will advise you of this when you attempt to run it at Step 1 in the preceding task. Follow the instructions to enable System Restore and then start over to create the restore point.

# Preparing Your Hard Disks

If you're using an existing disk with lots of data as your capture and edit drive, you should *defragment* the drive before installing Movie Maker. During normal disk operation, Windows copies and deletes files all over the drive, sometimes splitting longer files and placing them in widely separated places on your hard drive when writing them to disk. Defragmenting the drive reunites all file components and packs the files efficiently together on the drive, opening up large contiguous spaces to enable smooth capture and fast editing of your video.

Before defragmenting, delete all unnecessary files on the drive, especially larger files, since they take up space and can slow the defragmenting process significantly. I usually use Windows Explorer for this job, and XP provides a tool called Disk Cleanup that can delete temporary files, which can really add up.

Once you've deleted as many files as you can, it's time to defragment them. Note that the Windows Disk Defragmenter utility has an Analyze tool that lets you analyze the drive to see if it needs defragmenting. Skip that test and defragment anyway, just to be sure that your disk is in optimal condition.

## To delete files using Disk Cleanup:

1. Click Start > Accessories > System Tools > Disk Cleanup.

   Windows will analyze your hard drive (**Figure 1.11**) and calculate how much space you can save by using the utility (**Figure 1.12**).

2. Choose the files to delete and whether to compress old files; then click OK.

   Windows deletes and compresses as directed.

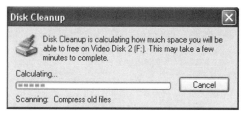

**Figure 1.11** Removing extraneous files before defragmenting your disks saves time and space. Disk Cleanup is a great tool for this.

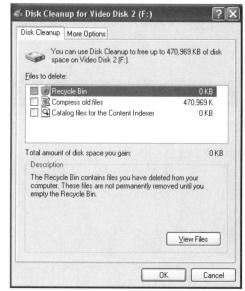

**Figure 1.12** The Disk Cleanup tool keeps track of unnecessary files so that you can delete them.

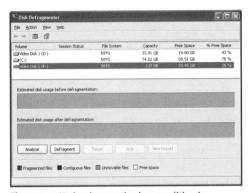

**Figure 1.13** No book on authoring or editing is complete without a visit to the Disk Defragmenter. Click Analyze to see how big a mess you actually have on your disk.

## To defragment your drives:

1. Click Start > Accessories > System Tools > Disk Defragmenter.

   Windows opens the Disk Defragmenter application window (**Figure 1.13**).

2. Choose the disk to defragment by clicking it in the application window; then click Defragment. If you've deleted all the files discussed above, you should defragment your system drive (usually c:\) and also defragment your capture drive (usually d:\ or later) to create large open spaces for capture and editing.

   Go get a cup of coffee. You're pretty much done, but if you care to watch, here's what you should be seeing: Before defragmenting, the program analyzes disk usage. Though you can't see it in the black-and-white screen shots, most of the small lines surrounded by white spaces are fragmented files that will be conjoined during the defragmentation process (**Figure 1.14**).

*continues on next page*

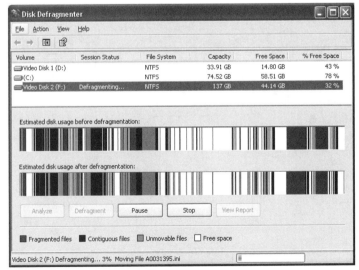

**Figure 1.14** Hmmm...lots of space on the disk, but no huge open spaces to capture my video. That slows down video capture and subsequent editing, as the disk has to hunt for places to store the video.

**PREPARING YOUR HARD DISKS**

The defragmented disk is now ready for video capture and editing (**Figure 1.15**). Note that the files are now efficiently packed, leaving plenty of contiguous disk space.

## ✔ Tips

■ Depending upon how much data is on the disk and the size of the drive, defragmenting can take anywhere from 30 seconds to several hours. Keep this in mind before starting this operation.

■ Turn off all background programs and don't use the computer when defragmenting the drive. If any program writes data to disk while the system is defragmenting, the Disk Defragmenter may need to stop and restart, extending the completion time significantly.

■ Large files slow the disk defragmentation process significantly. Before defragmenting, I usually search for and delete all unnecessary audio and video files (since they're among the largest files on the drive).

■ Defragmenting can make a significant difference in performance. In one test I did for *PC Magazine,* defragmenting the system disk improved application performance by 5 percent, whereas adding an additional 512 MB of memory produced no performance boost.

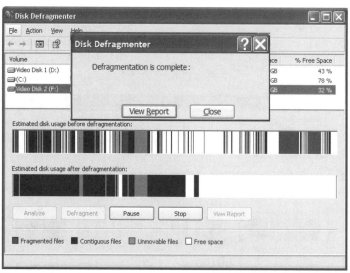

**Figure 1.15** Hooty, hoo! Look at all that clear space on the disk. I think I'll remake *Gone with the Wind.* (I know, frankly, you don't give a darn.) You're now ready to install Movie Maker and get started.

# CREATING WATCHABLE VIDEO

A video editor is like a hammer. Knowing how to hammer nails, straight and true, is a noble skill, but it doesn't guarantee you can build a sturdy house. Similarly, knowing how to capture your video and add transitions and titles and perhaps a special effect or two doesn't guarantee your video is *watchable*—that family and friends will be interested in watching it for more than two or three minutes without squirming in their chairs.

My goal with this book is not only to show you the capabilities of Movie Maker, our metaphorical hammer, but to help you create watchable videos. This involves a range of skills, such as using the proper camcorder settings; framing your shots correctly; shooting the right shots; and capturing, trimming, and weaving your scenes into a polished video production.

Don't fret. I'm not talking Hollywood movies, MTV videos, or 60-second commercials here. If you're like me, you probably shoot most, if not all, of your videos of friends and family for viewing by that same group and have minimal or no commercial aspirations.

So this chapter doesn't throw a lot of advanced theory your way—just a small set of fundamentals that will change the way you shoot and edit, and hopefully increase your enjoyment of the process. It should also greatly improve the perceived quality of your video.

# What *Is* Watchable Video?

For better or for worse, what's on television today defines what's "watchable." Next time you're watching television, pay attention to the following elements.

First, in most shows, note the relative lack of camera motion. Specifically, while the show shifts from camera to camera, there is very little *panning* (moving the camera from side to side) or *fast zooming* (changing the zoom magnification either into or away from the subject). You'll almost never see the shaking that evidences a hand-held camera.

Second, note how transitions are used as the behind-the-scenes producer shifts from camera to camera. *Transitions* are visual effects that help smooth the change from shot to shot. Inside of a scene, or within a series of shots from a single location during a single time period, most directors simply *cut* between the various clips. One camera angle stops, and the other starts.

When television shows use a transition to alert the viewer that the time or location is about to change, it's almost always a simple *dissolve* (an effect that briefly merges the current clip with the next clip and then displays the second) or *fade to black*. On kids' shows and "zany" sitcoms, you may see more "artistic" transitions, but they're not random. Typically, the effect relates to the subject matter of the show—for instance, a crocodile dragging the first clip over the second in *Crocodile Hunter*.

Finally, note the pace of change. Few, if any, shows (or movies) display a static screen for longer than 10 or 15 seconds. News and sports shows use multiple text streams to keep viewers' eyes occupied, along with frequent background updates and cuts to reporters in the field, while sitcoms and other shows change cameras and camera angles frequently.

So here's the bar: videos worth watching use stable shots filmed from multiple angles and don't introduce random special effects, but they still manage to introduce some element of change every 5 to 15 seconds. If you want to produce watchable video, that's your target.

You really can't produce watchable video without shooting well and capturing well. For the most part, this chapter discusses how to shoot well, while the remainder of the book covers the editing side.

# Watchable Video Guidelines

The good news is the building blocks of TV-quality video are very accessible. You simply need to follow a few guidelines (see the sidebar).

## Shooting for success

A key point to keep in mind in creating watchable video is the goal of your movie. Let's start with one proposition: that not all occasions demand the same level of attention in either shooting or editing. Sometimes you bring the camera just to capture the day or the event and really just want to have fun without the pressure of creating a masterpiece. Still, you want the video you shoot to look as good as possible, so you definitely want to use the proper camera settings and compose your shots carefully.

Other times, for weddings, significant birthdays and anniversaries, graduations and other events, you want to weave in advanced shot combinations that captivate and impress your viewers. You may even want to develop a short list of shots so that your video can follow a definite storyline. This takes a bit more planning up front and more editing time at the back.

So you don't need to concern yourself with advanced shot composition each time you dust off your camera. You should gain a fundamental knowledge of the basics that will improve all of your videos. Then you should learn some more advanced techniques, for those special occasions where you want to spread your creative wings.

Let's start at the top of the guidelines and then work our way through the other elements.

## Guidelines for Creating Watchable Video

- Use a feature-rich video editor
- Develop strong nonlinear editing skills
- Choose the right camera settings
- Apply basic shot composition
- Apply advanced shot composition

## Definitions 101

Here are some terms that are critical to video production. I'll try to stick with the following definitions in this chapter and throughout the book to ensure that we're speaking a common language.

**Shot composition.** Composition is the arrangement of the primary subjects on the screen. The goal is to present the most aesthetically pleasing image possible without exceeding the ambitions and time constraints of your project.

**Shooting, taping, or videotaping.** These terms all refer to the process of pointing your camera, pressing the red Record button, and recording on tape. I may slip up sometimes and use the term *filming*, a definite faux pas since we're using a DV or other tape-based camcorder that doesn't have film, but the process meant is the same.

**Scene (during shooting).** During shooting, the scene is the key area where the action takes place. In a crime drama, the murder scene takes place in the bedroom or boardroom or library. In a football movie, you'll have locker room scenes (tasteful, of course), scenes on the field, and finally the tickertape parade scene, in the center of town.

**Shot.** A shot typically is described in terms of what you're doing with the camera when you're shooting a particular scene. So in a long shot, the camera is very far from the subject (unless you're at the race track, of course), while in a close-up shot, the camera is close to the subject. An establishing or wide shot typically shows the entire scene so that the viewer understands the environment relevant to that footage. You'll learn more about the different types of shots later in this chapter.

**Scene (during editing).** During editing, a scene is a discrete chunk of video composed of one or more shots. Typically, during editing, you identify the scenes you want to use in the final project and then assemble them with your video editor.

**Clip.** A clip is a generic term for a chunk of audio or video that you're editing in Movie Maker's Movie window. It is often used interchangeably with *scene*.

**Sequence.** A sequence is a group of scenes pieced together. In a wedding video, for instance, you might have a sequence for the rehearsal dinner, a sequence for the ceremony, and a sequence for the reception. You piece these sequences together into a finished movie.

**Movie.** A movie is the end product of your shooting and editing—what you end up with after you've pieced together the various scenes and added all the transitions, titles, and special effects; it's the creative fruit you serve up to your audience.

**Video.** Typically refers to what's transferred from your camcorder to your computer. Video is also used interchangeably with the term *movie*.

## Using a Feature-Rich Video Editor

The video editor serves two primary functions in the creation of watchable video. First, it provides an accessible workspace for cutting up your raw footage into the most watchable segments and then piecing them together into a compelling movie.

Second, the video editor provides a multitude of elements for introducing change into your videos to satisfy the MTV-nurtured attention spans of viewers. For example, Movie Maker can supply intra-scene transitions, special effects, and offers a range of interesting title effects. Finally, MovieMaker's AutoMovie function, discussed in Chapter 14, converts your videos to MTV-style music videos and is an excellent tool for enhancing many common videos.

USING A FEATURE-RICH VIDEO EDITOR

# Developing Strong Nonlinear Editing Skills

A great tool, like our metaphorical hammer, does little good if you don't know how to use it. The rest of this book will give you the details. Even while you're shooting, however, you should understand Movie Maker's most valuable capability so that you can make the best use of this tool.

Simply stated, Movie Maker, like all computer-based video editors, is a nonlinear tool, which means that you can move video scenes around freely, like checkers on a checkerboard. Consider **Figure 2.1**. At the upper left is the Contents pane, which contains the scenes in the order that I shot them and later captured them on my hard disk. At the bottom is the Storyboard, where I can assemble all the scenes that I want in the final movie. (I'm jumping ahead a bit here on the interface side; if you want to bone up on Movie Maker's interface elements, you can take a quick look at "The Movie Maker Interface" in Chapter 3.)

**Figure 2.1** One of Movie Maker's best features is that it's nonlinear, so you can cut and paste videos from anywhere to anywhere.

This is the beginning of a video I'm creating with footage shot at the Fiddler's Convention here in Galax, where I live. This is the opening sequence that introduces the viewer to the yearly, world-famous gathering. Later sequences will highlight individual bands and music and instrument types, like bluegrass and mandolins, and some of the country dancing I shot at the event.

As you can see in the Movie Maker Storyboard, Scene 1 shows an announcer introducing a band on stage. The next scene is the sign at the entrance to the Fiddler's Convention, which I shot first on the way in, so that the viewer instantly knows what the video is about.

Next, using the song from the background music in the first scene, I display several other scenes that visually illustrate the magnitude of the festival: the hundreds of parked trailers and tents spread over about 20 acres, the thousands of people in the stands and milling about. (To make everything work together seamlessly, I use the Continuity system, described later in this chapter.)

Going to the Fiddler's Convention, I knew that I would need these shots to complete the video, but it wasn't convenient to shoot them all immediately upon my entrance. Hey, I was being dragged around by two little girls who didn't give a hoot about continuity. No problem, though, because whenever I get the shots—later that night or even the next day—I can cut and paste them in Movie Maker wherever and whenever I need them.

If you've never edited video before, you will find this is a huge paradigm shift that really unleashes significant creative potential. As you'll discover throughout this chapter and later in the book, Movie Maker's nonlinear nature is absolutely key to creating watchable videos.

That said, it all starts with the camera. So let's focus on that aspect of creating watchable video.

# Choosing the Right Camera Settings

If you produced camcorders and sold them to untrained consumers, your primary goal, if you wanted to sell a lot of them, would probably be to allow your customers to produce the best possible videos right out of the box—no tweaking of controls required. Camcorder manufacturers are a bright group, and this is pretty much what they've attempted to do.

Still, in certain instances, you can improve the quality of your video if you tune the controls to match your surroundings and the goals of the shot. In addition, there are certain camera features you should always use, and some to avoid at all costs.

Finally, two realities of consumer camcorders—lighting and audio—have their own sets of challenges, which you should know about up front. This section briefly addresses these issues, and then we move on to shot composition.

## It's all about exposure

No, this isn't a section about Madonna or Justin Timberlake; it's about the exposure setting on your camera, which controls how much light gets to the charged coupled device (CCD) that captures the image. Virtually all consumer camcorders have automatic exposure settings that work well most of the time.

However, they also feature special *programmed auto-exposure (AE)* modes that can improve video quality in well-defined shooting conditions. For example, most Sony camcorders have the following programmed AE modes for specific shooting conditions:

◆ Spotlight prevents faces from being excessively white.

◆ Portrait sharpens close-up images and softens the background.

◆ Sports captures crisp images of fast-moving subjects.

◆ Beach & Ski prevents faces from appearing dark against the generally lighter background.

◆ Sunset Moon optimizes shooting controls for low-light conditions.

◆ Landscape focuses solely on far-away objects, softening any objects in the foreground.

Many DV cameras also have settings for backlit conditions, which, like the Beach and Ski mode, can prevent faces from appearing overly dark. In my experience, these modes work very well in their defined roles, improving image quality over fully automatic settings. For this reason, you should definitely identify the modes available on your camera and learn how to switch to them for the defined conditions.

## The skinny on night-shot modes

Most DV cameras offer one or two low-light modes, which fall into two categories. The first is an infrared-assisted mode that creates a greenish "night vision goggles" effect. This is very effective for capturing sleeping children or nocturnal animals, but you lose all the color in the shot—the image's colors consist of shades of green.

The other mode doesn't use infrared, but slows the shutter speed dramatically to ensure that sufficient light gets to the CCD. This preserves color, but even minimal motion produces extreme blurriness that usually makes the video unusable.

Depending upon your goal, either or both modes work just fine. However, don't confuse either as a mechanism for boosting light under low-light conditions. That is, if you're shooting video at a quiet dinner party or dark restaurant, neither mode will improve your results. You need to either boost the ambient light in the room by turning on some lights or get a light for your video camera.

## The white balance issue

White balance is kind of like bad cholesterol. It's not something you think about often, but whenever it comes up, it's generally negative news.

White balance is a problem because cameras perceive the color white differently based upon the light source, whether florescent or incandescent light or sunlight. All cameras perform white balancing automatically, but under some circumstances, such as shooting in sunlight, under florescent lights, or under rapidly changing lighting conditions, the auto-sensing mechanisms may not be accurate, so you run a pretty significant risk that the colors will be off.

For example, I once forgot to white balance my camera during a trip to Zoo Atlanta, and all of the video had a blue tone. Or when I switched from outdoor shooting to indoor shooting at a wedding without white balancing, all whites appeared slightly pinkish, including the bride's wedding dress, which was a big hit, let me tell you.

Both problems could have been prevented with proper white balancing. The procedure is similar for most cameras: you zoom the camera into a white object like a wall, wedding dress, or piece of paper and press the white-balance button. Alternatively, many cameras have white-balance presets for indoor and outdoor shoots. Check your camera's documentation for details.

If this all sounds overly technical, you can also simply stay in automatic white-balance mode and point the camera at a white object for about 10 seconds or so whenever lighting conditions change, such as when you move into direct sunlight from the shade or move indoors from outside. This will give the automatic white-balance mechanism the best chance of operating correctly.

## Automatic versus manual focus

Automatic focus is generally effective for keeping the video image sharp and in focus. Under certain conditions such as the following, however, manual focus produces superior results:

◆ Shooting a stationary subject from a tripod (where focus can inadvertently drift if the subject momentarily moves out of the picture).

◆ Shooting under low-light conditions (where the camera can lose focus and repeatedly adjust the focus back and forth to find it).

◆ Shooting through a window (where the camera may focus on the glass, rather than the objects behind the glass).

Check your camera's documentation to learn how to disable automatic focus and how to operate the manual focus controls.

## When to use image stabilization

Image stabilization is a feature that minimizes minor hand shaking and other camera motion such as might occur while walking or riding in a car. While not a panacea, image stabilization provides some benefit and should be used whenever you're not shooting from a tripod. When shooting from a tripod, however, most camera vendors recommend disabling this feature. Check your camera's documentation for the recommendations regarding image stabilization and to learn how to enable and disable this mode.

## Other settings

Here are other controls to consider before shooting, along with some suggestions for using the best setting.

- **Date.** DV cameras imprint the date and time of each shot in the video, and Movie Maker uses this information to detect scenes in the video. It's a great feature that makes setting the time and date on your camera a priority.

- **12-bit audio versus 16-bit audio.** Use 16-bit audio; 12-bit audio was created so that you could lay down two tracks of audio simultaneously while shooting, a capability that most cameras don't offer. The 16-bit audio setting creates larger files, so it requires more space on your hard disk. However, the additional data delivers better quality.

- **Digital zoom.** Unlike optical zoom, which uses the camera's lens to produce additional detail when zooming in, digital zoom simply zooms into the digital image, which creates obvious pixilation (jaggies) at extreme settings. Most pros disable digital zoom, and you should, too.

- **Standard play (SP) versus long play (LP).** With DV camcorders, you can record up to 90 minutes of video on a 60-minute tape using LP mode, which uses a slower tape recording speed (12.56 mm per second compared to 18.812 mm per second for standard play) to pack more video onto the same tape. The same video signal is stored in each mode; it's just that LP mode stores the same video on less tape, which is theoretically less safe. For example, if an inch of tape is damaged in LP mode, you'd lose 50 percent more video than you would in SP mode. Some pundits state that the slower tape speed actually decreases your chances for error, but also that LP modes are implemented slightly differently on different camcorders and shouldn't be used if the tape may later be played back on a different camera. For me, this was much more of an issue when DV tapes cost $25; now that they're under $4 in bulk, SP is probably a safer choice.

- **16:9 aspect ratio versus 4:3 aspect ratio.** Use 16:9 only if you have a widescreen television that can play it without distortion. Note that 16:9 video played on a normal TV will appear squashed.

- **Digital effects.** Many cameras offer digital effects such as sepia, mosaic, fade from black, and fade to black, plus primitive titling capabilities. You can produce these with much greater precision using Movie Maker, so disable these effects on your camcorder.

## The realities of shooting with consumer camcorders

There are two realities about shooting with DV camcorders, particularly inexpensive consumer models. First, most camcorders produce suboptimal quality in anything other than extremely bright conditions. Second, it's very difficult to capture clear, crisp audio using solely the camcorder's microphone unless you're very close to the subject. Fortunately, you can minimize or resolve both problems with some advance planning and/or some inexpensive accessories.

Let's look at the lighting problem first. This is a particular issue for me because my wife favors cozy, intimate family celebrations with minimal lighting, preferably candlelight. Unfortunately, under these conditions, it's impossible to shoot video that looks even remotely good. For example, **Figure 2.2** was taken at a wedding reception without ancillary lighting, and the subject's faces are very indistinct because of the low light.

Of course, under candlelight, the problem is obvious. The low-light issue is much more insidious under normal room lighting, which generally is still too dark for high-quality images. Here, however, the image on your LCD panel may look fine, and you won't discover that your images are too dark until you've captured your video on disk or viewed it on a television screen. Either way, it's too late to address the problem.

**Figure 2.2** Unless you're shooting participants in the witness protection program, poor lighting like this produces unacceptable images.

**Figure 2.3** Lights like this one from Sony can go a long way toward reducing low-light quality issues.

Basically, there are two ways to solve the lighting problem. First, you can turn on every light in the room, sacrificing short-term intimacy for the long-term quality of your memories of the event. This generally works well in most homes, where lighting is plentiful, so long as you can get your spouse to agree.

In darker reception halls, restaurants, and similar venues, where you can't control the lighting, your best option is to purchase a video light like the Sony HVL-20DW2 shown in **Figure 2.3** (assuming your camcorder doesn't have a light, of course). This particular model attaches to the accessory shoe on top of the camera and draws power from the camcorder's battery. Alternatively, you can get a light that uses separate batteries.

Note that capturing good-quality video under low-light conditions is a serious, serious issue, probably mentioned more in most camcorder reviews than any other deficit. Unfortunately, short of spending $3,000 for a camcorder that takes pictures in low light, there is no simple solution. Ignore it, and it will repeatedly degrade the quality of your indoor shots; take the steps discussed here, and you can minimize this problem.

CHOOSING THE RIGHT CAMERA SETTINGS

## Improving audio quality

As you would expect, the problem with camcorder-based audio starts with the microphone. First, since it's located on the camera body, it can easily pick up a host of operator noises such as the clicking of the zoom controls. More serious is the pickup pattern of the microphone, which defines the area from which the microphone gathers sound.

**Figure 2.4** Microphones like this one from Sony help capture better audio when the audio source is distant from the camera.

Typically, DV camcorders use microphones that prioritize all sounds in front of the camera equally. This pattern works well if you're shooting a group of people equidistant from the camera, but is useless if you're shooting a lecturer or speaker at the front of the room or anyone far away from the camera.

Here, you also have two options: either get closer to the speaker or purchase a separate microphone. For the latter, the options are almost limitless, but the easiest and cheapest alternatives are microphones that sit on the camera body itself, like the Sony ECM-MSD1 (**Figure 2.4**).

The MSD1 offers a narrower, front-focused pickup pattern that ignores ambient noise and captures audio primarily from the direction in which the camera is pointing. These types of microphones are also called shotgun or gun microphones.

These types of microphones probably won't help if you are shooting a lecturer from the back of the room. However, at a birthday party or wedding, you can shoot someone 10 to 15 feet away and clearly hear what the person is saying, which is almost impossible using solely the microphone on the camera body.

CHOOSING THE RIGHT CAMERA SETTINGS

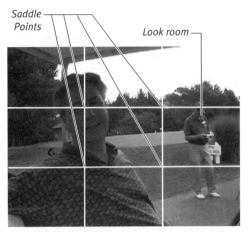

Saddle Points

Look room

**Figure 2.5** The rule of thirds. My golf buddy's head is located at the upper-left saddle point in the video frame, providing the necessary look room.

Look room

**Figure 2.6** My other buddy is facing the opposite direction, so I placed him at the upper-right saddle point. Note how the eyes are above the top third of the frame.

# Applying Basic Shot Composition

Once you get the camera settings down and deal with audio and lighting, it's time to start thinking about shot composition, which is the art of placing your subjects in the frame to create the most aesthetically pleasing image.

Here are four basic techniques to keep in mind while shooting. After you read this section, watch for them on TV and in the movies. Once you see how consistently the pros use these techniques, you'll be surprised that you never noticed them before.

## The rule of thirds

According to the rule of thirds, you should divide each image into a tic-tac-toe grid, like that shown in **Figure 2.5,** and place the primary subject of the frame at one of the four saddle points, or intersections of the four lines. This rule has its roots in Greek architecture and Renaissance art and is based on the belief that certain shapes and proportions are more pleasing to the eye than others.

When you are shooting a subject that isn't moving, the image looks best when the open space is located in front of where the subject is facing, as shown in Figure 2.5 and **Figure 2.6**. This is called providing look room or nose room.

When your primary subject is moving, place your subject in the back third of the frame, leaving lead room in the front. In **Figure 2.7**, my daughter is skating from left to right, so the lead room is on the viewer's right. Similarly, in **Figure 2.8**, my other daughter is moving from right to left, so the lead room is on the viewer's left.

A corollary to the rule of thirds is that the eyes should always be at or above the top third of the video. This holds true regardless if the shot is taken from close up and includes the face only, or from farther back, as in **Figures 2.5** to **2.8**.

Like all rules of aesthetics, the rule of thirds isn't fixed in stone; sometimes you simply have to shoot what looks appropriate at the time. For example, if the background is direction-neutral, I find it hard to apply the rule of thirds when shooting a subject looking straight at me, as in **Figure 2.9**.

That said, it's clear that the "center the image in the camera" instruction we learned back with our first Instamatic is not universally appropriate. Though it's impossible to apply the rule of thirds to every frame in your video, especially with moving subjects, use it as a guide, and you'll find your videos more aesthetically pleasing.

## Motion techniques

One of the most striking differences between professional and amateur video is the amount and quality of the motion in the video. When you watch most television shows or movies, you'll notice two facts related to motion. First, most shots are either totally stable or have only slight, virtually unnoticeable motion. Second, if there is significant motion, it's very smooth.

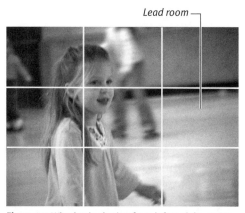

Lead room

**Figure 2.7** Whatley is skating from left to right, so I try to keep her in the back left of the frame, to provide lead room.

Lead room

**Figure 2.8** Rose is skating (well, shuffling, actually) from right to left, so the lead room is on the other side.

**Figure 2.9** I find it hard to apply the rule of thirds on a subject facing directly at me, unless there's another object in the background that dictates it. Here the background is neutral, so this buddy is framed in the middle.

In contrast, most amateur videos are shot from unstable platforms that shake continuously, with fast zooms (using the camera's zoom controls to zoom into or out of the image), pans (moving the camera from side to side), and tilts (moving the camera up and down).

Obviously, the pros have multiple cameras and better equipment, making their jobs a lot easier. Still, if you follow these five rules, you can produce very similar results.

◆ Shoot from a stable platform. I'm not going to tell you to shoot with a tripod because I know it's impractical most of the time. However, you can buy an inexpensive monopod (a one-legged tripod) at Wal-Mart for under $20 that will hold your camera at a steady height, making it much simpler to reduce the shake in the video. Folded up, it's only slightly longer than an umbrella, so it's easy to carry around. Even with a monopod, you should lean against something solid, like a wall, tree, or fence, whenever possible.

If you're shooting without a tripod or monopod, find the most comfortable sustainable position for the camera; usually this is about chest high, holding the camera with both hands and sighting with the viewfinder. If your camera has a shoulder strap, see if you can use this strap to support the weight of the camcorder when you're shooting. One of the best approaches is to simply lay the camera on a fixed object, like a desk, table, or shelf.

*continues on next page*

**APPLYING BASIC SHOT COMPOSITION**

◆ Zoom, pan, or tilt only to follow the action, not for dramatic effect. Don't try to slowly zoom into your wife's face as she watches your daughter's gymnastics meet; frame the close-up shot and then start shooting. Don't pan from skyscraper to skyscraper in downtown Manhattan; shoot one building, stop, reframe the next building, and start shooting again (or cut the panning sequences between buildings during editing).

◆ Whenever possible, rehearse the necessary camera motion beforehand. This approach works exceptionally well at sporting events like baseball games or gymnastics meets, where the athlete has to follow a designated path, whether to first base or to the vault spring. While you're waiting for your child, practice with other children. Not only does this promote the smoothness of your camera motion, but it also helps ensure that obstacles don't obscure your line of sight during that critical moment.

◆ For all shots that have motion, start at a stable position for a few seconds whenever possible, and hold the final shot for a few seconds to ensure that you have sufficient footage for editing.

◆ Use your waist for panning and tilting shots, not your hands or your feet. That is, to pan across a scene, hold the camera steady and swivel at the waist across the scene. To tilt up and down, hold the camera steady and bend forward and backward at the waist.

## The Continuity system

Briefly, the Continuity system is a style of editing whose goal is to present a scene so that the cuts from scene to scene are unnoticeable to the viewer—that is, the progression of shots within the scene is logical, without any discontinuities that jar the viewer. It's a pretty complex system with lots of rules, so for our purposes here we'll focus on its absolutely critical points.

Most importantly, you need to start each sequence with an establishing shot that presents the watcher with a complete view of the setting. Then you can move into medium shots and close-ups, with periodic reestablishing shots to keep the viewer grounded. (See the sidebar "Taxonomy of Shots" later in this chapter for definitions of these types of shots.)

This sequence of shots is shown in **Figure 2.10**, taken from a television interview I participated in several years ago at a trade show. This was a two-camera shoot, so it's unlike what most of us do day to day, but the technique is instructive.

The first shot is the establishing shot: two guys talking with the stage and people walking around behind us clear to the viewer. This gives the viewer a feel for the environment. This is Camera 1. Next is a medium shot of me with a title, on Camera 2. Then Camera 1 tightens the framing to a medium two-shot of the friendly interviewer and me (note the adherence to the rule of thirds in the medium shot of me, but not in either the wide shot or the medium two-shot).

What's particularly instructive is the difference between the establishing shot and the medium two-shot. They look very similar, but in the establishing shot, you can clearly tell what's going on in the background—folks walking around with bags; must be a trade show. In the medium two-shot, you see only body parts walking around, and the environment is much less comprehensible to the viewer. That's okay, since the establishing shot already clued the viewer to what's going on. In addition, the camera person periodically shifted back to a wider shot with this camera so that viewers entering in midstream would understand the context.

The clear lesson is this: Start every sequence with an establishing shot, or series of shots, that presents the environment to the viewer. Then shoot progressively closer so that you get scenes that present the detail you want without confusing the viewer. Next time you watch ESPN Sports Center or the evening news, notice how the video follows this progression.

Establishing shot   Medium shot   Medium Two shot

**Figure 2.10** The Continuity system in action. The first shot is an establishing shot that clearly shows we're at a trade show. The next is a cut to a medium shot and then to a medium two-shot.

Let's apply this theory to our typical one-camera shoot, using the Fiddler's Convention video mentioned earlier. As shown in **Figure 2.11**, I start with a medium shot of the announcer, breaking the rules, but only for a second. Call this my nod to the *Tom Jones Show*, which always started with Tom's hand on the microphone before he broke into "It's Not Unusual." Always liked that dramatic effect.

However, the first shot is on the screen for only a moment or two, primarily to introduce the audio background track of the announcer and the band playing on the stage. Then I cut to the Fiddler's Convention sign, so the viewer immediately knows what's going on; then several wide shots showing the stage from the background, the acres of trailers and tents, and the thousands of folks in the stands; and then the stage.

After this, I can start adding medium shots and close-ups of the band members and interesting attendees because I've set the stage with the wide shot. Let's apply this approach to some common situations.

- **Birthday party.** Start with exterior shots of the house and interior shots of the party room showing all participants and decorations. Then move to medium shots of guests and the birthday celebrant.

- **Soccer game.** Set the stage with wide shots of the field, showing both goals, the location of both teams, and the grandstands. Then start working in views of your star forward, the team, the coach, and other participants.

- **Dance recital or play.** Use exterior shots of the gymnasium or theater to set the stage; then shoot the entire gym or stage to show the complete environment. Then add medium shots of the participants and, later, close-ups.

**Figure 2.11** In my first video of the Fiddler's Convention, I used a series of wide shots to introduce the spectacle to the viewer before transitioning to medium shots of the band.

Remember to shoot an establishing shot each time you change the physical location of the scene. For example, if you're shooting a family wedding, you shouldn't shift from a scene in the chapel to a scene in the reception hall without an establishing shot of the reception hall. It also helps to shoot closing wide shots that you can fade to black during editing so that the viewer understands one sequence is ending and another is starting.

Once again, the lovely aspect of digital video is the nonlinear nature of the editing process. You don't have to shoot the establishing shots first; you can shoot them later and cut and paste them in at the proper location.

## The Continuity system for audio

The Continuity rule for audio is a bit cerebral, but it's exceptionally important so bear with me for a moment. I'll use an example to illustrate the point.

Assume that you're at a wedding reception. You want to show people dancing and having a good time, so you shoot a bunch of shots of everyone dancing—say 10 minutes worth taken over a 30-minute period.

You start editing and quickly realize that no one will watch 10 minutes of dancing, so you start trimming away footage to get down to a more palatable 4 minutes. Here's the problem: Since the band or DJ didn't play the same song all night, most shots of the revelers have different songs playing in the background. Though your viewers can accept visual cuts from person to person without a sense of discontinuity, audio cuts are a different matter—that is, cutting from 5 seconds of one song to 5 seconds of another song is a big red flag that signals a discontinuity.

To avoid this, when shooting, make sure that you capture at least one complete song that you can use as background for the entire finished dance sequence. Then, as described in "Advanced Timeline Editing" in Chapter 9, you can use that song as the background for the entire 4 minutes and cut and paste bits of other shots to complete the sequence.

In essence, you're fooling the audience into thinking that you took all of the shots during one song, simulating a multiple camera shoot with one camera, which is incredibly effective. Sure, problems can arise—for example, if you choose a disco song and have footage of people slow dancing—but overall, this is a very powerful technique, with broad application.

For example, in the Fiddler's Convention video, I used the audio from the first scene as the background for the entire first sequence. In addition to the wide shots, I came back to medium and close-up shots of the band and pasted in other bits of people listening, dancing, and generally having a good time. These are all the shots I would use to convey the atmosphere of the event, and provide the visual context for later sequences. But because I captured one entire song on tape and used it to create essentially a music video, the presentation is much more polished than if I had pasted the same scenes together with disparate audio tracks, revealing to my viewers that the scenes aren't really continuous.

At a recent wedding, I kept the camera running during both the entry and exit processionals, which took about 10 minutes each. Then, using one song from each processional as the background, I condensed each sequence to about 2 minutes, which was much more palatable to viewers.

# Applying Advanced Shot Composition

Advanced shot compositions typically involve different types of shots and shot combinations. You've seen them hundreds of times on TV; they're easy to implement and look very polished. Here's how to use some in your own movies.

## Medium shot, point-of-view shot, reaction shot

**Figure 2.12** starts with a medium shot of my wife and daughter, obviously staring at something. What is it, you find yourself asking. Then I cut to a point-of-view shot, which shows the action in the eyes of my daughter: her point of view. Then, as the horse draws nearer to her, she smiles in delight; that's the reaction shot.

As with all of the shots we're discussing, it's important to recognize that these shots were filmed out of order. I shot about 2 minutes of video before a horse carriage ride and pieced together these 15 or 20 seconds before we got on the carriage to show how Whatley was enjoying the day.

I used the background audio from the first and third shots for the entire sequence to preserve audio continuity. Then I pasted a shot of the horse, taken later, into the middle to show Whatley's point of view. It looks like I have two cameras to most untrained eyes, which was the effect I was seeking, but I had only my trusty Sony DCR-PC1.

Think, for a moment, about the unlimited potential for these types of shots. You're at a softball game and your daughter gets a hit. You catch the line drive on video and then want to switch to the crowd cheering and your spouse smiling like a fool.

But you can't physically move the camera fast enough to catch all this action. Thinking in advance, while other kids were at bat, you took several shots of the crowd cheering and your spouse smiling. You also took several shots of your spouse pensively watching the action, just to use when piecing together this video.

During editing, you start with the pensive shots of the spouse, then the line drive, and then the crowd and proud spouse shots. If you use the audio from the actual line drive for the whole sequence, it will look like you had multiple cameras working the entire game. It's not hard, it's not time consuming; you just need to plan ahead.

*Medium shot*　　　　*Point-of-view shot*　　　　*Reaction shot*

**Figure 2.12** What's Whatley staring at? A horse? How delightful.

## Over-the-shoulder shot, point-of-view shot

An over-the-shoulder shot is what you see on the left in **Figure 2.13**, a shot that includes the back of one of the subjects and the focus of the subject's attention. It's also an establishing shot, because it shows the elephant's environment at Zoo Atlanta.

Then you switch to a point-of-view shot that shows in detail what your subject is looking at. This is a great combination for involving your primary subject in your sequence while following the rules of continuity discussed earlier.

*Over-the-shoulder shot*　　　　　　　*Point-of-view shot*

**Figure 2.13** Using the over-the-shoulder shot as an establishing shot; then cutting to a point-of-view shot of the elephant.

# Cutaways

A cutaway is a shot that relates to the primary subject of the video, but isn't the primary subject. For example, when ESPN interviews the winning coach after a football game, the coach might attribute the win to a goal-line stand late in the fourth quarter. During the interview, while the coach is still talking, ESPN switches to a view of the play and then cuts back to the coach once the play is done.

Or maybe it's the weatherperson describing the wonderful spring-like weather that just descended in mid December. The shot starts with the weatherperson, and then cutaways show joggers running in shorts, couples sunning on the grass, and babies crawling on blankets. Then back to the weatherperson for tomorrow's forecast.

Here's what I like about cutaways. Number one, they allow you to show the flavor of the entire event. Rather than simply keeping the camera on little Sally during the softball game, you shoot the coaches cajoling, the parents praising, the shortstop shuffling, an uproar from the umpire—all the shots that make baseball such a compelling game.

Second, cutaways can serve as patches for badly shot video that you can't cut from your sequence, as may occur when you're capturing an entire song, speech, or sermon to use as the background track for your audio as described earlier.

For example, **Figure 2.14** shows six images of a shot from the Fiddler's Convention. Much of the fun action occurs away from the stage, and this dynamic duo had generated an amazing amount of dancing, shuffling, and stomping. The main subjects of the video sequence were the two performers; all other shots not directly of them were cutaways.

**Figure 2.14** Using cutaways. The primary subject here is the two-person band; the cutaways are the folks dancing.

Following the audio continuity system described previously, I filmed one entire song, moving from one side of the scene to the other while recording, and catching some of the dancing action as I went. Then I hung around for two other songs, shooting different, additional dance sequences.

Because I moved around while filming the background song, there was an awful lot of unusable footage and bad framing. Wherever necessary, however, I just pasted in a dance sequence to hide the bad footage, allowing me to produce one fairly cohesive 4-minute song.

Similarly, for a wedding video, you might want pictures of the proud parents watching the ceremonial first dance. So you shoot the entire ceremonial dance and later shoot the proud parents beaming at something else; you can then use these shots of the parents as cutaways to patch into the dance sequence.

My rule for cutaways is that you can never get enough of them. If your goal is advanced shot composition, spend a lot of time shooting subjects other than your primary ones.

APPLYING ADVANCED SHOT COMPOSITION

## Taxonomy of Shots

Here's a list of shots and some suggestions for when to use them.

◆ **Establishing shot.** Any shot that provides the viewer with a visual overview of the environment of the shot.

◆ **Long shot.** Any shot that doesn't cut out any body part of the primary subject. For example, **Figure 2.15** is a long shot that shows a lovely straight left arm but a disturbing hint of a reverse pivot. This is about the shortest long shot you'll see; shots from farther away are also called medium or extreme long shots. Long shots are good for showing action and as establishing shots and are also called wide shots.

◆ **Medium shot.** Any shot that cuts away a portion of the primary subject, up to a close-up, which shows only the upper shoulders and face. These shots are also called mid-shots. Medium shots are good for introducing the viewer to the character and should be used before a close-up.

**Figure 2.15** Here's a long shot that adheres to the rule of thirds. For those who care about such things, I parred this short par-three hole (that's my story and I'm sticking to it).

◆ **Close-up shot.** Any shot that shows only the shoulders and head, or closer in. These shots are good primarily for reaction shots. Use close-ups sparingly, for effect only; during most shoots, a medium shot is a much better choice to show people talking.

◆ **Over-the-shoulder shot.** Shows the upper shoulder of a subject and the primary subject of the video.

◆ **Point-of-view shot.** Shows the point of view of the immediately preceding subject on the screen.

◆ **Reaction shot.** Shows a subject's reaction to the immediately preceding shot.

# GETTING STARTED WITH MOVIE MAKER

3

As a journalist who specializes in video-related topics, I get a lot of email asking basic questions about digital video, editing, and video production in general. Sometimes, late at night when I'm answering these queries I fantasize about bundling them together on my www.doceo.com Web site. I could label them the Jan-FAQs (pretty catchy, eh?), attract a gazillion eyeballs from interested readers, start accepting advertising, and then sell the whole thing to Donald Trump.

Until then, however, it strikes me that since Movie Maker is the prototypical "first video editor" used by many editing newbies; many readers of this book may share some of the same questions. So this chapter begins with an abridged version of the Jan-FAQs to make sure we're all on the same page when it comes to terms and terminology. Then it introduces the Movie Maker interface and discusses how and where to set project defaults. Finally, it concludes with a brief look at how to plan and organize your Movie Maker projects.

# The Jan-FAQs

On one level, making movies sounds kind of easy. You shoot your video, capture it on your computer, edit it into a polished production, and then spit it out for your viewers to adore. Then you start thinking about details like formats and resolutions and codecs and frame rates and DV and MPEG-2 and authoring for DVD, and it's pretty easy to get sidetracked by the details.

The good news is, it really can be as easy as it sounds. The bad news is that you need to learn a bit about digital movie making before getting started. You don't need a semester course; reading the next few sections should make the rest of the book a lot easier to understand. I know this stuff seems basic, but the devil can be in the details.

## What is video, anyway?

Video is a synchronized stream of frames and audio. In the United States, which uses the NTSC (National Television Systems Committee) standard, video on your television displays 30 frames a second. Europe uses a different standard that displays 25 frames per second, while most films you see in theatres are shot and displayed at 24 frames per second.

Interestingly, video can be created from digital photographs and other nonvideo sources. When displaying a photograph on United States TV, however, the production system creates 30 frames per second of that still image to broadcast over the airwaves. Movie Maker performs a similar function when you add still images to your video productions.

THE JAN-FAQs

720 pixels

480 pixels

**Figure 3.1** Santa comes a calling in this 720x480 frame from a DV camera.

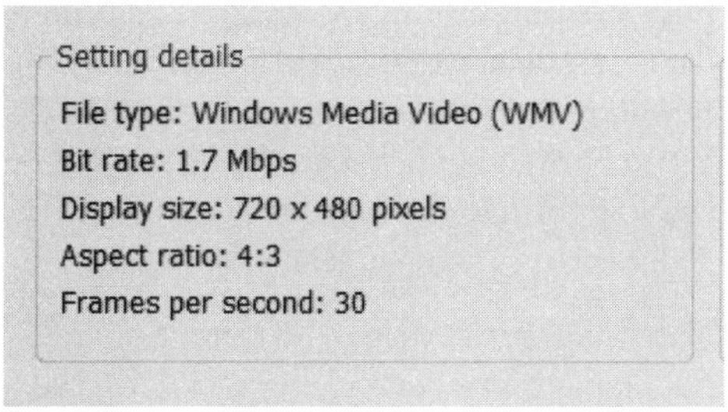

Setting details

File type: Windows Media Video (WMV)

Bit rate: 1.7 Mbps

Display size: 720 x 480 pixels

Aspect ratio: 4:3

Frames per second: 30

**Figure 3.2** The five characteristics Movie Maker uses to define a digital video file.

# What is digital video?

Okay, promise me you'll stand on one leg as you read this.

Digital video is any video played on a computer or other digital device. To be honest, analog video has always been kind of magic to me, and I've never really been good at defining it, other than saying it's the type of video broadcast over television sets and stored on VHS and Hi8 camcorders.

However, digital video suits my "left brain, fallen-CPA" thought processes to a Mr. T, precisely because it is so endearingly definable. For example, all digital video files are composed of *pixels*, or picture elements, each with its own defined color. Stack enough pixels across and up and down and you get a video *frame*, which is what appears ever so briefly on your computer monitor.

Each frame has a *resolution*, which simply defines the number of pixels across and up and down. For example, DV, the primary format used on digital camcorders, has a resolution of 720 pixels across and 480 pixels up and down, a resolution commonly referred to as 720x480. That's shown in the frame recording when Santa came a-calling in **Figure 3.1**.

As you can see in **Figure 3.2**, which shows a segment of the Movie Maker output screen, Movie Maker defines digital video files using four characteristics in addition to resolution, referred to as display size in the figure. Let's go through them.

THE JAN-FAQS

## File types

Movie Maker supports four file types to varying degrees. At a high level, a file type identifies the standard or protocol under which the file was created, which further defines which programs can edit and play the file. This sounds, and is, really technical, but fortunately you don't need to delve into file types too deeply because Windows and Movie Maker take care of them behind the scenes.

What *is* important to know is that Movie Maker can input and output Windows Media Video (files with a .wmv extension) and Audio Video Interleaved (.avi) files, both standards created by Microsoft. You'll primarily use WMV files for burning to CD-ROM, playing back from your hard drive, sending via email, or posting to a Web site. In contrast, when you capture video from your DV camcorder, you'll usually store it in an AVI file.

In addition to these two file types, Movie Maker can import many files created under the MPEG (Moving Pictures Experts Group) standard; these files have a variety of extensions, including .mpg, .m1v, and .mpeg. Movie Maker can't, however, output in MPEG format.

Movie Maker's inability to output MPEG files is significant because MPEG is the file type used in DVD production, which means that while you can use videos produced in Movie Maker in DVDs, you'll need a separate program, typically called an *authoring* program to actually create and burn the DVD.

Movie Maker can also import (but not output) files that use Active Streaming Format (ASF), an older Microsoft standard that's now infrequently used. Since Windows Media Video Format has completely superseded the ASF format, the inability to output in ASF format isn't a big deal.

Note that Movie Maker can't input or output Apple QuickTime files, which have the .mov extension.

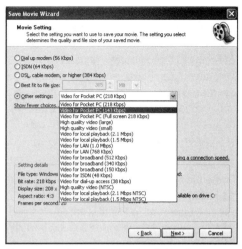

**Figure 3.3** Movie Maker uses wizards like these to shield you from technical details.

*16:9 display*

*4:3 display*

**Figure 3.4** Consider shooting and editing your DV in 16:9 mode if your TV looks like that on the top, but stick to 4:3 for most traditionally shaped TVs like that on the bottom.

# Bit rates

The bit rate is a measure of how much data is associated with *one second* of video. In Figure 3.2, you see the bit rate 1.7 Mbps. Mbps stands for megabits per second, which means that this digital video file has 1.7 megabits of data per second of video.

Bit rate is important because you typically want to tune the files you produce to suit the way the person watching the video will access them. For example, 1.7 Mbps is a fairly substantial bit rate, appropriate for files played back from a hard drive or CD-ROM drive. However, if you posted that file to a Web site to be played by viewers connecting via 28.8-Kbps or 56-Kbps (kilobits per second) modems, your viewers might feel as though the video file took forever to play. So when you're posting a file, one produced at a much lower bit rate, say 28 Kbps, is better.

Don't sweat it, however, because Movie Maker makes it very simple to assign a bit rate. Using the Save Movie wizard, shown in **Figure 3.3**, all you need to do is pick a device or connection, and Movie Maker will set the optimal bit rate.

# Aspect ratios

Aspect ratio is a much simpler concept than bit rate. Many camcorders support two aspect ratios for shooting: 4:3 and 16:9. The first, 4:3, is appropriate when shooting video for display on televisions that have a slightly rectangular viewing area—the traditional shape of many TV screens (**Figure 3.4**). If you have a widescreen television set, however, you can shoot, edit, and output in the 16:9 aspect ratio. Note that Movie Maker can produce movies in both 16:9 and 4:3 aspect ratios.

THE JAN-FAQS

## Frames per second

Frames per second (fps) is a measure of the number of frames per second that are stored in the digital video file and displayed during playback. The starting point is always 30 fps because the video you're capturing (in the US, anyway), adheres to the NTSC standard which has 30 frames per second. However, when you're producing files for the Web, Movie Maker may include fewer than 30 frames per second, usually 15 or fewer, because this improves the overall quality of the video. More on how frame rate impacts quality in the discussion of compression that follows.

So, what's the net/net on digital video? Any time you see a file on your computer, you should know that it has five characteristics that largely define it. These are file type, bit rate, resolution (display size), aspect ratio, and frames per second. So now when I discuss a Windows Media File produced at 320x240 resolution, 4:3 aspect ratio, 15 frames per second and an 800-Kbps bit rate, you'll know exactly what I'm talking about.

## What is video compression and how does it relate to file type?

Excellent question—glad you brought this up. Video compression, quite simply, is any technology that shrinks digital video files for storage or transmission. Video compression technology always includes two components: an encoder, which compresses the file, and a decoder, which decompresses and displays the file.

Because they are equal parts encoding and decoding, all compression technologies are also referred to as codecs, for code/decode, or compress/decompress, depending upon whom you ask. Pretty much any time you see video on the computer, it's compressed, since uncompressed digital video is too large to be easily stored or displayed on a computer.

Here's where it gets a touch complicated. Some file types, like WMV and MPEG, come with their own compression technologies. For this reason, all WMV files are compressed with Windows Media Video codecs, and all MPEG files are compressed with MPEG compression technologies.

However, the AVI file type supports multiple compression technologies, as does the QuickTime format. So if you see an AVI file sitting on your hard disk, it could actually be encoded using any number of supported compression technologies, including the DV format, which is the compression format used by most digital camcorders.

Movie Maker does a good job of shielding you from these details, and it's hard to imagine a scenario where the distinction between file type and codec will be important. Still, when you talk about WMV and MPEG, remember that they are both file types and compression technologies.

In contrast, AVI is strictly a file type that can use an assortment of codecs. If you are capturing from a DV camcorder, virtually every time you see an AVI file, it will use the DV codec, but this isn't exclusively true.

## Why do files on the Internet often look so bad?

All video compression technologies are *lossy* in nature. This means that they discard certain pixel-related information while they are being compressed, and they display a facsimile of the original image during decompression, but not the original image itself. This is exactly like the JPEG still-image technology used on most digital cameras.

However, digital cameras don't perform very much compression, so they can produce very high-quality images. Unfortunately, video files played over the Internet have to be compressed a great deal, or viewers will wait forever to watch them.

The key concept to remember with all lossy compression technologies is that the more you compress, the more information you lose and the worse the image looks. For example, the left side of **Figure 3.5** shows

the original JPEG image as captured by my brand-spanking-new Canon Digital Rebel (love that camera), which uses about 7:1 compression (compressing an image ordinarily about 18 MB in size down to about 2.6 MB). On the right is the same image, produced at about 60:1 compression, which absolutely destroys image quality.

This isn't to say that JPEG compression isn't a fine technology, since it's actually pretty competent. Rather, any time you compress an image or video file to a fraction of its original size with a lossy compression technology, quality is going to suffer.

To reduce the amount of compression applied to my videos, I reduce the resolution from 720x240 to 320x240 or less, and I reduce the frame rate from 30 to 15 fps. Still, at bit rates like 28 or 56 Kbps, the amount of compression required is still very significant, which is why most video distributed at modem speeds on the Internet looks pretty awful.

*Original Image (about 7:1 compression)*      *Highly compressed image (about 60:1)*

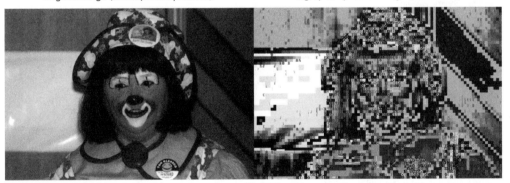

**Figure 3.5** The more you compress, the more you lose, with JPEG still-image technology and all video compression technologies.

## What about audio compression?

Another good question. While video gets all the headlines, audio compression generally accompanies video compression step by step. However, since audio files are much smaller than video files to start with, less compression is necessary. Still, rest assured that while you're choosing the output for your WMV files in Movie Maker, the program is compressing both audio and video.

## What is DV video and how does it differ from FireWire?

I've touched on this question, but let's bang the point home. DV is a codec, or compression technology. DV camcorders store video in DV format on those little matchbox-sized tapes, and then the DV files are transferred to the computer during capture.

FireWire is a data transfer technology used to send the DV files from camcorder to computer. It's also known as IEEE 1394, the Institute of Electrical and Electronic Engineers standard, and as i.LINK on Sony camcorders.

## What's nonlinear editing?

Ouch, now you're going for the throat! I'll do my best.

In the beginning, all analog tapes were edited on linear systems. Most linear systems involved at least four components: A, B, and C decks and the editing system itself (**Figure 3.6**). The A and B decks contained the source videos, and the C deck stored the edited video.

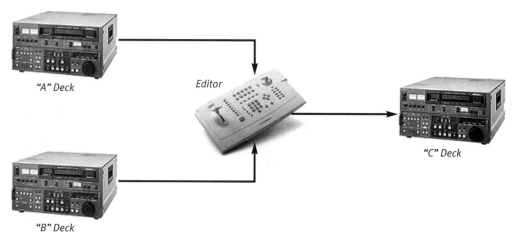

"A" Deck     Editor     "C" Deck

"B" Deck

**Figure 3.6** Profile of a linear editing system.

Imagine that you shot three sequences and later decided to cut the middle sequence. Using a linear editor, you would copy (or *dub* in video speak) the first sequence from the A deck to the C deck and then skip ahead to the start of the third sequence on the A deck and copy that to the C deck. To create a transition effect between two clips, you would place the source tapes on the A and B decks, run the video through the editing system, and store the result on deck C.

This process sounds complicated and expensive because it is. Worse than that, every edit results in another dub of the original source video. As when you photocopy a photocopy, this redubbing gradually reduces the quality of the video, producing what's commonly caused "generation loss."

In addition, because production is linear, each change requires you to start the process over. While the editing system can keep track of your edits, the only way to produce the finished tape smoothly is to start the process from the beginning and run the final tape again.

In contrast, all digital video editors, including Movie Maker, are *nonlinear*. This means that you can cut and paste bits and pieces of video as desired, just like you do with paragraphs in Microsoft Word, without any of the generation loss that comes with tape-to-tape copying, and without having to rebuild from scratch. If you find a spelling error in the closing credits, for example, you simply change the text, click the Render button, and walk away.

Basically, a nonlinear editor can do everything a linear editor can do, with the following advantages:

◆ Since your video is digital, once you capture it, you're done flipping tapes in and out, and you can use any captured video anywhere in the production, irrespective of where and when you shot it.

◆ Once your files are digital, no generation loss will occur when you apply effects.

◆ Since your project is nonlinear, and all your files are digital, changing details toward the end of the project is no big deal.

**THE JAN-FAQs**

## So what can I do using Movie Maker?

Now that you have some basic DV-related terms under your belt, we can move on to a more direct discussion of Movie Maker.

Movie Maker is a nonlinear editor. As with all editors, producing a video in Movie Maker involves basically three phases: importing, editing, and rendering and outputting (**Figure 3.7**).

**The import phase.** This phase involves bringing your source content into Movie Maker. Movie Maker can *capture* video from analog and digital camcorders, VHS decks, Web cameras, and other sources of video, or *import* assets already on your hard disks, assuming that it's one of the four supported file types (MPEG, AVI, WMV and ASF).

You can also import still images from your digital camera or scanner, and even images downloaded from the Web, into your video projects. Movie Maker will convert these to video when you're ready to render your project.

When you import video into a project, Movie Maker automatically adds any audio in that file to the production. You can also add audio from a number of different sources to supplement or replace the audio in the original file, and even create a narration track to add to the video.

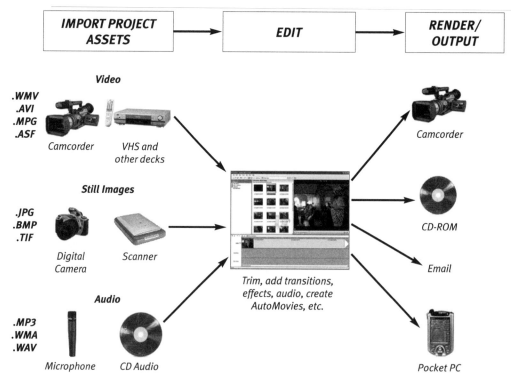

**Figure 3.7** Movie Maker's three-step workflow: import, edit, and render/output.

Note that while Movie Maker can't directly import audio from a CD-ROM, Microsoft's Windows Media Player can, producing files that you can then import into Movie Maker.

Note that Movie Maker imports all audio, video, and still image contents into their own *collections*, discussed later in this chapter in "Creating and Managing Collections." Once you start working with any piece of content, Movie Maker starts a *project*, where it stores information about the location of all content and the edits you've performed.

**The editing phase.** After you import all project assets, you can edit them—that is, you can cut, paste, and trim, omitting all segments you don't want in the final production. Then you can add transitions *between* videos or still images and add video effects and titles to all visual assets. Movie Maker has a special feature called AutoMovie that can combine your source video footage and a background audio track you've selected and automatically create a music video.

**The rendering and output phase.** When you're finished editing your project and consider it complete, the next step is to render it. Rendering is the process of implementing all the edit decisions you made in the project. Movie Maker starts with the source files you imported and pieces them together, then adds all the transitions, titles, and effects you selected during editing, and then produces what Movie Maker calls a *movie*.

From there, you can *output* the movie back to the camcorder so you can watch it on TV, or you can burn it on a CD-ROM, attach it to an email message, or produce a file you can post to a Web site. Note that Movie Maker can produce only two file types: Windows Media Video and AVI files (and only AVI files using the DV codec).

Note that like most nonlinear editors, Movie Maker is *nondestructive* (despite all those nasty rumors you've heard about Microsoft). This means that it does not edit, delete, or otherwise modify any of the files that you've imported into the project. Rather, during rendering, it reads the information from those files and uses that data to create a new file that incorporates all of your edits.

Note also that the project file does not actually contain copies of any of the audio, video, or still image content you've included in the project. This keeps the project files pretty small, but also means that you can't delete any of this content until after you output the final movie.

## What about producing DVDs?

As mentioned earlier, Movie Maker can't produce MPEG files and doesn't offer DVD authoring capabilities. You can, however, use files created in Movie Maker in a DVD project by exporting the videos from Movie Maker and then reimporting them into an authoring program like Sonic Solutions' MyDVD. Appendix A provides an overview of the process for producing DVDs with MyDVD 5.

If you're producing video for import into MyDVD or other authoring programs, it's best to output the file in AVI format using the DV codec. This preserves the quality of your video and provides a standard file type recognized by virtually all DVD authoring programs.

THE JAN-FAQS

# The Movie Maker Interface

The Movie Maker interface is where you'll spend virtually all of your time with the program. While you'll launch wizards for capturing your videos, described in Chapters 4 and 5, and for final output, described in Chapters 15 and 16, you'll perform all other import and edit work in this space. As you can see in **Figure 3.8**, there are four major windows.

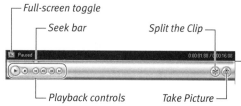

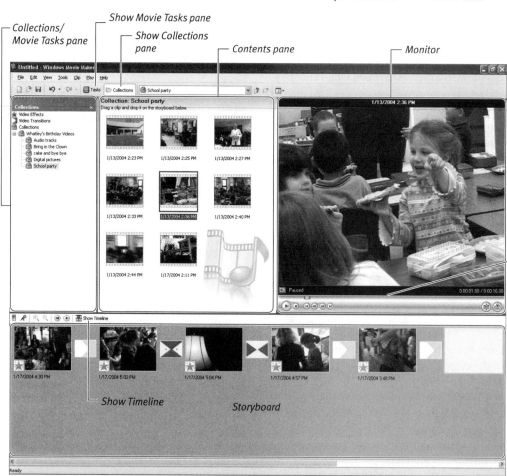

**Figure 3.8** Movie Maker's main interface.

**Figure 3.9** The Movie Tasks pane, a helpful tool for working your way through a project.

◆ **Collections/Movie Tasks pane:** This pane toggles between two views. Figure 3.8 shows the Collections pane, which lists collections of video, still image, and audio content, as well as transitions and other video effects. When you toggle to the Movie Tasks pane (**Figure 3.9**), Movie Maker displays a list of tasks commonly associated with video production, including capturing and importing, editing, and rendering the finished movie. To start any activity, you simply click on the task. This pane also provides tips for many of these activities. Note the controls shown in Figure 3.8 for switching between the Collections pane and the Movie Tasks pane.

◆ **Contents pane:** This pane displays the *clips* contained in the selected collection. If the selected collection contains videos, as shown in Figure 3.8, you'll see thumbnails of the various scenes in the video. If you select the Transitions collection, you'll see thumbnail images of the various transitions in the collection.

◆ **Monitor:** The Monitor serves a number of critical functions. First, click any *clip* in the Contents pane, and it appears in the Monitor. Second, when you're editing your project and want to preview your work, you'll see it in the Monitor window, which is why I'll probably slip up and call it the Preview window from time to time. During either operation, you can control viewing with the playback controls, pull the Seek bar to the desired frame, or toggle the view to full screen. At the bottom right of the Monitor, you'll also find controls for splitting a clip and for taking a picture.

THE MOVIE MAKER INTERFACE

◆ **Storyboard/Timeline:** This window also has two views, which you toggle with the control at the top of the window. Figure 3.8 shows Movie Maker with the Storyboard view displayed; this view shows each clip included in the project in a separate window. **Figure 3.10** shows the same clips in the Timeline, a longitudinal view that shows separate *tracks* for video, transitions, audio, audio/music (background music or narration), and title overlays (titles). Chapter 9 describes how to work in the Storyboard and Timeline.

## ✔ Tips

■ If you click the Show Collections button twice, the Contents pane will expand into the Collections/Movie Tasks pane **(Figure 3.11)**. Click either the Show Movie Tasks Pane or Show Collections Pane button to open either window.

■ Spend a few seconds toggling between the Movie Tasks pane and Collections views, and extend the Contents pane as described in the preceding tip. Once you do this once or twice, you'll stop yourself asking yourself, "Now where were those movie tasks?"

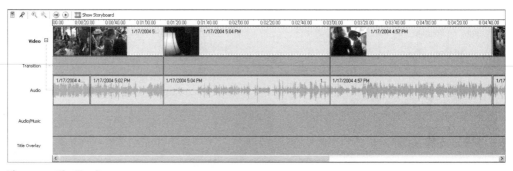

**Figure 3.10** The Timeline.

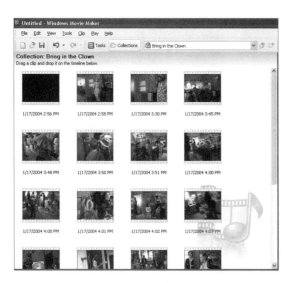

**Figure 3.11** You can expand the Contents pane over the Movie Tasks and Collections panes for more room.

## Other interface details

Let's spend a few moments examining other details of the Movie Maker interface. **Figure 3.12** shows the main toolbar at the top of the Movie Maker interface. The buttons on the left should be familiar to anyone who's worked in Word or any other Windows program; you click them to start a new project, open and save projects, and undo and redo actions.

Movie Maker stores your last 10 actions, which you can undo and then redo using the namesake buttons. For completeness, Figure 3.12 also shows the Show Movie Tasks Pane and Show Collections Pane buttons, which are described in the previous section.

Note the Choose Collection list box and the buttons it contains. You can use these to navigate through and select collections as an alternative to using the Collections pane. We'll explore these functions in the next section, "Creating and Managing Collections."

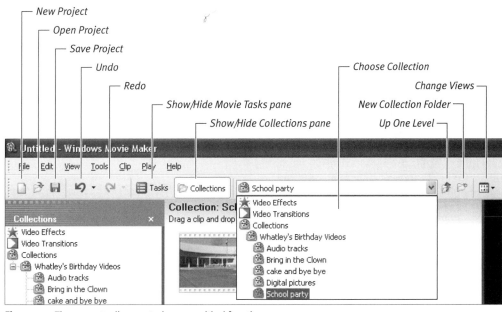

**Figure 3.12** The upper toolbar controls many critical functions.

# Creating and Managing Collections

Managing your collections is a major part of project management, so let's dive into it. Operations are a touch idiosyncratic, but easy enough to deal with once you understand what's going on.

From my perspective, project management is easiest when all collections related to your project are grouped together, as shown in **Figure 3.13**. This makes all of your project assets easy to find, and all of your collections easy to delete when you've finished the project.

Consolidating related assets and collections is simple when you import audio and still image assets because you can create and insert a collection anywhere in the collections tree, and Movie Maker will load the assets into that collection. In contrast, when you capture and import video, Movie Maker always creates a new collection, and that collection is always on the root of the collections tree. Not a huge deal, though—you can always rename the new collection as desired and drag it to any location in the tree, as you'll see in "To move a collection" later in this chapter.

I'll fully explore importing audio, video, and still image assets in their respective chapters. For now, here's a quick overview of the process so you can visualize the optimal project organization before getting started.

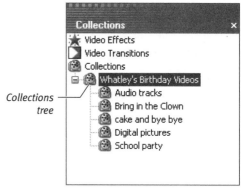

*Collections tree*

**Figure 3.13** The collections tree, where you organize all project collections.

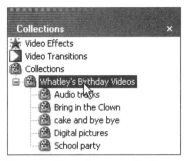

**Figure 3.14** To create a new collection, click the collection from which the new collection should branch.

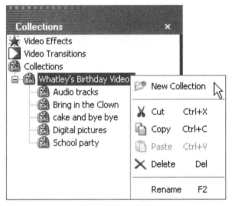

**Figure 3.15** Then right-click and choose New Collection.

**Figure 3.16** Movie Maker adds the new collection.

## To create a new collection:

1. Click the collections tree root or any collection (**Figure 3.14**).

2. Do *one of the following:*

   ▲ Right-click and choose New Collection (**Figure 3.15**).

   ▲ On the right side of the main toolbar, click the New Collection Folder button (see Figure 3.12).

   Movie Maker inserts a new collection titled New Collection (**Figure 3.16**).

3. While the New Collection name field is active, as shown in Figure 3.16, type a name for the collection.

## To rename a collection:

**1.** Do *one of the following:*

▲ Slowly click the collection twice.

▲ Click the collection; then right-click and choose Rename.

The collection name field becomes active (see Figure 3.16).

**2.** Type the desired name and press Enter on your keyboard.

Movie Maker renames the collection (**Figure 3.17**).

## ✔ Tip

■ You cannot rename the video effects, video transitions, or root collection on the collections tree.

## To import audio and still images into a collection:

**1.** Click the collection you wan to import into (**Figure 3.18**).

**2.** Do *one of the following:*

▲ From the main menu, choose File > Import into Collections (**Figure 3.19**).

▲ Press Ctrl+I.

Movie Maker opens the Import File window (**Figure 3.20**).

**3.** Select the audio and still image content to insert and click Import.

Movie Maker imports the audio and still images into that collection (**Figure 3.21**).

**Figure 3.17** You can then easily rename a collection.

**Figure 3.18** To import images or audio into a collection, select the collection.

**Figure 3.19** Then from the File menu, choose Import into Collections

**Figure 3.20** The Import File dialog box.

## ✔ Tips

- If you prefer, you can import content using commands in the Capture Video section of the Tasks pane (see Figure 3.9). To import content into a specific collection, first choose the collection using the Choose Collection list box (see Figure 3.12); then import the content.

- You can import additional still-image or audio content into an existing collection, so you don't have to start a new collection each time you import these types of content. In contrast, Movie Maker starts a new collection for each video file that you import.

- You can combine multiple video collections into one after capture or import by dragging the video files from each collection into the target collection.

- You can combine all three types of content in the same collection.

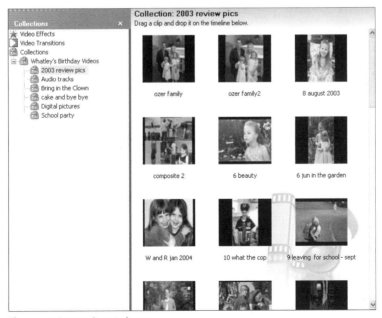

**Figure 3.21** Images inserted.

## To import video into a collection:

1. Do *one of the following:*

   ▲ From the main menu, choose
   File > Import into Collections
   (see Figure 3.19).

   ▲ Press Ctrl+I.

   Movie Maker opens the Import File
   window (**Figure 3.22**).

2. Select the video files to insert and
   click Import.

   Movie Maker imports the video file into
   a new collection on the root of the collections tree (**Figure 3.23**).

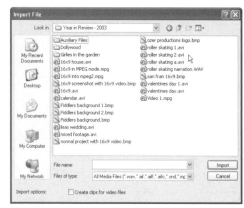

**Figure 3.22** Importing video also starts with the
Import File dialog.

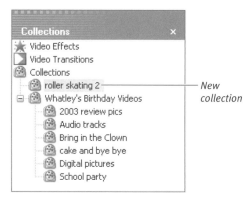

*New
collection*

**Figure 3.23** But all imported video
collections end up on the root of the
collections tree.

**Figure 3.24** Just select the new collection and drag it.

**Figure 3.25** Drag the collection to the target collection, which will become highlighted.

**Figure 3.26** Release the mouse button to drop the new collection in the existing one.

## To move a collection:

1. Click the collection to make it active (**Figure 3.24**).

2. Drag the collection to the target collection (**Figure 3.25**).

   Movie Maker highlights the target collection.

3. Release the mouse button.

   Movie Maker moves the collection to the new location (**Figure 3.26**).

## ✔ Tips

- You can import multiple video files simultaneously, and Movie Maker will create a separate collection for each video file.

- Movie Maker can split an imported video file into separate *clips* using a number of different techniques depending upon file type. This process is discussed in "Creating Clips in Video Files" in Chapter 8.

## To delete a collection:

1. Click the collection you want to delete.

2. Do *one of the following*:
   ▲ Right-click and choose Delete (**Figure 3.27**).
   ▲ Press the Delete key on your keyboard.
   ▲ From the main menu, choose Edit > Delete (**Figure 3.28**).
   Movie Maker deletes the collection.

### ✔ Tips

- Note that the assets remain untouched; Movie Maker simply removes any reference to the files in the Collections pane.

- If you delete a collection that has assets already used in the project, the assets are preserved in the project.

## To cut/copy and paste a collection:

1. Click the collection you want to cut, copy or paste.

2. Do *one of the following*:
   ▲ Right-click and choose Cut or Copy (**Figure 3.29**).
   ▲ Press Ctrl+X (Cut) or Ctrl+C (copy).
   ▲ From the main menu, choose Edit > Cut or Copy (**Figure 3.30**).

3. Click the new location (**Figure 3.31**).

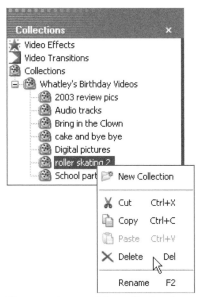

**Figure 3.27** You can delete collections by right-clicking and choosing Delete.

**Figure 3.28** You can also choose Delete from the Edit menu.

**Figure 3.29** Cut and Copy commands are accessible from the right-click menu.

Figure 3.30
Cut and Copy are also accessible from the Edit menu.

Figure 3.31 Click the new location.

Figure 3.32 Right-click and choose Paste.

4. Do *one of the following:*

▲ Right-click and choose Paste (**Figure 3.32**).

▲ Press Ctrl+V.

▲ From the Movie Maker menu, choose Edit > Paste.

Movie Maker pastes the collection into the new location (**Figure 3.33**). If you choose Copy, it leaves the original collection where it was; if you choose Cut, it deletes the original collection.

## ✔ Tip

■ Copying collections is useful when you frequently reuse the same project assets. In a business setting, for instance, if you use the same graphics and audio tracks in all productions, copying is an easy way to move those assets from project to project.

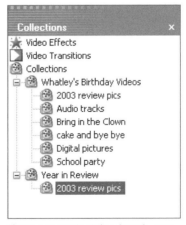

Figure 3.33 Movie Maker does the rest.

# Customizing Your Collection Views

After you import a still image or audio file into a collection, Movie Maker defaults to Thumbnails view, displaying each of these assets separately. For example, Figure 3.31 shows a collection of still images, each with its own thumbnail image.

In addition, when you import video into Movie Maker, you'll likely subdivide each video into separate clips using techniques discussed in "Creating Clips in Video Files" in Chapter 8. Once displayed in a collection, each clip will also have its own thumbnail image.

Though the thumbnails help, you're still confronted with multiple assets in each collection. Many times, particularly with video, it's helpful to rename clips in your collection so that you can find relevant clips more quickly during editing.

Movie Maker provides a Details view as well as a Thumbnails view, plus six different ways to sort content in each collection. All will be useful down the road when you're trying to find that one critical piece of content that will make or break your production.

### To rename content in the collection:

1. Do *one of the following:*
   ▲ Click the text beneath the thumbnail twice slowly.
   ▲ Click the thumbnail; then right-click and choose Rename.

   The text beneath the thumbnail becomes active (**Figure 3.34**).

2. Type the desired name and press Enter on your keyboard.

   Movie Maker renames the item (**Figure 3.35**).

**Figure 3.34** Renaming clips and other content makes them easy to find during editing.

**Figure 3.35** Clip renamed.

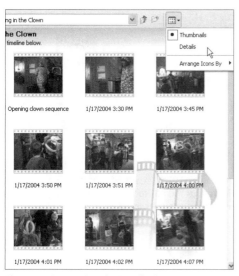

**Figure 3.36** Accessing the Details view.

## To switch between Thumbnails and Details views:

◆ On the main toolbar, click the Views button and choose Details (**Figure 3.36**).

Movie Maker switches to Details view (**Figure 3.37**).

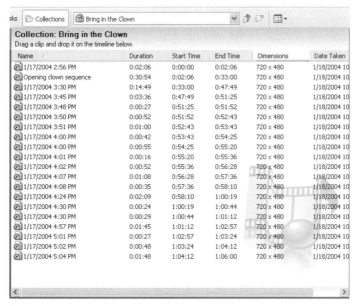

**Figure 3.37** Details view.

## To arrange icons in the collection:

1. On the main toolbar, click the Views button and choose Arrange Icons By (**Figure 3.38**).

2. Choose the desired parameter to arrange the icons.

   Movie Maker arranges the icons based upon the selected parameter.

## ✔ Tip

■ In Details view, you can sort items in a collection by clicking the title of the column you want to sort on. For example, **Figure 3.39** shows the 2003 Reviews Pics collection, which contains pictures of my daughters taken over the preceding year. To sort by Date Taken, click that heading; Movie Maker will display the images in chronological order, starting with the oldest (with the arrow pointing up). To reverse the order and display the newest first, click the heading again.

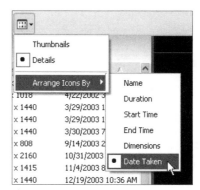

**Figure 3.38** You can sort collections using any of the parameters listed in this menu.

**Collection: 2003 review pics**
Drag a clip and drop it on the timeline below.

| Name | Duration | Start Time | End Time | Dimensions | Date Taken |
|---|---|---|---|---|---|
| ozer family | 0:00:00 | 0:00:00 | 0:00:00 | 950 x 1144 | 4/22/2002 3:54 PM |
| ozer family2 | 0:00:00 | 0:00:00 | 0:00:00 | 984 x 1018 | 4/22/2002 3:54 PM |
| 4 girliess with michell2 | 0:00:00 | 0:00:00 | 0:00:00 | 2160 x 1440 | 3/29/2003 10:10 PM |
| 4 girlies with Michelle | 0:00:00 | 0:00:00 | 0:00:00 | 2160 x 1440 | 3/29/2003 10:10 PM |
| 4 girlies in front of cake | 0:00:00 | 0:00:00 | 0:00:00 | 2160 x 1440 | 3/30/2003 7:28 PM |
| 6 beauty | 0:00:00 | 0:00:00 | 0:00:00 | 1212 x 808 | 9/14/2003 2:29 PM |
| 10 what the cop | 0:00:00 | 0:00:00 | 0:00:00 | 1440 x 2160 | 10/31/2003 4:21 PM |

**Figure 3.39** Or click any heading in Details view to sort based on that parameter.

**Figure 3.40**
Close a branch by clicking the minus sign.

**Figure 3.41**
Branch closed.

**Figure 3.42**
Click the plus sign to reopen a branch.

**Figure 3.43**
There's the branch again.

## To contract and expand branches on the collections tree:

1. To contract a branch, hiding it from view, click the minus sign to the left of the collection branch (**Figure 3.40**).

   Movie Maker contracts the branch (**Figure 3.41**).

2. To expand a branch, click the plus sign to the left of the collection branch (**Figure 3.42**).

   Movie Maker expands the branch (**Figure 3.43**).

### ✔ Tips

■ Unfortunately, there is no way to contract or expand all branches at once. Still, Movie Maker's branched collection view is a great feature that really simplifies working with complex or multiple projects.

■ Movie Maker sorts collections using numbers first and then letters. You can circumvent this approach by adding a space before the text in a collection name to bring it to the top of the list. As you would expect, multiple collections with spaces in front of the names are sorted first numerically and then alphabetically—so if you need to, you can add two or more spaces to make collection rise to the top, and so on, and so on.

CUSTOMIZING YOUR COLLECTION VIEWS

# Customizing Movie Maker's Panes

One of Movie Maker's unique strengths is a highly flexible interface that you can customize for every phase of production. For example, when you're working with your collections, you can expand the Collections pane to show as many clips as possible. When editing, you can expand or shrink the Storyboard or Timeline to better suit your needs, or expand the Monitor to display your video larger than life.

Here's how it works. All four windows are separated by a thin blue line. Simply hover your pointer over the blue line, and it turns into a two-headed pointer you can use to drag and either expand or shrink the window.

Let's start with the screen shown in **Figure 3.44**.

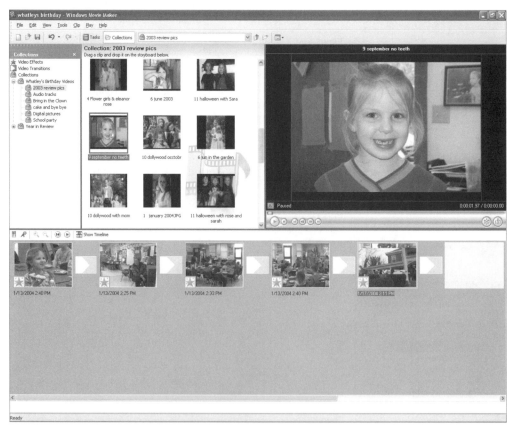

**Figure 3.44** Let's make the Contents pane larger so we can see more pictures.

*Drag pointer* ──

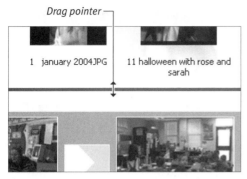

**Figure 3.45** Hover the pointer over the blue line separating each pane, and it sprouts another arrow, indicating you can drag the pane.

## To adjust window size:

1. Hover your mouse over the blue line separating the two windows you want to adjust (**Figure 3.45**).

   Your pointer changes to a two-headed arrow.

2. Drag the window to the appropriate size.

3. Repeat as desired.

   Movie Maker resizes the interface (**Figure 3.46**). Note that I expanded the Collections pane to the maximum by dragging it down and to the right. Note how this shrinks the Monitor but expands the number of thumbnails available in the Storyboard.

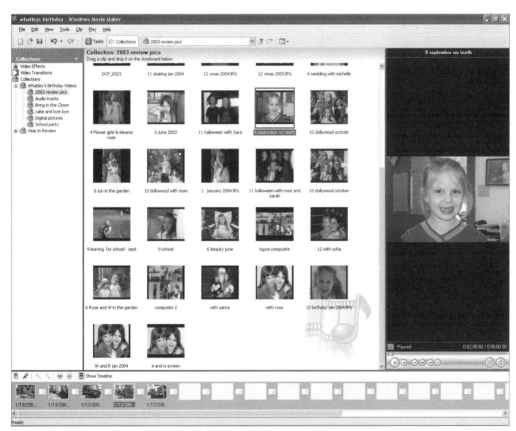

**Figure 3.46** Ah, much more space for seeing what's in the Contents pane and renaming the pictures as necessary.

# Setting Project Defaults

There are several project defaults you should set before getting started. Most important, from my perspective, is the location of the files created by Movie Maker when rendering your project. Like most Microsoft programs, Movie Maker likes to bury these somewhere deep in the Documents and Settings folder, where they're nearly impossible to find and delete.

I prefer to keep all project assets in one folder on my main video drive, so I'll show you how to change the default here; you then need to make sure you select the same drive during capture. I'll also show you several other housekeeping options to consider.

## To set general and advanced options:

1. From the main Movie Maker menu, choose Tools > Options.

   Movie Maker opens the Options dialog box open to the General tab (**Figure 3.47**).

2. Click the Browse button to change the Temporary Storage location.

   As you can see in Figure 3.47, I've already changed this to a folder on my F: drive that's named for the occasion. I'll capture and import all video and other assets into that folder, which makes them easy to find and either delete or reuse.

3. If desired, select the Open Last Project on Startup check box to have Movie Maker automatically open the project you last worked on when you again run Movie Maker.

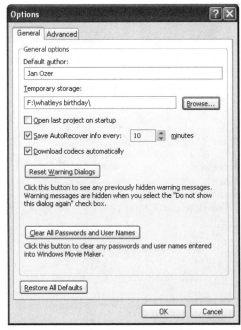

**Figure 3.47** General options for project defaults.

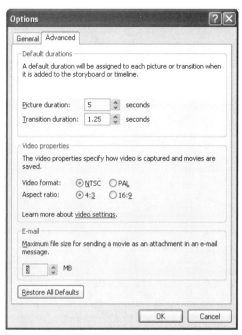

**Figure 3.48** Advanced options for project defaults.

**4.** If desired, select the Save AutoRecover Info Every check box and change the duration by using the arrow keys or directly entering a new duration.

Editing without AutoRecover turned on is like driving without a seatbelt. Do so at your own risk.

**5.** If desired, select the Download Codecs Automatically check box.

New codecs are often necessary to either display a file produced elsewhere or produce certain output files. I leave this checked.

**6.** If desired, click Reset Warning Dialogs to reveal any previously hidden messages.

This will re-enable any of Movie Maker's warning dialog boxes that you've disabled.

**7.** If desired, click Clear All Passwords and User Names.

When uploading files to a Web site, you can enter user names and passwords that Movie Maker retains for your convenience. Clicking this button clears this information so other computer users can't upload videos without reentering this data.

**8.** If desired, click Restore All Defaults to restore the General options to their original settings.

**9.** Click the Advanced tab in the Options dialog box to access advanced options (**Figure 3.48**).

*continues on next page*

SETTING PROJECT DEFAULTS

**10.** If desired, adjust the default durations for pictures and transitions by typing a new duration or adjusting the value using the arrow keys to the right.

These are default values applied to any picture or transition inserted into the project. You can adjust these values manually on the Timeline.

Note that if you change the default value for either pictures or transitions in mid project, the change is applied prospectively only. New pictures or transitions added to the project will use the new values, but Movie Maker will not change the duration for pictures or transitions already inserted into the project, even if they were inserted using the previous default duration.

**11.** If desired, change the Video Properties settings to the appropriate values.

In general, Movie Maker can ascertain these values from video captured or imported into the project. Changing these values to the incorrect settings will distort your video. For example, if you shoot your video at an aspect ratio of 4:3 and change the aspect ratio to 16:9, Movie Maker will squeeze the video vertically to make it fit (**Figure 3.49**).

I would leave these setting along unless you're sure they're wrong (for example, if you're shooting with a PAL camcorder and know it, and the format is set to NTSC) or if the video looks distorted upon output.

**12.** If desired, change the Maximum file size for email attachments by typing a new value, or adjusting the value using the arrow keys to the right.

Movie Maker uses this value to set encoding parameters for videos produced for distribution via email. Most Internet service providers (ISPs) have an attachment limit, usually in the range of 1 to 5 MB. If you try to send an email attachment larger than this limit, the ISP won't send it.

If you know the limit set by your ISP, adjust the value to that limit. Otherwise, leave this value at 1 MB.

**13.** If desired, click Restore All Defaults to restore Advanced options to their original settings.

### ✔ Tip

■ Once you change an option, Movie Maker retains the new setting in all subsequent new projects.

*4:3 original displayed at 4:3*          *4:3 original displayed at 16:9*

**Figure 3.49** You'd smile too if you could eat that much cookie without worrying about your waistline. On the left is the video as it should look; on the right, you can see the squeezed appearance the comes from displaying 4:3 video at 16:9.

# Part II: Gathering Your Assets

# Capturing DV

I've been a big fan of the digital video (DV) format since I acquired a DV camcorder back in 1996. Not only was the quality better than my Hi8 camcorder, capture was also much simpler. And since DV camcorders record the time and date of each shot, Windows Movie Maker can divide captured video into scenes, making it easier to find the clips to include in the project.

Just to get our terms straight, the term *video capture* was coined in the olden days, when transferring analog video from camcorder to computer required a "capture card" that converted the analog signal to digital and then compressed the video so it would fit on disk. Today, all that occurs on the DV camcorder, which stores the video on tape as a digital file rather than in analog format. This makes capture from a DV camcorder more like a file transfer; and some even refer to the process as a file import. Call it what you will, getting DV video from your camcorder to your computer is a snap.

The same cable that carries the DV video to your computer lets you control the camera, so you can start, stop, rewind, and fast-forward your DV camera within Movie Maker—a useful capability unavailable with most analog camcorders. All these factors make DV capture fast, painless, and highly functional.

# Connecting for DV Capture

Before setting up for DV capture, quickly review the section "Preparing Your Hard Disks" in Chapter 1.

I'm assuming that you have a FireWire connector or card installed in your computer. If you don't, start there, and make sure it's up and running. Don't spend too much money on the connector; for your purposes, virtually all cards will serve equally well, from the $19 variety on up, and they all plug into an available PCI card slot inside your PC. Choosing one with at least two ports will allow you to connect both your camcorder and a FireWire hard drive, if you need additional storage space for your captured video.

### To connect a camera and computer for DV capture:

1. Plug in your DV camcorder to AC power. Battery power should work, but it doesn't work with all cameras.

2. Make sure that the camcorder is in VCR, VTR, or Play mode.

3. Connect your FireWire cable to the camera's DV connector (**Figure 4.1**). Virtually all cameras use a tiny four-pin connector like that shown on the left side of **Figure 4.2**.

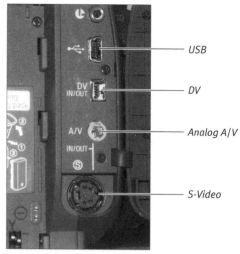

**Figure 4.1** The DV port on the Canon GL2 camera. Note the single analog A/V connector for composite video and both audio channels.

**Figure 4.2** A four-pin (on the left) to six-pin DV cable. DV cables also come with dual four-pin and dual six-pin connectors.

**Figure 4.3** The typical six-pin DV connector, which looks like either connector on the left, is found on most—but not all—computers.

4. Connect the FireWire cable to your computer using either of the FireWire connectors shown on the left in **Figure 4.3**, and using the larger six-pin connector shown on the right in Figure 4.2.

Note that while most computers use a six-pin port, some computers (like my Dell Latitude D800 laptop) use a four-pin connector identical to that in most cameras. So identify which connector your computer has *before* buying a cable, which comes in three varieties: four-pin to six-pin, four-pin to four-pin, and six-pin to six-pin.

You're now ready to run Windows Movie Maker and enter Capture mode.

✔ **Tip**

■ Speaking of buying a cable, basic FireWire cables are priced between $12 and $50, depending on brand and store. If you're buying, check out `www.cables.com`, which offers a complete line of FireWire cables at very reasonable prices.

## FireWire to the Rescue

FireWire technology was invented by Apple Computer and then standardized by the Institute of Electrical and Electronic Engineers as IEEE 1394. Sony's name for FireWire is i.LINK and companies refer to the connectors as FireWire, DV, or IEEE 1394. Whatever the name, they should work together seamlessly.

Some newer DV cameras, like the Canon GL2, have Universal Serial Bus (USB) ports to transfer still images from camera to computer, but USB can't transfer DV video—it can only transfer still images. To capture DV, ignore this connector (and the traditional analog connectors) and find the FireWire port.

**CONNECTING FOR DV CAPTURE**

## File System Format Limitations

Windows XP lets you format your hard disks using one of three file system formats: NTFS (Windows NT File System), FAT 32 (32-bit File Allocation Table), and FAT 16 (16-bit File Allocation Table).

Most systems purchased with XP installed use the NTFS file system, which is the fastest and most flexible. For example, although you can capture files of any size using files formatted with NTFS (up to the capacity of the disk itself, of course), FAT 16 disks can't capture files larger than 2 GB (about 9-1/2 minutes of video), and FAT 32 formatted disks are limited to 4 GB (about 18 minutes).

The only way to change the file system is to delete all the data on your hard disk and reformat the disk, a definite pain when the disk is your system drive (usually C). However, if you purchase a second disk drive just for video, which is highly advised, be sure to format it using the NTFS file system.

To determine the file system format used for a particular hard disk, select the disk in Windows Explorer, right-click, and choose Properties. This will open the dialog shown in **Figure 4.4**.

To format any disk other than your system disk with NTFS, select the disk in Windows Explorer, right-click, and choose Format, which will open the Format Video Disk dialog (**Figure 4.5**). Remember: do this only if you're ready to delete all the data on the drive.

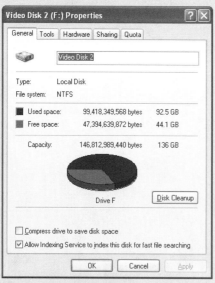

**Figure 4.4** The Video Disk Properties dialog identifies the file system used on that disk.

**Figure 4.5** Here's how you format your hard disks. Note that formatting deletes all data on the disk.

# Time Code: What You Need to Know

As you shoot, your DV camcorder stamps each frame with a sequential time code that looks like this:

`01:02:03.04`

Here's what it stands for:

*Hours:minutes:seconds.frames*

Time code enables your DV camcorder and programs like Movie Maker to locate and access any particular frame on the DV tape.

Note that DV tapes don't come with time code embedded; these codes are stored on the tape by the camera as you shoot. Ideally, time code is consecutive from start to finish, so each frame is unique. If there is a break in time code, the camera starts counting again at 00:00:00.01, which means duplicate time codes and potential confusion.

Breaks can occur, for example, when you watch video that you've recorded and play past the end point of the recorded video. If you start recording anew from that point, the camera restarts the time code from the beginning.

Movie Maker handles time code breaks fairly well, but other programs don't—especially higher-end programs that use continuous time code for features like batch capture. For this reason, it's good practice to maintain a continuous time code on each recorded tape. You can accomplish this in one of two ways:

◆ Put each tape in your DV camcorder with the lens cap on and record from start to finish. Then rewind and start your normal shooting, which will overwrite the previously recorded frames but maintain the time code structure.

◆ Whenever you film with your DV camcorder, be sure you don't start beyond the last previously written time code segment. This will be apparent if you see nothing but lines in the time code field.

# Capturing DV

DV capture is a simple, wizard-driven operation that is slightly different depending upon whether you're capturing the entire tape or just bits and pieces from a tape. Let's examine both scenarios, starting with capturing the entire tape.

### To capture an entire DV tape:

1. Do *one of the following*:
   - ▲ In the Movie Tasks pane, click Capture from Video Device (**Figure 4.6**).
   - ▲ From the main menu, choose File > Capture Video (**Figure 4.7**).
   - ▲ Press Ctrl+R.

   Movie Maker opens the Video Capture wizard (**Figure 4.8**).

   Note that if Movie Maker can't detect the camera, you'll see the error message displayed in **Figure 4.9**.

2. Enter a file name for the captured video file or use the name assigned by Movie Maker.

**Figure 4.6** Start the capture process here...

**Figure 4.7** ...or here.

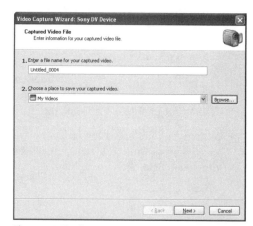

**Figure 4.8** The first pane of the Video Capture wizard. I find life easier when I place all captured videos in a folder on the root in my capture drive.

**Figure 4.9** Here's what you see if your camcorder isn't turned on or the cable isn't connected.

CAPTURING DV

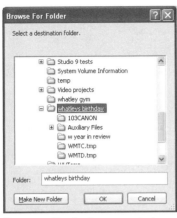

**Figure 4.10** Here's where you select a different capture folder.

3. Either accept the default storage location for the video or click the Browse button to select another folder (**Figure 4.10**).

4. Click Next to advance to the next screen. The wizard displays the Video Setting pane (**Figure 4.11**).

5. Select the video setting you want to use (see the "Capture Format Strategies" sidebar later in this chapter for more information).

6. Click Next to advance to the next screen. The wizard displays the Capture Method pane (**Figure 4.12**).

7. Check the Capture the Entire Tape Automatically check box.

8. If desired, click the Show Preview During Capture check box.

   Enabling the preview will affect performance only on slower computers (like Pentium III and slower computers). If you have a Pentium 4 computer, you should be able to preview and capture without difficulty.

*continues on next page*

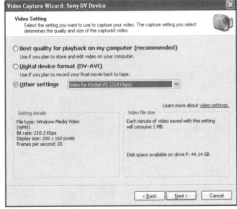

**Figure 4.11** The second pane of the Video Capture wizard, where you choose your capture format and other settings.

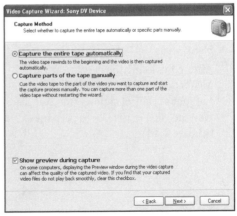

**Figure 4.12** Here's the jumping off point between capturing the entire tape or just bits and pieces.

**9.** Click Next to advance to the next pane.

The wizard advances to the DV Capture in Progress pane and begins automatically rewinding and capturing the entire tape (**Figure 4.13**). You can stop the capture process at any time, and Movie Maker will open the dialog box shown in **Figure 4.14**. As you can see, you can elect to store the video captured up to that point and stop the capture, or resume capturing the entire tape.

**10.** If desired, select the Create Clips When Wizard Finishes option (Figure 4.13).

If you check this option, Movie Maker breaks the captured file into separate clips based upon time codes on the DV tape. If there are no time stamps, Movie Maker will split the file into clips by identifying significant changes in content from frame to frame.

One of the great things about Movie Maker is that unlike other similar programs, you can still capture an entire DV tape automatically even when you have tapes containing breaks in the time codes or with significant unused portions toward the end. With other programs, you might be forced to capture manually (as described in the next task), but Movie Maker can automatically capture the recorded content and ignore any blank areas.

After completing the capture, Movie Maker will create a new collection on the root of the collections tree and display the clips in the Contents pane (**Figure 4.15**).

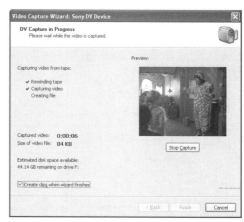

**Figure 4.13** Movie Maker capturing the entire tape. Note the Create Clips When Wizard Finishes check box, which tells Movie Maker to detect different scenes in the video and present each scene as a separate clip in the Contents pane.

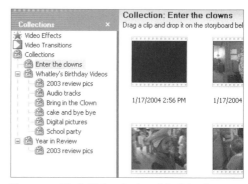

**Figure 4.14** Movie Maker displays this dialog box when you stop the capture process.

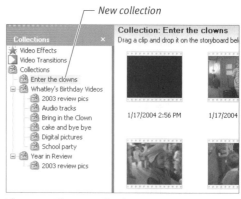

**Figure 4.15** The new collection.

CAPTURING DV

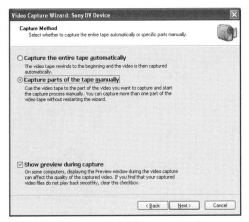

**Figure 4.16** Select the option here to manually capture sections of the tape.

## To manually capture parts of a DV tape:

1. Do *one of the following:*
   ▲ In the Movie Tasks pane, click Capture from Video Device (Figure 4.6).
   ▲ From the Movie Maker menu, choose File > Capture Video (Figure 4.7).
   ▲ Press Ctrl+R.
   Movie Maker opens the Video Capture wizard (Figure 4.8).
   If Movie Maker can't detect the camera, you'll see the error message displayed in Figure 4.9.

2. Enter a file name for the captured video file or use the name assigned by Movie Maker.

3. Either accept the default storage location for the video or click the Browse button to select another folder (Figure 4.10).

4. Click Next to advance to the next menu.
   Movie Maker displays the Video Setting screen (Figure 4.11).

5. Select the video setting you want (see the "Capture Format Strategies" sidebar later in this chapter for more information).

6. Click Next to advance to the next menu.
   Movie Maker displays the wizard's Capture Method screen (**Figure 4.16**).

7. Check the Capture Parts of the Tape Manually check box.

*continues on next page*

**CAPTURING DV**

**8.** If desired, click the Show Preview During Capture check box.

If your computer is older, it may not be fast enough to capture and store the video and update the Preview window at the same time, which usually means it will drop frames during capture, which degrades the quality of the captured video.

That's because when Movie Maker drops frames, it has to duplicate frames to make up the difference. For example, if during capture, Movie Maker captured frames 1,2,3 and 4, but dropped 5, 6 and 7, it would repeat frame 4 three extra times, which looks very jerky during playback.

**9.** Click Next.

Movie Maker opens the Capture Video screen (**Figure 4.17**).

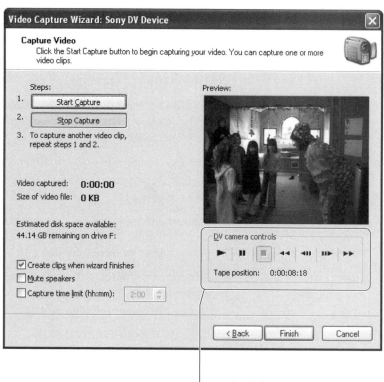

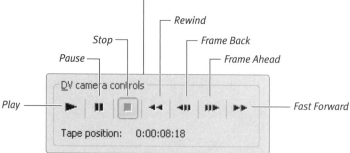

**Figure 4.17** The manual capture screen. Use the playback controls to move to the first frame you want captured and click Start Capture.

Figure 4.18 Click Stop Capture to stop the capture, and repeat the process as desired.

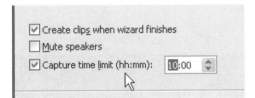

Figure 4.19 Setting the time limit for capture lets you start the capture and then walk away.

10. Use the DV camera controls to cue the video to the initial frame to be captured and to pause the tape.

11. Click Start Capture.

Movie Maker starts playing the DV tape and starts capturing.

12. Click Stop Capture to stop the capture (**Figure 4.18**).

13. Repeat Steps 10 through 12 until you've captured all the clips you want from that tape.

14. If desired, click the Create Clips When Wizard Finishes option.

If you select this option, Movie Maker will break the captured file into separate clips based upon time codes on the DV tape. If there are no time stamps, Movie Maker will split the file into clips by identifying significant changes in content from frame to frame.

15. If desired, click the Mute Speakers check box to mute the audio during capture.

16. If desired, click the Capture Time Limit check box and set the duration to the desired value (**Figure 4.19**).

Movie Maker will capture video for the selected duration for all subsequent captures while this check box is enabled.

After completing the captures, Movie Maker will create a new collection in the root of the collections tree and display the clips in the Contents pane (Figure 4.15).

# Viewing Your Captured Video

If you're like me, the first thing you want to do after capturing is watch the video. Fortunately, Movie Maker makes this extremely easy.

### To view your captured video:

1. In the Contents pane, do *one of the following*:

   ▲ Double-click the clip you want to play.

   ▲ Click the clip and use playback controls in the Monitor to start playback (**Figure 4.20**).

   Movie Maker plays the selected clip.

2. Use the controls beneath the Monitor to stop, go back to the start, jump to the end, or move through the video frame by frame.

### ✔ Tip

■ If you captured your video using scene detection and the Contents pane contains multiple clips, the Monitor stops playing at the end of each clip. To jump to the next clip, press the right arrow key. To start and stop playback, press the spacebar—one of Movie Maker's most valuable keyboard shortcuts.

**Figure 4.20** Quite a flair for the dramatic, eh? Click the clip you want to play and use controls in the Monitor to start and stop playback.

## Capture Format Strategies

When it comes to capture format, Movie Maker provides two options: Windows Media Video (WMV) and AVI using the DV codec. Which should you use?

Well, if you're ultimately outputting the video back to your DV camera, the choice is obvious, you have to capture, edit, and output in DV.

Otherwise, the optimal format depends upon your ultimate goal for the video. If you plan to include the video in a DVD or some other high-quality output format, I would capture and edit in DV format.

In addition, if you intend to edit the video extensively, using lots of titles, transitions and special effects, I would also capture in DV format, even if you're ultimately outputting at much lower resolution. Capturing in DV introduces the best-quality footage into the editing process, which produces the best possible output.

On the other hand, if you are capturing for immediate playback with minimal editing, I would capture using the setting appropriate for the distribution medium you'll use. That is, if you're capturing for output to a Pocket PC with no editing, by all means use that preset.

I would almost never choose Best Quality for Playback on my Computer, the capture setting recommended by Microsoft. This captures video at 320x240 resolution, which will look postage-stamp-sized on most bigger monitors. If I were capturing for immediate playback on my computer and hard disk space wasn't an issue, I would use the High Quality Video preset (**Figure 4.21**), which, as shown in **Figure 4.22,** captures at 640x480 resolution, 30 frames per second.

If disk space is an issue, try the Video for Local Playback preset (**Figure 4.23**), which captures at 14 MB per minute, storing about 70 minutes of video per gigabyte of disk space.

For other uses, scan through the presets and choose the most suitable option.

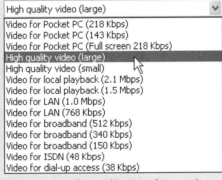

**Figure 4.21** I would use this preset for capturing video for immediate playback, but only if disk space wasn't a concern.

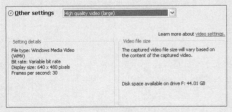

**Figure 4.22** Note the resolution and bit rate information.

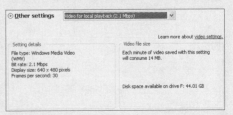

**Figure 4.23** If disk space were at a premium, I would use this preset.

# CAPTURING ANALOG VIDEO

Capturing analog video using Movie Maker is a little more complicated than using Movie Maker to capture DV, mainly because you may need to fine-tune certain input settings, such as the brightness or color of the incoming video.

In addition, while DV capture interfaces are relatively standard among different cameras and FireWire devices, analog capture devices and their software interfaces can be as different as snowflakes. So although Microsoft has attempted to present a standard approach for analog capture in Movie Maker, each capture device has unique elements, making it impossible to document the differences between the various devices. That said, most capture devices use a core set of similar controls, so what I show in this chapter should be a great start toward identifying similar controls on your own capture device. Use this chapter as a guide, and consult the manual or Help files that came with your analog capture card for fine-tuning.

In this chapter, we'll use Movie Maker to capture video from a camcorder and live video feed from a Web camera (Web cam).

# Connecting for Analog Capture

Although not quite as simple as setting up for DV capture, connecting for analog capture is pretty easy if you can follow color codes and fit square pegs into square holes (metaphorically speaking, of course). Before setting up for analog capture, quickly review the section "Preparing Your Hard Disks" in Chapter 1.

### To connect a camera and computer for analog capture:

1. Plug in your analog camcorder to AC power.

   (Battery power should work, but it doesn't always with some cameras.)

2. Make sure the camcorder is in VCR, VTR, or Play mode.

3. Connect your video cables to the camera by doing *one of the following* (**Figure 5.1**):

   ▲ If both your camera and analog capture device have S-Video connectors and you have the necessary cable (**Figure 5.2**), use the S-Video connector.

   ▲ If S-Video is not available and your analog camera or deck has a separate composite video port (Figure 5.1), use a cable like the one shown in **Figure 5.3**. In most instances, composite video connectors are yellow, and most three-headed cables are coded yellow (composite video), red (right audio), and white (left audio and mono audio). Follow the color coding at both ends and you'll speed installation.

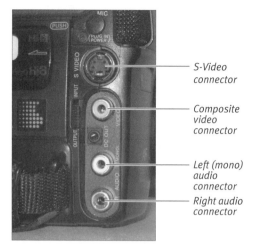

S-Video connector

Composite video connector

Left (mono) audio connector

Right audio connector

**Figure 5.1** The business end of my venerable Sony Hi8 camcorder has separate outputs for S-Video and composite analog video as well as stereo audio.

**Figure 5.2** An S-Video cable. Use S-Video whenever it's available, because you'll definitely get higher quality than with composite video.

**Figure 5.3** The typical three-headed analog cable with separate RCA connectors, for composite video and left and right audio. Fortunately, most are color-coded to help you make proper connections.

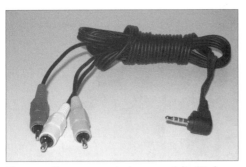

**Figure 5.4** If your camcorder has a specialty AV plug like that of the Canon GL2 shown in Figure 4.1 you'll need a specialty cable. Note the three rings on the single connector: one for each of the three outputs.

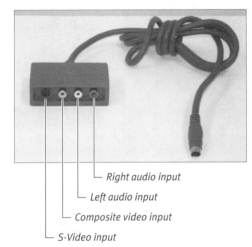

— Right audio input

— Left audio input

— Composite video input

— S-Video input

**Figure 5.5** The breakout box for the ATI All-in-Wonder graphics card. This accepts analog inputs; another cable (not shown) accepts outputs for writing back to tape.

▲ If S-Video is not available and your camera has a specialty A/V port (see Figure 4.1 in Chapter 4), you should have received a specialty cable that looks like that shown in **Figure 5.4**. Plug the single end into your camera.

**4.** Connect your audio cables to the camera by doing *one of the following:*

▲ If your camera has separate audio connectors (see Figure 5.1), connect a cable like that shown in Figure 5.3, being careful to match the colors of the connectors and output ports when applicable.

▲ If your camera has a specialty A/V port, you should have a specialty cable that looks like the one in Figure 5.4. Plug the single end into your camera.

**5.** Connect your video cable to the capture card in your computer.

Most capture cards have input ports and output ports. For example, the ATI All-In-Wonder 9000 PRO card installed in my HP Workstation xw4100 uses a separate breakout box for analog input with ports for S-Video and composite video and right and left audio (**Figure 5.5**). Note that the All-In-Wonder uses a separate port and cable for outputting productions back to analog tape. If you see two sets of analog connectors, either in a breakout box like the All-In-Wonder or on the bracket that's attached to the capture card itself (and is accessible on the back of the computer), check the product's documentation to determine which connector is input and which is output.

*continues on next page*

**CONNECTING FOR ANALOG CAPTURE**

**6.** Connect your audio cables to the computer by doing *one of the following:*

▲ If your analog capture card has separate audio inputs, use the audio input on your capture card.

▲ If your analog capture card doesn't have separate audio inputs, use your sound card's line-in connector (**Figure 5.6**).

Most computers have stereo audio inputs (Figure 5.6) rather than separate RCA connectors (Figures 5.3 and 5.4). To convert RCA inputs into stereo audio inputs, you'll need a Y-connector like the one shown in **Figure 5.7**, or a similar adapter. You can pick these up at Radio Shack or on the Web at www.cables.com.

You're now ready to run Movie Maker, set the proper software options, and start capturing.

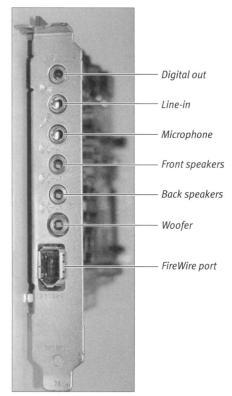

Digital out

Line-in

Microphone

Front speakers

Back speakers

Woofer

FireWire port

**Figure 5.6** The business end of a Creative Labs Audigy sound card. Use the line-in connector, not the microphone, for your analog input.

**Figure 5.7** A Y-connector converts the two RCA-type analog connectors to one stereo connector compatible with your sound card.

## Alternatives to Analog Capture

When capturing DV video, Movie Maker can store the video in DV format, a high-bandwidth, high-quality format ideal for high-quality editing and production. However, when capturing from analog sources, the only capture format is Windows Media Video, a more compact format that saves disk space but doesn't provide the same high quality as DV.

The quality difference between these two formats matters most when editing for output back to tape, which enables you to watch your videos on a television set, and when producing video for DVDs. If these are your goals, before buying an analog capture device, consider these three alternatives that allow you to capture and edit in DV format.

**Alternative 1:** Convert to DV first with your DV camera. Most mid- and higher-end DV cameras can convert analog footage to DV. To start, you connect the analog outputs from the analog camera to the analog inputs on the DV camera and then configure the DV camera to accept analog input. To actually record, you press Play on the analog device and Record on the DV camera. Once your footage is captured to DV tape, you can capture the DV tape to disk as described in Chapter 4. Note that first converting your VHS tape to DV also creates a more durable archival copy of your video than the one on the quickly eroding VHS tape you're probably currently using.

**Alternative 2:** Use your Digital 8 camera to convert 8mm and Hi8 tapes. Some (but not all) Digital 8 camcorders can convert analog tapes to DV format for capture. If you have a Digital 8 camcorder, check your documentation and see if you can output your analog tapes through the DV port.

**Alternative 3:** Buy a hardware device that converts analog video from your camcorder to DV format. In essence, these devices make your analog camera look like a DV camcorder to your computer, so you simply capture as described in Chapter 4. The only problem is cost; the Canopus ADVC-100 costs $299 (www.canopus.com), for instance, and the ADS Technologies PYRO A/V Link costs $199 (www.adstech.com).

CONNECTING FOR ANALOG CAPTURE

# Capturing Analog Video

When capturing DV video, Movie Maker can control the camera via FireWire, enabling a fully automatic capture mode. However, because analog camcorders and other analog video inputs don't offer similar controls over camera operation, all capture of analog video is manual.

In most instances, Movie Maker will capture high-quality video with no adjustments required. But if either the color or brightness of the captured video is sub-par, you may have to optimize the incoming video as discussed in "Tuning the Incoming Video Signal" later in this chapter.

When capturing from a new video source, which may be either a different analog tape or a different device altogether, it's best to capture a short segment and then immediately play the video back to make sure that the incoming audio and video quality is acceptable. If it is, go forth and conquer, and capture the rest of your segments. If it isn't, read "Tuning the Incoming Video Signal" later in this chapter.

### To capture analog video:

1. Do *one of the following:*
   ▲ In the Movie Tasks pane, click Capture from Video Device (**Figure 5.8**).
   ▲ From the Movie Maker menu, choose File > Capture Video (**Figure 5.9**).
   ▲ Press Ctrl+R.
   Movie Maker opens the Video Capture wizard (**Figure 5.10**).

**Figure 5.8** Start the capture process here.

**Figure 5.9** Or you can start the capture process here.

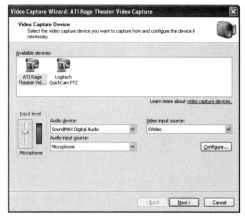

**Figure 5.10** This is what you see when you have multiple capture devices. Click the desired capture device with your pointer.

**Figure 5.11** Then choose the target audio device.

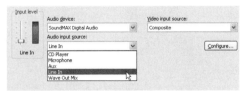

**Figure 5.12** Choose the appropriate input source.

**Figure 5.13** Then choose your video input source. Choose S-Video over composite if it's available.

**Figure 5.14** Then adjust the incoming audio so that the signal hovers around the 75-percent mark.

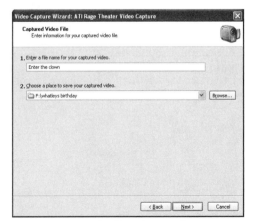

**Figure 5.15** Naming the file and storage location. I always like a central storage location for all project assets in an easy-to-find folder on my video capture drive.

**2.** If there are multiple available devices, click the desired capture device with your pointer.

In this example, I'll capture from my camcorder using the Rage Theater Video, which is the software for All-in-Wonder. Later in this chapter, in "Capturing Live Video," I'll use the Logitech QuickCam.

**3.** From the Audio Device drop-down list, choose the appropriate device (**Figure 5.11**).

Your choices again will vary depending on the capture device you use. For capture devices that don't support analog input, you may need to use the system sound card.

**4.** In the Audio Input Source drop-down list, choose the appropriate source (**Figure 5.12**).

Typically, when capturing from a system sound card, this will be Line In.

**5.** In the Video Input Source drop-down list, choose the appropriate input (**Figure 5.13**).

When available, always use S-Video, since it delivers a higher quality video stream than composite input, optimizing the quality of your captured video.

**6.** Press play on your camcorder to start playback, and adjust the audio input level so that the audio meter occasionally reaches into the yellow bar but never into the red (**Figure 5.14**). Be sure to test both high- and low-volume regions of the clip.

**7.** Click Next to advance to the next screen of the wizard.

Movie Maker displays the Captured Video File screen (**Figure 5.15**).

*continues on next page*

**CAPTURING ANALOG VIDEO**

**8.** Enter a file name for the captured video file or use the name assigned by Movie Maker.

**9.** Either accept the default storage location for the video or click the Browse button and select another folder.

**10.** Click Next to advance to the next screen. Movie Maker displays the wizard's Video Setting window (**Figure 5.16**).

**11.** Select the video setting you want to use (see the "Capture Format Strategies" sidebar later in this chapter for more information).

**12.** Click Next to advance to the next screen. Movie Maker opens the Capture Video window.

**13.** Use the camera playback controls to cue the video to approximately 20 seconds before the initial frame you want to capture.

**14.** Press Play on your camcorder to start the video playing.

At this point, you should see video playing in the Preview window (**Figure 5.17**). If you don't, something is wrong with your setup. Check your cables first to make sure they're connected to the right input and outputs and then check your capture card's documentation to make sure that it is properly installed.

**Figure 5.16** If I'm capturing to edit the video, I'll always go with the High Quality Video (Large) setting, since it offers the best quality that Movie Maker can produce.

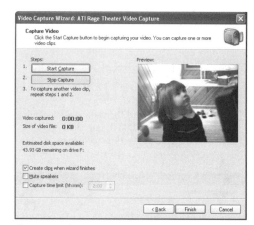

**Figure 5.17** The Capture Video screen ready to capture. Click Start Capture to start capture.

CAPTURING ANALOG VIDEO

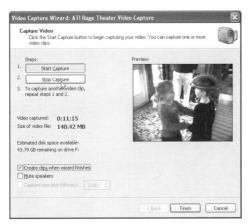

**Figure 5.18** Click Stop Capture to stop. When you're all done capturing, click Finish to exit the Video Capture wizard.

**15.** Watch the Preview window and click Start Capture approximately 10 to 15 seconds before you actually want capture to start.

Some capture devices take a few seconds to start capturing; so starting early ensures that you capture the desired frames and provides additional frames for fade-in and fade-out or for interscene transitions during editing.

**16.** Watch the Preview window and click Stop Capture approximately 10 to 15 seconds after the last target frame appears (**Figure 5.18**).

**17.** Repeat Steps 13 through 16 until you've captured all the target clips from that tape.

**18.** If desired, select Create Clips When Wizard Finishes (Figure 5.18).

If you select this option, Movie Maker will break the captured file into separate clips by identifying significant changes in content from frame to frame.

**19.** If desired, click the Mute Speakers check box to mute the audio during capture.

**20.** If desired, click the Capture Time Limit check box and adjust the duration to the desired value.

Movie Maker will capture video at the selected duration for all subsequent captures while the check box is enabled.

*continues on next page*

**21.** When you've finished capturing all scenes, click Finish on the bottom right.

After completing the captures, Movie Maker will create a new collection on the root of the collections tree and display the clips in the Contents pane (**Figure 5.19**).

### ✔ Tip

■ Hearing audio while you're capturing is no guarantee that the audio has been properly captured (and you may not hear it—I didn't using the All-in-Wonder capture card). Audio capture can fail for a number of reasons, so it's wise to be in the habit of playing back the first one or two files you capture to make sure that audio is present, and that the quality and volume are acceptable.

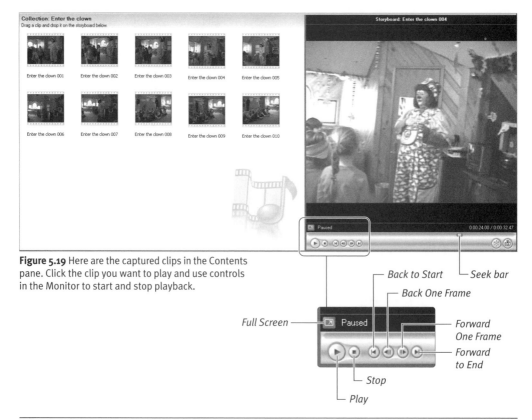

**Figure 5.19** Here are the captured clips in the Contents pane. Click the clip you want to play and use controls in the Monitor to start and stop playback.

Back to Start
Seek bar
Back One Frame
Full Screen
Forward One Frame
Forward to End
Stop
Play

# Viewing Your Captured Video

If you're like me, the first thing you want to do after capture is to watch the video. Fortunately, Movie Maker makes this extremely easy.

### To view your captured video:

1. In the Contents pane (Figure 5.19), do *one of the following:*

   ▲ Double-click the clip you want to play.

   ▲ Select the clip you want to play and use the playback controls in the Monitor to start playback.

   Movie Maker plays the selected clip.

2. Use the controls beneath the Monitor to stop, go back to the start, jump to the end, or move through the video frame by frame.

### ✔ Tip

■ If you captured using scene detection and the Contents pane contains multiple clips, the Monitor stops playing at the end of each clip. To jump to the next clip, press the right arrow key. To start and stop playback, press the spacebar— one of Movie Maker's most valuable keyboard shortcuts.

VIEWING YOUR CAPTURED VIDEO

# Tuning the Incoming Video Signal

Because DV video is digitized by the camera, video capture is a simple file transfer from camera to computer. In contrast, analog capture involves an analog-to-digital conversion, which is something like a negotiation between two parties speaking a common language with slightly different accents.

This is how it works. The analog camera outputs an analog signal that it perceives as representing reality, adjusting the brightness, color, and contrast accordingly. Then, using factory preset values, the analog capture card looks for and captures a signal that it perceives as representing reality. Seldom do the two realities match.

This is a long way of saying that if you're going to capture analog video, most of the time you will have to mess with the analog input controls to get the video looking right. I'll walk you through the controls used by the ATI All-in-Wonder 900 Pro, which will look similar, but not identical, to the analog configuration controls provided by other analog capture cards.

Note that the adjustment procedure is typically an iterative process that starts only if and when you have a problem. That is, first you notice a problem with your video, then you adjust the video, then you capture some more to make sure you fixed the problem, and then you continue to adjust until you get it right.

**Figure 5.20** Here's where you access the video adjustments.

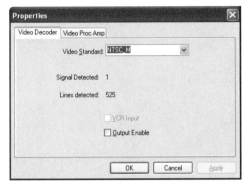

**Figure 5.21** Not much to do here; I'll jump to the Video Proc Amp in a moment.

**Figure 5.22** The Properties screen for different devices will look different, depending on the device you use, although it will usually include a core set of similar adjustments. (This screen reflects the properties of the Logitech QuickCam.)

## To adjust incoming video:

1. Do *one of the following:*
   - ▲ In the Movie Tasks pane, click Capture from Video Device (Figure 5.8).
   - ▲ From the Movie Maker menu, choose File > Capture Video (Figure 5.9).
   - ▲ Press Ctrl+R.

   Movie Maker opens the Video Capture wizard (Figure 5.10).

2. If there are multiple devices available, choose the desired capture device.

3. Click the Configure button beneath the Video Input Source menu (Figure 5.10).

   Movie Maker opens the Configure Video Capture Device dialog box (**Figure 5.20**).

4. Click the Camera Settings button to open the Properties screen (**Figure 5.21**).

   This screen will look different, depending on the analog capture device you use. For example, **Figure 5.22** shows the Properties screen for the Logitech QuickCam, which obviously is different from the screen in Figure 5.21. When tuning the incoming video, it's important to find the controls that adjust the brightness, contrast, and other characteristics. For the All-in-Wonder capture card, these controls are located on the Video Proc Amp tab.

   *continues on next page*

TUNING THE INCOMING VIDEO SIGNAL

**5.** At the top of the Properties screen, click the Proc Amp tab (Figure 5.21).

Movie Maker displays the video adjustment controls (**Figure 5.23**). Note that Movie Maker does not display video in the Monitor while you're adjusting the incoming parameters. For this reason, you have to modify the settings and attempt to correct the color or brightness issue and then advance to the Capture Video screen to preview the effect of your changes.

**6.** Adjust the controls as necessary.

It's always helpful to note the adjusted values used during correction so that you can re-create your results if necessary.

**7.** Click OK to close the Properties screen.

**8.** Click OK to close the Configure Video Capture Device screen (Figure 5.20).

The first screen of the Video Capture wizard should still be displayed (Figure 5.10).

**9.** Click Next to advance to the wizard's Captured Video File screen.

**10.** Click Next to advance to the Video Setting screen.

**11.** Click next to advance to the Capture Video screen.

**12.** Press Play on your camcorder to start the video playing. Watch the video in the Preview window to determine if the adjustments made in Step 6 have corrected the problems with the video. If so, proceed to capture; if not, repeat Steps 3 through 12 until the problem is resolved.

To be totally certain your adjustments are effective, you should capture some video and play it in the Monitor window. Sometimes, you can observe significant changes between the color and brightness during preview and the color and brightness of the actual captured video.

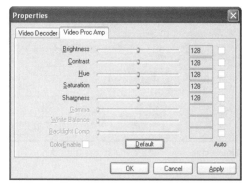

**Figure 5.23** Here's where I adjust the brightness and color for video captured with ATI's All-in-Wonder card.

TUNING THE INCOMING VIDEO SIGNAL

✔ **Tips**

■ While Movie Maker has good controls for adjusting clip brightness after capture, controls for adjusting color, hue, and saturation are minimal. This makes it very important that you correct any color imperfections during capture.

■ If you have radically different scenes on tape, you should adjust color and brightness for each scene.

## Capture Format Strategies

When capturing analog video, your only option is capture in Windows Media Video (WMV) format. Which setting should you use?

This depends upon your ultimate goal for the video. If you plan to include the video in a DVD or write it back to tape, use the High Quality Video (Large) setting (**Figure 5.24**). This introduces the best-quality footage into the editing process, which produces the best possible output.

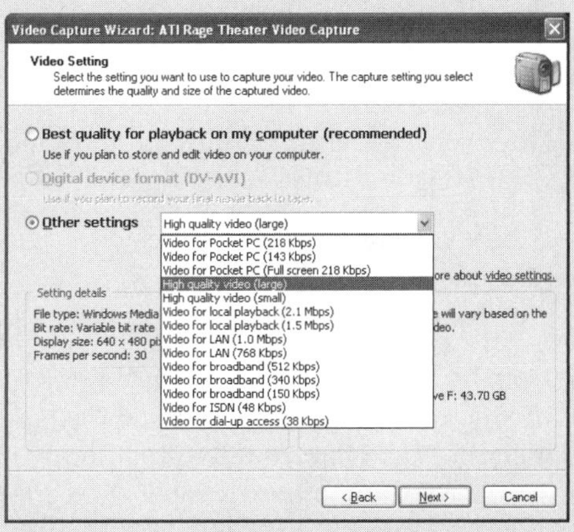

On the other hand, if you are capturing for immediate playback with minimal editing, I would capture using the setting appropriate for your target distribution medium. That is, if you're capturing for output to a Pocket PC with no editing, by all means use that preset.

I would almost never choose Best Quality for Playback on My Computer, the capture

**Figure 5.24** This is the setting I like when capturing to edit (as opposed to immediately distributing the video).

setting recommended by Microsoft. This captures video at 320 x 240 resolution, which will look postage-stamp-sized on most bigger monitors.

If you're capturing for immediate playback on your computer and hard disk space isn't an issue, use the High Quality Video preset. If disk space is an issue, use the Video for Local Playback preset (shown on the list of available presets in Figure 5.24), which captures at 14 MB per minute, storing about 70 minutes of video per gigabyte of disk space.

For other uses, scan through the presets and choose the most suitable option.

# Capturing Live Video

Capturing live is convenient for short videos, like those you might send via e-mail, where you don't want to take the time to tape and then capture. You can capture live from any device that can output an analog video signal, including DV cameras (connected via the analog outputs), analog cameras, and Web cameras (Web cams).

Here I'll capture a short video with the Logitech QuickCam orbit, a sexy stalk of a camera that captures both high-quality video and audio.

### To capture live video:

1. Do *one of the following:*

   ▲ In the Movie Tasks pane, click Capture from Video Device (Figure 5.8).

   ▲ From the Movie Maker menu, choose File > Capture Video (Figure 5.9).

   ▲ Press Ctrl+R.

   Movie Maker opens the Video Capture wizard (Figure 5.10).

2. If there are multiple devices available, click the desired capture device with your pointer (**Figure 5.25**).

3. From the Audio Device drop-down list, choose the appropriate device, and then from the Audio Input Source drop-down list, choose the appropriate input source. Adjust the input levels.

4. Click Next to advance to the next window.

   Movie Maker displays the Captured Video File screen (**Figure 5.26**).

5. Enter the file name and storage location.

**Figure 5.25** Let's capture some live video with the Logitech QuickCam Orbit. Choose the capture device and then the audio and video settings.

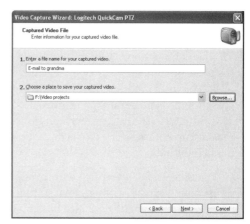

**Figure 5.26** Again, name the file and location.

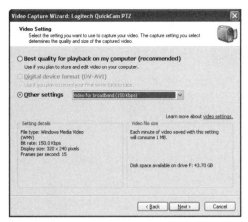

**Figure 5.27** This video is for e-mailing, so 1 MB for about 1 minute is about right.

**Figure 5.28** Here I am, surrounded by my dual muses: calendar on my right, BowFlex on my left. Which is it going to be tonight: deadlines or deltoids?

**6.** Click Next to advance to the next window. Movie Maker displays the Video Setting screen (**Figure 5.27**).

**7.** Select the video setting you want to use. There is no e-mail setting, but I'll use the Video for Broadband setting, so my 60-second message will be just a bit more than 1 MB in size.

**8.** Click Next to advance to the next window. Movie Maker opens the Capture Video screen (**Figure 5.28**). If you're capturing from a Web cam like I am here, you should see video right away. If you're capturing from a camcorder, place the camcorder in camera mode (or whichever mode you use for shooting video), and you should see video in the Preview window. If you don't, check the cables and then the documentation for your capture card. Note that you don't need to be recording to tape to make this work; you just need to be in camera mode so that the camcorder is sending a signal to the viewfinder and/or LCD panel and out the analog cables.

**9.** Get yourself arranged and click Start Capture when you're ready to begin.

**10.** When the live video is complete, click Stop Capture.

**11.** When you've finished capturing all scenes, click Finish at the bottom right. After completing the captures, Movie Maker will create a new collection on the root of the collections tree and display the clips in the Contents pane.

*continues on next page*

## ✔ Tips

- When recording live, make sure the camera is a reasonable distance from your face—at least four or five feet. Otherwise, the camera tends to distort the image, for example, exaggerating the size of your nose, eyes, and eyebrows.

- When recording live and compressing down to fairly low data rates, you'll get the best results with a clean background free of clutter. Avoid bookshelves, Venetian blinds, trees, plants, and finely detailed wallpaper, all of which have unnecessary detail that makes it hard for the Windows Media Video codecs to compress the video at high quality.

- Note that most camcorders timeout in camera mode if you don't start recording within a specified time, such as 5 minutes. If you can't find and disable this setting, you may have to press the Record button and record to tape to keep the camera going for the duration of the live capture. Then, of course, you can simply use the tape for something else.

# WORKING WITH STILL IMAGES

As much as I enjoy video, I often carry my digital still camera either as an adjunct to or instead of my DV camera. There are many reasons, most of them pretty obvious.

For example, I can't afford the digital flat panels that reportedly adorn the walls of Chez William Gates, so I need printed pictures to hide the cracks and peeling wallpaper. Second, as much as the grandparents enjoy videos of my kids, they also want printed photographs, now produced with my digital camera and either an Epson printer or a service like www.snapfish.com.

In addition, digital-image slide shows are easier to produce and often have the same impact as video, especially when adorned with background music, pan and scan motion, and narration. You can build slide shows in Movie Maker (see "Editing Still Images" in Chapter 9) or use Microsoft Plus! Photo Story (see Appendix B).

Those planning to use Movie Maker in combination with their digital still images need master only a few straightforward skills. The first is knowing how to grab a still image from a movie imported into Movie Maker. The second is knowing how to prepare a digital image for use in Movie Maker. This chapter shows you how to do both and then shows you how to scan images for use in Movie Maker.

# Capturing Still Images

Movie Maker makes it simple to grab still images from captured video, both from the Contents pane and the Timeline. After capture, Movie Maker inserts the image in the collection containing the source video and lets you save the actual file in any desired location on your hard disk.

One of the high points of my daughter Whatley's birthday party was near the end, when the clown created swords and helmets from balloons, converting the heretofore peaceful six-year-olds into a whirling mass of armed animosity. And this was *before* the sugar rush from the cake, candy, and Coca-Cola. Let's grab a picture of little sister Rosie attacking her defenseless mother.

For the purposes of this section, I'll assume that you've already captured the video and that it's sitting in a collection.

### To capture still images from the Contents pane:

**1.** Select the clip that contains the frame you want to use.

Movie Maker highlights the clip and displays the initial frame of the clip in the Monitor (**Figure 6.1**).

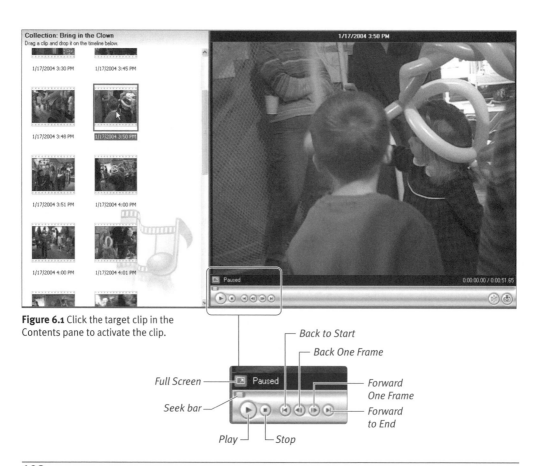

**Figure 6.1** Click the target clip in the Contents pane to activate the clip.

Full Screen
Seek bar
Play
Stop
Back to Start
Back One Frame
Forward One Frame
Forward to End

1/17/2004 3:50 PM

0:00:17.38 / 0:00:51.65

Take Picture

*Take Picture button* —

**Figure 6.2** Take THAT, mommy! Click the button to take a picture.

2. Use the Playback controls to advance to the target frame and pause the video.

3. At the bottom right corner of the Monitor, click the Take Picture button (**Figure 6.2**).

   Movie Maker grabs the frame and opens the Save Picture As dialog box.

4. Navigate to the storage location for the file.

5. Name the file as desired (**Figure 6.3**).

6. Click Save to save the file.

   Movie Maker saves the file and inserts the frame into the collection (**Figure 6.4**).

*continues on next page*

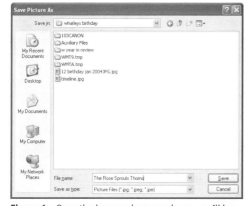

**Figure 6.3** Save the image where you know you'll be able to find it (your only format option is JPEG).

Collection: Bring in the Clown
Drag a clip and drop it on the timeline below.

1/17/2004 4:57 PM    1/17/2004 5:01 PM

1/17/2004 5:02 PM    1/17/2004 5:04 PM

1_17_2004 4_30 PM_0001    1_17_2004 3_50 PM_0001

— *New image*

The Rose Sprouts Thorns

**Figure 6.4** Movie Maker conveniently adds the grabbed frame to the collection.

CAPTURING STILL IMAGES

**109**

### ✔ Tips

- The resolution of the frame captured by Movie Maker depends upon the size of the original video and the source. If you grab the frame from the Contents pane, Movie Maker stores the image at the original resolution of the video file, up to 640x480. If you grab it from the Timeline, Movie Maker grabs the image at 320x240, irrespective of the actual resolution of the file.

- In all instances, Movie Maker stores the file in JPEG format.

## About Deinterlacing

Take a quick look at **Figure 6.5**. On the left, you should see horizontal lines that look like slices throughout the video, most noticeably on hard edges like the balloons and Rose's collar. On the right, these lines are pretty much gone.

*continues on next page*

**Figure 6.5** Those lines on the left are interlacing artifacts that most image editors can filter out, as PhotoImpact did on the right.

## About Deinterlacing *continued*

Que pasa? NTSC television uses what's called *interlacing* to present the smoothest possible video, which works like this. Rather than capturing at 30 frames per second, the camera captures 60 fields per second. Two fields together create one frame; so, in essence, 30 frames are still being captured. The first field in a frame contains all the odd lines (1, 3, 5, 7, and so on), while the second field in the frame contains all the even lines (2, 4, 6, 8, and so on). During playback, the television displays 60 fields per second, rather than 30 frames, so motion appears smoother on the television screen.

Interlacing works great on TV, but it can cause problems when you attempt to match two fields together to create a frame, which is what happens when Movie Maker grabs a frame. Specifically, if there is motion within the video, the two fields shot 1/60 of a second apart simply don't match up, producing the slicing artifacts you see on the left.

The answer? Most good image editors have a deinterlace filter like the one offered in Ulead's PhotoImpact image editor program (**Figure 6.6**), which I used to remove the lines from the image on the right in Figure 6.5. You won't see these slicing artifacts on every screen capture, but they're enough of a problem that if you plan to use lots of screen grabs, you need an image editor with an effective deinterlace filter.

Unfortunately, Movie Maker is one of the few programs that doesn't offer deinterlacing capabilities as part of its screen-grab function. If and when you move on to another video editor, you'll likely see this problem disappear.

**Figure 6.6** To get to the deinterlace filter in PhotoImpact, for instance, choose Effect from the main menu and then choose Video > DeInterlace.

# Editing Still Images

Okay. The question on the table is this: Your digital camera takes shots at a princely resolution of, say, 2160x1440 pixels. DV video resolution is 720x480, and Movie Maker can output video at a maximum resolution of 640x480. How do you resolve the difference?

To answer this question, let's first get a bird's-eye view of how Movie Maker works with still images; then we'll identify the optimal technique for preparing your images so that you can insert them into a Movie Maker project.

## How Movie Maker works with images

Movie Maker takes an admirably laissez-faire attitude toward images, basically displaying them as you place them in the movie. It does not try to fill the screen with your image, stretching it horizontally or vertically, or trim your image to fit; it simply adjusts your image larger or smaller to fit the screen without changing the aspect ratio. If this means that your image doesn't completely fill the frame, so be it. At least there's no distortion.

Movie Maker also provides good visual cues to help you predict what your image will look like when it's finally produced. Let's take a look at **Figure 6.7** to get a sense of how this works.

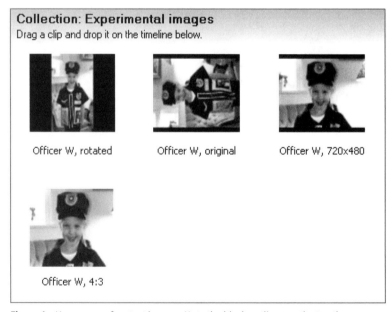

**Figure 6.7** Here are our four test images. Note the black outlines on the top three.

Officer W, Original, is the original 2160x1440-pixel image, shot by turning the camera to the side to capture a landscape view. Office W, Rotated, is the same image rotated 90 degrees to the left so that Whatley is standing straight up.

If you click Officer W, Rotated to preview the image in the Player, you see large areas of black to Whatley's left and right, which is precisely the way it would appear in the final DVD or video (**Figure 6.8**). This is Movie Maker's way of telling you that the image doesn't match the final resolution of your project, and Movie Maker is not going to squish or otherwise distort the video to make it appear full screen. Note that these same black areas show up in the Contents pane, providing the same message.

## Optimizing Officer W

The obvious question is what image resolution must you use to totally fill the Monitor window and eliminate those black bars? Since picture resolutions vary immensely among different cameras, the answer isn't a particular resolution, but a specific aspect ratio, which must be 4:3.

What this means is that for every 4 horizontal pixels, you must grab 3 vertical pixels. In the case of Officer W, Rotated, the capture resolution is 1400 pixels across and 1050 pixels high. If you divide 1400 by 4, you get 350. Multiply 350 by 3, and you get 1050.

**Figure 6.8** Movie Maker won't shrink or distort your image, but the black space on the left and right is wasted screen space.

It's a pain, but keep a calculator open on your desktop when you're grabbing still images. Once you find the optimal horizontal resolution for your images, divide by 4, multiply by 3, and you've calculated the ideal height. Or find an image editor like Ulead Systems' excellent PhotoImpact XL, which does the math for you (**Figure 6.9**). The little lock icon in the top tool panel constrains the Crop tool to the selected shape, Computer/TV (4:3).

The other obvious question is why you don't capture at an aspect ratio or 4:2.66, which is the aspect ratio for 720x480 pixels, the resolution of the DV video I captured for this project. The complete answer is long, confusing, and involves arcane differences between how computers and televisions display video data.

The quick, empirical answer is this. If you capture at the 4:2.66 aspect ratio and enter the result, Movie Maker tells you via black bars at the top and bottom of the screen that you're not totally filling the screen. For example, in Figure 6.7, the image Officer W, 720 x 480, shows small bars on the top and bottom. In contrast, Officer W, 4:3, shows no black bars at all, indicating that 4:3 is the best resolution for cropping still images for use in a Movie Maker project.

## ✔ Tip

- Always cut out the relevant portion in the shape of the desired aspect ratio. Never change the aspect ratio of an image or resize an image to make it fit a specific area.

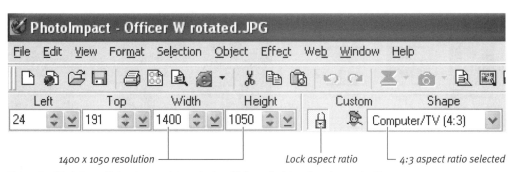

Figure 6.9 PhotoImpact's lovely cropping controls, which can lock to a target aspect ratio.

**Figure 6.10** To engage your scanner using PhotoImpact, for instance, choose File from the main menu and then choose Scanner > *scanner name*.

**Figure 6.11** Here's the Visioneer control panel, which probably won't be identical to yours, but contains the same basic parameters.

# Scanning Photographs

While I'm most likely considered an "early adopter" of digital pictures, I still have many traditional photographs I enjoy integrating into my Movie Maker productions. The dynamic duo I use to integrate them is a Visioneer scanner and the omnipresent PhotoImpact XL image editing software.

Most of you will use a different combination of hardware and software, so I'll stick to the high-level points to consider when scanning and prepping your images. I'm assuming you have the scanner connected to your computer, the proper drivers installed, and your photograph inserted in the scanner. I'm also assuming you understand, in general, how to scan images. The focus here is how to scan images for use in a Movie Maker project.

## To scan photographs for Movie Maker:

1. Use the appropriate software controls to engage your scanner. If you're using PhotoImpact, choose File from the main menu and then choose Scanner > *scanner name* (**Figure 6.10**).

   Your scanner control software should open (**Figure 6.11**).

   *continues on next page*

2. If the program offers pre-scan cropping tools, crop around the area you intend to display in the video file (**Figure 6.12**).

Remember that ultimately you will crop the image to a 4:3 aspect ratio, so attempt to capture as close to 4:3 as possible. For example, note on the bottom left of Figure 6.12 that I've set the scanned image size to 4 inches by 3 inches, a 4:3 aspect ratio.

If you're scanning the image for a DVD or to transfer back to DV tape, note that televisions don't display the outer edges of video, instead cropping between 5 percent and 8 percent of the video on all four sides in what's called an *overscan*. For this reason, don't crop too tightly around the target area; leave a little leeway for overscan.

In addition, if you plan to use the image in a program with pan and scan capabilities, like Microsoft Plus! Photo Story, leave a bit of extra room on all sides for additional creative flexibility (see Appendix B for more information on Plus! Photo Story).

3. Set the scan mode to 24-bit color.

4. Set the capture resolution to the highest optical scan resolution enabled by the scanner.

This is normally a specification provided with the scanner, and it produces the best possible scanned image quality. My oldish Visioneer maxes out at 600x1200 resolution, so I'm scanning at 600 dpi (Figure 6.12).

**Figure 6.12** First, scan only the relevant portion of the image, leaving room for overscan.

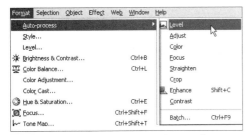

**Figure 6.13** Then adjust your image in your photo editor. I like the automatic adjustments best.

**Figure 6.14** Time to crop again to a 4:3 resolution.

**5.** Press the appropriate button to scan the image.

Since I'm scanning from within PhotoImpact, the image appears within the program. If you're using a separate program for scanning, load the newly scanned image into your image editing program.

**6.** Touch up your image as desired.

Entire books have been written on post-scanning image restoration so I'll largely skip over this point. My one comment is that most programs, PhotoImpact included, offer automated processing, which in my experience produces results that are vastly superior to what I could do manually (**Figure 6.13**).

**7.** Using the program's cropping control, crop your image down to a perfect 4:3 image resolution.

You can perform this cropping most easily when you're using a program like PhotoImpact that lets you lock the aspect ratio. Otherwise, you'll have to do the math yourself. Specifically, once you find the optimal horizontal resolution for your images, divide by 4, multiply by 3, and you've calculated the ideal height. For example, in **Figure 6.14** the optimal width is 2200. Divide by 4 to get 550, and then multiply by 3 to get 1650. Note that the results need to be exact, or you won't be able to produce a perfect 640 x 480 image in Step 8.

*continues on next page*

8. Using the program's Image Size screen, resize the image to 640×480 (**Figure 6.15**).

   Be sure not to change the aspect ratio (note the Keep Aspect Ratio check box checked in Figure 6.15), and use the highest possible rescaling method offered by the program.

9. Save the image in BMP or TIF format, the two most widely supported uncompressed formats that Movie Maker can import.

   **Figure 6.16** shows the image safely imported into Movie Maker; the absence of black edges indicate a perfect fit.

### ✔ Tip

■ If you plan to print or otherwise use the scanned image, you may want to retain a high-resolution copy after Step 6. At the final 640×480 resolution, the image doesn't have enough data to reproduce well for any application other than onscreen viewing and video.

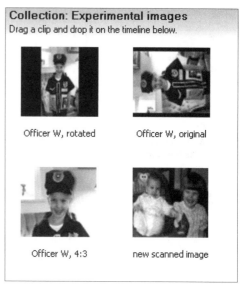

**Figure 6.16** No black around the image means it's perfectly sized.

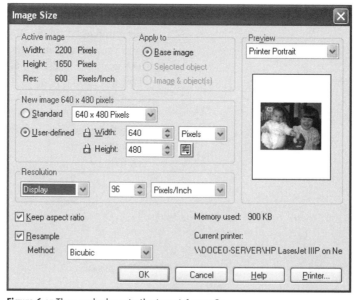

**Figure 6.15** Then scale down to the target 640 × 480.

*(Sidebar, left margin:)* **SCANNING PHOTOGRAPHS**

# IMPORTING MUSIC

You already know that Movie Maker can import a range of audio formats, including Windows Media Audio (WMA), MP3, and WAV (see "To import audio and still images into a collection" in Chapter 3 for more information). But for many of you, importing music into the collection isn't the hard part. Rather, it's getting the music you currently have on CDs, cassettes, or records into a digital file so that you can import it into a Movie Maker project.

This chapter begins by showing you how to rip CD tracks using Microsoft's free Windows Media Player. Then it shows you how to connect a cassette player or stereo receiver to your computer so that you can capture analog audio using Microsoft's Plus! Analog Recorder, a component of Microsoft's Plus! Digital Media Edition product.

If you use another program to rip your CDs or convert your analog assets, be sure to store your audio files in a format that Movie Maker can import, such as MP3, WAV, or WMA.

# Ripping Audio Tracks

Ripping audio tracks sounds violent, but it's really just the process of copying digital audio tracks from a CD and converting them to a different digital format that Movie Maker can import. That's why Windows Media Player calls the process *copying*. Very much like DV capture, it's fast, high-quality, and simple, with few configuration options to set.

Most configuration decisions are dictated by whether you're ripping the audio solely for use in a video project or for more general use. For example, if you have an MP3 player and an extensive music library, you'll probably convert all your music to MP3 format and store the songs in your library.

On the other hand, if you're ripping CDs strictly for video production, you may want to use the Windows Media Audio format and store the files in the same project folder as the video. I'll try to cover both options—ripping for a specific video production and ripping for your music library—in the tasks that follow.

All computers that ship with Windows XP installed also include Windows Media Player. If Windows Media Player isn't loaded on your computer, you can download the program for free here: www.microsoft.com/windows/windowsmedia/download/default.asp

*Windows Media Player*

**Figure 7.1** Click here to run Windows Media Player.

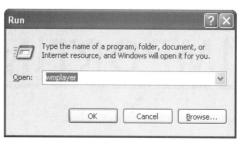

**Figure 7.2** Or choose Start > Run and type wmplayer.

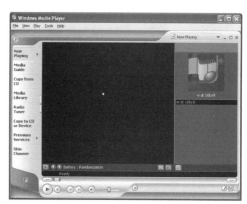

**Figure 7.3** Here's Windows Media Player, the free Microsoft product we'll use to rip the CD tracks.

**Figure 7.4** To access ripping or copying options, choose Tools > Options from the Options window.

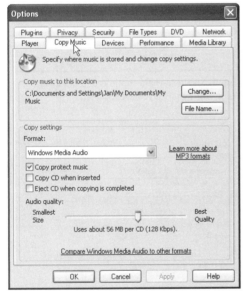

**Figure 7.5** Here is where you will set your Copy Music options.

## To choose your CD copying options:

1. To start Windows Media Player, do *one of the following:*

   ▲ Choose Start > Programs > Accessories > Entertainment > Windows Media Player.

   ▲ Double-click the Windows Media Player icon on the Windows taskbar (**Figure 7.1**) or desktop.

   ▲ Choose Start > Run and then, in the Run dialog box that appears, type wmplayer and click OK (**Figure 7.2**).

   Windows XP runs Windows Media Player (**Figure 7.3**).

2. From Windows Media Player's main menu, choose Tools > Options (**Figure 7.4**).

   The Options dialog box opens.

   Note that Windows Media Player hides the menu bar at the top of the player in default viewing mode (the bar that contains the File, View, Play, Tools, and other menus), so it may not be visible when you first look at the program. To make the menus appear, hover your mouse above the top of the interface.

3. Click the Copy Music tab (**Figure 7.5**).

4. If you want to change the default storage location, click the Change button in the Copy Music to This Location section of the dialog box.

   If you're ripping the tracks specifically for a video production, consider changing the location to the video storage folder. On the other hand, if you're adding these tracks to your Windows Media Player music library, just store them as you usually would.

*continues on next page*

RIPPING AUDIO TRACKS

**5.** If you want to change the naming convention used by Windows Media Player to store the music files, click the File Name button.

The File Name Options dialog box appears (**Figure 7.6**). Change the options if desired.

**6.** After you've made your changes, click OK to close the File Name Options dialog box and return to the Options dialog box (Figure 7.5).

**7.** In the Format list box on the Copy Music tab, do *one of the following:*

▲ If you're copying audio files solely for use in a specific video production, choose Windows Media Audio Lossless (**Figure 7.7**).

This option provides the best quality, but also the largest file size, so be prepared to delete the files after production. Note that if you choose this option, you won't have to adjust the Audio Quality slider because Windows Media Player will automatically select Best Quality.

▲ If you're copying files to include in a music library, make sure you choose the same format that you used for all the other songs in your library.

**8.** Deselect the Copy Protect Music check box if you want to be able to play your music on other computers in your home or office.

Don't get me wrong—I'm a great believer in protecting music copyrights, but checking this box severely limits where you can listen to your music, and it can render the files useless if you ever have to reinstall your operating system.

**9.** If desired, change the Copy CD When Inserted and Eject CD When Copying Is Completed options.

**10.** Click OK to close the Options dialog box.

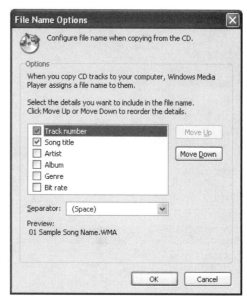

**Figure 7.6** The file name options determine how Windows Media Player names a file.

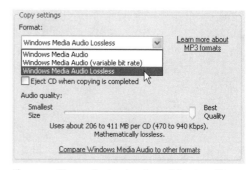

**Figure 7.7** Choose the lossless format (best quality, largest file size) for files you're using specifically for a video (and can later delete).

**Figure 7.8** To copy tracks from a CD, start with the Audio CD dialog box.

## To copy tracks from a CD:

1. Place a CD in the CD drive.

   Windows XP opens the Audio CD dialog box (**Figure 7.8**).

2. Select Play Audio CD Using Windows Media Player in the section, What Do You Want Windows to Do?

3. Click OK.

   Windows Media Player opens to the Now Playing tab.

4. On the left side of the Windows Media Player interface, select the Copy from CD tab (**Figure 7.9**).

   Note that if your computer is connected to the Internet, Windows Media Player will automatically check with an online database to identify the CD-ROM and populate most of the information you see in Figure 7.9. If your computer is not connected, you'll see generic titles like "track 1" and "unknown artist."

*continues on next page*

**Figure 7.9** Windows Media Player checks an online database to name your files for you, a nice convenience.

5. Using the check boxes to the left of the songs, select the songs you want to copy.

   I'm opening my production using the Cars' "Good Times Roll"—perfect for a six-year-old's birthday party. This is the only track I'll copy from this CD.

6. In the toolbar above the CD tracks, select the Copy Music radio button.

   Windows Media Player starts copying the selected track and changes the Copy Music button to Stop Copy, so you can stop the copy process (**Figure 7.10**). Unless you stop the process, Windows Media Player copies the tracks, converts them to the selected format, and pastes them in the target location.

**Figure 7.10** Let the good times roll! There goes Windows Media Player, converting the file.

# Converting Analog Audio to Digital

Many video producers have music in analog format that they want to include in their Movie Maker projects. To use music stored in analog format, you must convert it to digital files. One excellent tool for this task is Microsoft's Plus! Analog Recorder, a component of the Microsoft Plus! Digital Media Edition (DME), available for $19.95 at www.microsoft.com/windows/plus/DME/dmehome.asp. The Plus! suite also includes Photo Story, a cool tool for creating slide shows (see Appendix B for more information).

If you use another tool to rip your CDs, make sure you save the audio in a format that Movie Maker can import—and think of WMA as the default format.

As with video capture, two tasks are associated with audio capture: connecting the hardware and running the software. I'll start by showing you how to connect the hardware, which should be an identical process irrespective of the program you use to convert your audio. Then I'll show you how to capture the analog audio with the Plus! Analog Recorder. I'm assuming you've already installed the software.

## To connect for analog audio capture:

1. Identify the audio output connectors on your analog source device or on the receiver to which the device is connected.

   The preferred outputs for most consumer devices are dual audio output ports, called *RCA outputs* (**Figure 7.11**), which are usually colored red for right and white for left. Use these if available because they're designed for audio transfer and theoretically should produce a higher-quality signal than the stereo headphone jack; otherwise, connect via the stereo headphone jack.

2. Connect the cable to the analog output.

   If connecting via the RCA output ports, you'll need either a dual RCA to Stereo (1/8-inch) cable like that shown in **Figure 7.12** or a dual stereo cable (both ends look like the left side of Figure 7.12) and a Y connector like that shown in **Figure 7.13**.

   If connecting via the stereo headphone jack, you'll need a dual stereo (1/8-inch) cable like that shown in **Figure 7.14**.

3. Connect the cable to your sound card's line-in connector (**Figure 7.15**).

   Note that connecting via the microphone connector will produce an inferior result. Find the line-in connector, even if it takes a trip to the user manual to be sure.

**Figure 7.11** Dual RCA audio outputs (in the center Audio Out panel) are a good thing.

**Figure 7.12** Connect the dual connectors on the left to your analog source device.

**Figure 7.13** If your cable has dual RCA connectors on both sides, you need a Y connector like this. Hello, Radio Shack!

**Figure 7.14** Use a dual stereo cable like this one to connect a headphone jack to your sound card.

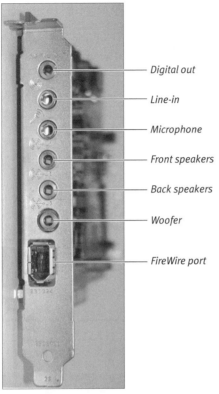

**Digital out**

**Line-in**

**Microphone**

**Front speakers**

**Back speakers**

**Woofer**

**FireWire port**

**Figure 7.15** The business end of a Sound Blaster Audigy Card.

## To determine if incoming volume will be sufficient:

1. Click Start > Programs > Microsoft Plus! Digital Media Edition > Plus! Analog Recorder.

   Windows runs the Plus! Analog Recorder (**Figure 7.16**).

2. Click Next to move to the next screen.

3. Choose the appropriate device from the Sound Device drop-down list (**Figure 7.17**).

4. Choose the appropriate channel from the Input Channel drop-down list.

*continues on next page*

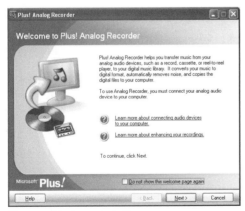

**Figure 7.16** Let's get started!

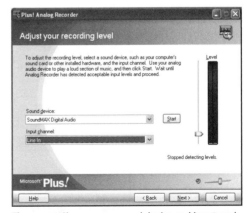

**Figure 7.17** Choose your sound device and input, and Plus! Analog Recorder will check your audio volume for you.

CONVERTING ANALOG AUDIO TO DIGITAL

**5.** Begin playing the audio from your sound device and then on Plus! Analog Recorder, click the Start button, located to the right of the Sound Device drop-down list.

Plus! Analog Recorder tests the incoming sound to determine whether volume is sufficient. If it isn't, you'll see the message shown in **Figure 7.18**; follow the direction in the error message and check that the cables are properly connected and

that you've selected the proper sound device and input channel. Do not proceed until you run this test and see the message "Detected acceptable levels" on the recording screen.

**6.** Click Next.

The Record Your Music window appears (**Figure 7.19**). Continue to the next task to capture the audio.

**Figure 7.18** Ruh-roh, Scooby-Doo. We've got problems. Time to check your cables and configuration.

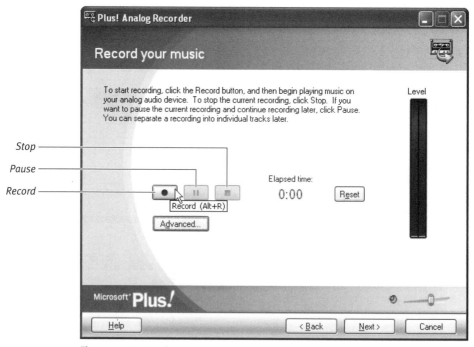

**Figure 7.19** Here's where we start the actual recording.

**Figure 7.20** Limit recording time here and you can start the process and walk away.

## To capture analog audio:

1. In Plus! Analog Recorder's Record Your Music window (Figure 7.19), click the Advanced button.

   The Advanced Recording Options dialog box appears (**Figure 7.20**).

2. Do *one of the following:*

   ▲ If you're recording music from a cassette or record and you want the individual tracks separated, make sure the Automatically Detect and Split Tracks check box is enabled (the default setting). See the Tip that follows at the end of this task for more information.

   ▲ If you're recording songs or other content that you don't want broken into tracks, uncheck the Automatically Detect and Split Tracks check box.

3. Enter the maximum recording time if you don't plan to hang around your computer while the music is being captured.

   Plus! Analog Recorder will stop recording after the specified period.

4. Click OK to return to the Record Your Music window.

5. Cue the audio to approximately 30 seconds before the target segment and start playing it.

   *continues on next page*

**CONVERTING ANALOG AUDIO TO DIGITAL**

**6.** In the Record Your Music window, click the Record button approximately 10 seconds before the target content begins to play.

**7.** Click Stop after you've recorded your content.

**8.** Click Next.

The Review and Name Your Tracks dialog box appears (**Figure 7.21**). Continue to the next task to review and name your track.

### ✔ Tip

■ Note that on some materials, automatically detecting tracks may not work effectively. For example, scratchy records may not register silence between tracks, or short periods of silence in the songs may be falsely recognized as track breaks. In these instances, it might be more efficient to capture tracks individually or record the album or cassette without track detection enabled and then manually split the tracks.

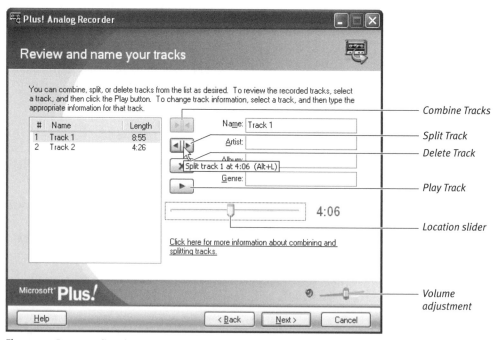

**Figure 7.21** Post-recording cleanup.

## To review, name, and optimize your music track:

**1.** In the Review and Name Your Tracks window (Figure 7.21), do *one or more of the following:*

▲ To split a track, select the track in the track list, move the Location slider to the target split point, and click the Split Track icon.

▲ To combine tracks, select the tracks in the track list while holding down the Shift key and click the Combine Tracks icon.

▲ To name the track, select the track and enter the name, artist, album, and genre in their respective fields.

**2.** Click Next to move to the Clean Your Tracks window (**Figure 7.22**).

**3.** To filter the "pops" and "hiss" from a track, select the track in the track list and select the appropriate check boxes. Preview the filtering by clicking Play and moving to different locations in the audio file via the Location slider.

Note that filtering can sometimes produce more harm than good, so preview extensively before deciding to apply either filter.

*continues on next page*

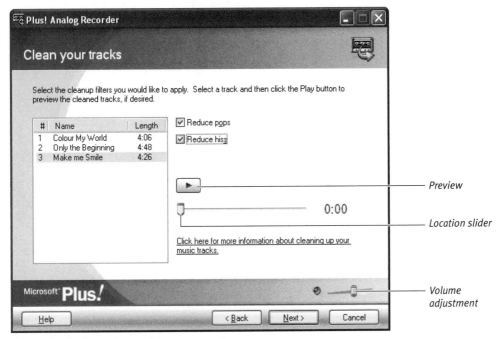

**Figure 7.22** Filtering options to clean up your audio.

CONVERTING ANALOG AUDIO TO DIGITAL

**4.** Click Next to move to the Select Settings and Save Tracks window (**Figure 7.23**).

**5.** Accept the default storage location, or click the Change button to change to a preferred location.

If you're converting analog audio specifically for a video production, consider changing the location to the video storage folder. If you're adding these tracks to your Windows Media Player music library, store them where you normally would.

**6.** If desired, click the Advanced button to change the conventions used by Plus! Analog Recorder when it names the files.

File name and storage options are shown in **Figure 7.24**. Change the options if desired.

**7.** In the Select Settings and Save Tracks window (Figure 7.23), make sure the Protect Content option is not selected if you want to be able to play your music on other computers in your home or office.

As mentioned earlier, checking this box makes your music unplayable on any other computer and can make the files useless if you have to reinstall the operating system at any future point.

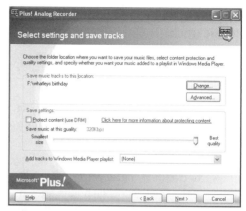

**Figure 7.23** Choosing the file location and encoding settings.

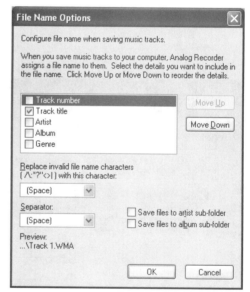

**Figure 7.24** These options are very helpful when producing tracks for your media library, but not really relevant for video production.

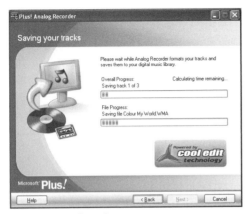

**Figure 7.25** Finally underway.

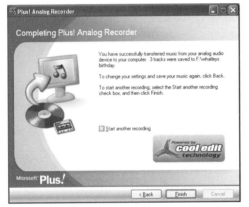

**Figure 7.26** The fat lady has sung. Let's move on to the next stage of video production.

**8.** In the Save Settings section, do *one of the following:*

- ▲ If you're converting analog audio files solely for use in a specific video production, use your pointer to move the Quality slider to Best Quality. This setting provides the best quality, but also the largest file size, so consider deleting the file after you produce your final movie.

- ▲ If you're copying files for inclusion in a music library, adjust the quality slider to the same setting you used when producing other songs.

**9.** To add the tracks to a Windows Media Player playlist or create a new playlist, select from the drop-down list beside Add Tracks to Windows Media Player.

**10.** Click Next.

Plus! Analog Recorder starts saving your tracks, displaying the dialog box shown in **Figure 7.25**. Another dialog box will appear once the process is complete, allowing you to either start another recording or exit the program (**Figure 7.26**).

CONVERTING ANALOG AUDIO TO DIGITAL

# WORKING IN THE CONTENTS PANE

The Contents pane houses the assets contained in each collection. With some assets, such as audio and digital images, the Contents pane is merely a convenient spot for storing assets before importing them into a project.

With video, however, the Contents pane is also a very convenient place to decide, in the immortal words of Bob Seger, "what to leave in, what to leave out." Even though it's much more fun to consider the special effects, transitions, and titles that lie ahead, unmercifully cutting unnecessary video from the project is probably the single most important editing task, and the Contents pane is the ideal place to start.

This chapter discusses how Windows Movie Maker creates "clips" from your captured and imported videos, and how you can split, combine, cut, copy, and paste clips within the Contents pane. It concludes with a brief description of how to relink "lost" clips, or clips that you've moved or changed in some way after inserting them into a collection.

# Creating Clips in Video Files

In Chapters 3 and 4, you learned how to create clips during capture. Now you'll learn how to create clips when importing video that's already saved to disk. As you'll see, it all boils down to selecting one check box during the import process; however, the results will differ depending on the type of file you're working with.

For example, if you import a Windows Media Video file, Movie Maker creates a clip for each marker in the file. Markers are frames inserted by the producer of the file to provide instant access to the frame when the file is played in Media Player. They're a fairly obscure feature of Windows Media Video, so if you've never heard of them or seen them, you're definitely in the majority.

If no markers exist, Movie Maker creates a clip each time there is a substantial change between frames with a minimum duration of one second. For example, if you were shooting indoors and then started shooting outside, Movie Maker would identify this as a substantial change and create a separate clip. Movie Maker uses the same technique of detecting scene changes based on content changes to create clips when importing MPEG files.

In contrast, if you import DV video from a camcorder, Movie Maker uses time stamps embedded in the DV tape to detect when you turned the camera on and off during a shoot, and the program creates a clip each time you restart shooting.

Note that if you don't elect to detect clips when importing or capturing the video, you can create clips later in the Contents pane as discussed in "To create clips for video in the Contents pane" later in this chapter.

## About the Contents Pane

The Contents pane *represents* audio, video, and still-image assets imported into a collection, but not the asset itself. So if you cut, split, trim, bend, fold, and mutilate assets imported into the Contents pane, the underlying asset will not be affected.

For example, if you import a library of still images into the Contents pane and then delete several of them later, the original digital images are left untouched. Likewise, if you split or combine audio or video assets in the Contents pane, the original assets remain untouched on the disk.

When you import video into the Contents pane, Movie Maker can split the original video file into individual "clips." Once again, these clips exist only in Movie Maker; the original video is still one large video file sitting on your hard drive.

Finally, collections do not relate to specific projects; once you create a project, it stays in Movie Maker until you delete it. In addition, the assets themselves are not collection or project specific: You can import one audio, video, or still-image file into multiple collections.

**Figure 8.1** Click here to import video.

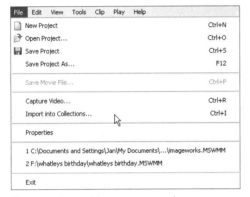

**Figure 8.2** Or use this menu command.

**Figure 8.3** Here's the Import File window. You know the drill: navigate to the appropriate folder and click the target file.

## To create clips while importing:

1. Do *one of the following* to start the video import process:
   - ▲ In the Movie Tasks pane, click Import Video (**Figure 8.1**).
   - ▲ From the Movie Maker main menu, choose File > Import into Collections (**Figure 8.2**).
   - ▲ Press Ctrl+I on your keyboard.

   Movie Maker opens the Import File dialog box (**Figure 8.3**).

2. Navigate to and select the video file you want to import.

   You can select multiple video files at one time, and Movie Maker will import each into a separate collection.

3. On the bottom left of the Import File dialog box, click the Create Clips for Video Files check box.

   *continues on next page*

**4.** Click the Import button.

Movie Maker starts importing the file, displaying the dialog box shown in **Figure 8.4**. As you would expect, the longer the file being imported, the longer Movie Maker takes to scan the file. On my HP Workstation xw4100, which has a 3.2-GHz Pentium 4 processor, Movie Maker takes about 5 minutes to scan a 60-minute DV file.

When scanning is complete, Movie Maker displays the imported clips in the Contents pane (**Figure 8.5**). It names the new collection after the name of the imported file and places all newly imported video collections on the root of the collections tree. See "To rename a collection" and "To move a collection" in Chapter 3 if you need to move or rename your collections.

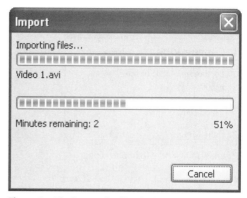

**Figure 8.4** The longer the file, the longer the wait.

### ✔ Tips

- Movie Maker can import the following video file types: .asf, .avi, .m1v, .mp2, .mp2v, .mpe, .mpeg, .mpg, .mpv2, .wm, and .wmv.

- If you click Cancel during clip detection, Movie Maker will display the clips that were detected before you clicked Cancel. The last clip will contain the undetected portion of the video file.

- Movie Maker names the clips according to the technique it uses to identify them. For example, if the technique is based on scene changes, it names the clip after the original file: 001, 002, 003, and so on. If the technique is based on splitting DV files according to their date and time codes, Movie Maker names each clip using the date and time the shot was taken.

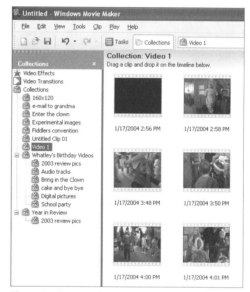

**Figure 8.5** Here are the separate clips.

Figure 8.6 For files you've already imported, choose Create Clips.

## To create clips for video in the Contents pane:

1. Select the target clip in the Contents pane.

2. Right-click and choose Create Clips (**Figure 8.6**).

   Movie Maker starts scanning the file, displaying the dialog box shown in **Figure 8.7**. When scanning is complete, Movie Maker displays the imported clips in the Contents pane (Figure 8.5), names the new collection after the imported file, and places all newly imported video collections on the root of the collections tree. See "To rename a collection" and "To move a collection" in Chapter 3 to move or rename your collections.

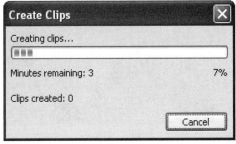

Figure 8.7 Again, waiting, waiting.

## To view clips in the Contents pane:

1. In the Contents pane, do *one of the following*:

   ▲ Double-click the clip you want to view.

   ▲ Click the clip you want to view and use the playback controls in the Monitor to start playback.

   Movie Maker plays the selected clip (**Figure 8.8**).

2. Use the controls beneath the Monitor to stop, go back to the start, jump to the end, or move through the video frame by frame.

## ✔ Tips

■ If the Contents pane contains multiple clips, the Monitor stops playing at the end of each clip. To jump to the next clip, press the right arrow key; to start and stop playback, press the spacebar.

■ If you want to play an audio file, the process is the same—follow the steps in this task. Still images will be displayed in the Monitor when you hover your cursor over them.

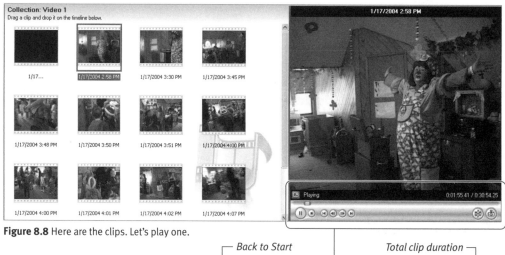

**Figure 8.8** Here are the clips. Let's play one.

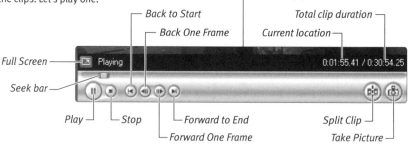

# What to Leave in, What to Leave Out

Because projects are so different from one another, it's difficult to generalize the type of footage you'll want to include or exclude. That said, the following are some general sequences that I'm planning for my birthday-party video:

1. **Setting the scene.** Includes exterior shots of the house and interior shots as establishing shots.

2. **Arrival.** People arriving, meeting and greeting, and getting set for the party.

3. **Entertainment.** The longest segment of the video (about 15 minutes), with video of the clown and crowd reactions to the magic act.

4. **Transition to cake scene.** Children having fun and then walking to the dining room.

5. **Cake scene.** Shots of Happy Birthday and blowing out the candles.

6. **Opening the presents.** The best part of the event, according to my daughter.

7. **Parting is such sweet sorrow.** Hugs, kisses, and goodbyes.

8. **Still-picture slide show.** Pictures taken during the event.

9. **Year-in-review pictures.** Pictures of my daughter taken since her last birthday.

The video I've imported thus far in the chapter contains footage destined for sequences 3, 4, and 5.

The first 46 minutes of this footage are focused on the clown, who performed primarily as a magician. From this, I'll grab two or three magic stunts in their entirety, plus the best shots I have of the crowd reacting to the show, to form the entertainment sequence. In the clown clips, I'll insert cutaway shots showing the crowd watching and laughing (see "Advanced Timeline Editing" in Chapter 9 for details). The magic acts will also provide the audio background and much of the video that I'll use in sequences 3 through 5 (see "The Continuity system for audio" in Chapter 2 for more information). Note that this sequence will be the most heavily edited sequence in my video.

My next task is to find scenes that work well in transitioning the video from the magic show to the cake scene. This sequence will contain about 20 to 30 discrete shots, lasting about 3 to 4 minutes. So I'll scan the video to find good short shots of kids having fun and later walking down the stairs to the dining room, and I'll delete the clips I won't use. I will try to limit the duration of any individual clip to between 5 and 10 seconds.

Finally, I'll use the cake sequence almost in its entirety for the obligatory "Happy Birthday" song and blowing out of the candles.

For all other sequences, I'm looking for the best short shots to piece together. I want to make sure to grab clips with the key attendees—family, best friends, richest neighbors—and eliminate clips that are either too long or contain bad camera work.

CREATING CLIPS IN VIDEO FILES

# Working with Audio and Video in the Contents Pane

In certain circumstances, Movie Maker's ability to create clips needs serious manual assistance. For example, when I was shooting the magic act, I shot for about 46 minutes, but I stopped and started the camera only once. Since Movie Maker uses time codes to split DV video, it produced only two clips during importing: one about 31 minutes long and one about 15 minutes. I'll definitely have to break these up manually to find the scenes I need.

Though you can perform this cutting on the Timeline, I find it easier to do in the Contents pane. I also find it useful to copy and paste clips, sometimes into different collections, sometimes into the same collection. Though I'll describe these procedures with video files, operation is identical for audio files.

### To split clips in the Contents pane:

1. Select the clip that you want to split. Movie Maker displays the clip in the Monitor (**Figure 8.9**).

2. Use the Monitor controls to move to the initial frame of the new sequence.

Split the clip into two clips at the current frame (Ctrl+L)

**Figure 8.9** Click the Split Clip button to split the clip into two clips.

**3.** Click the Split Clip button.

Movie Maker splits the clip and automatically inserts a name based on the name of the source clip, plus the suffix *(1)* and then *(2)* for subsequent clips (**Figure 8.10**).

To separate out a scene, use the Monitor controls to move to the frame after the last target frame in the sequence and split the clip again. For example, in **Figure 8.11**, I split the clip again, isolating the segment I named "Watching cutaway – children" and creating "1/17/2004 2:58 PM (2)."

**✔ Tip**

■ You can split a clip in the Contents pane or on the Timeline using the same basic procedures. Note that splitting a clip in one window does not affect the clips in the other window.

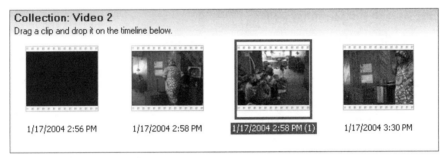

**Figure 8.10** Here we go, two clips.

**Figure 8.11** I split the clip again to create the discrete clip I'm targeting and rename it for later.

## To combine clips in the Contents pane:

1. Hold down the Shift or Ctrl key and click the clips you want to combine.

2. Right-click and choose Combine, or press Ctrl+M (**Figure 8.12**).

   Movie Maker combines the clips into a new clip, named after the clip that was shot first (**Figure 8.13**).

## ✔ Tip

■ Note that Movie Maker can combine only clips that are contiguous in the original file. If you select two clips that aren't contiguous, the Combine command will be dimmed.

## To delete clips in the Contents pane:

1. Touch the clip you want to delete.

2. Do *one of the following:*
   ▲ Right-click and choose Delete (**Figure 8.14**).
   ▲ Press the Delete key on your keyboard.
   ▲ From the main menu, choose Edit > Delete.

   Movie Maker deletes the clip. Note that the original assets on disk remain untouched; Movie Maker simply removes any reference to the clip in the Contents pane. If you delete a clip after using it in the Timeline, Movie Maker does not remove the clip from the Timeline.

**Figure 8.12** Select two contiguous files and click here to combine them. This will be grayed out if the clips aren't contiguous.

**Figure 8.13** The combined file. Note that the new name is that of the first clip in chronological order.

**Figure 8.14** Choose Delete to delete a clip, or press Delete on your keyboard.

**Figure 8.15**
Choose a command here to copy or cut a clip.

1/17/2004 2:58 PM        1/17/2004 2:58 PM

**Figure 8.16** Two identically named files in the Contents pane.

## To cut/copy and paste clips in the Contents pane:

1. Select the clip or clips.

2. Do *one of the following:*
   - ▲ Right-click and choose Cut or Copy (**Figure 8.15**).
   - ▲ Press Ctrl+X (Cut) or Ctrl+C (Copy) on your keyboard.
   - ▲ From the Movie Maker menu, choose Edit > Cut or Edit > Copy.

3. Select the new location (either within the same collection or in a different collection).

4. Do *one of the following:*
   - ▲ Right-click and choose Paste.
   - ▲ Press Ctrl+V.
   - ▲ From the Movie Maker menu, choose Edit > Paste.

   Movie Maker pastes the clip into the new location (**Figure 8.16**). If you chose Copy, it leaves the original clip where it was; if you chose Cut, it deletes the original clip. As you can see in Figure 8.16, Movie Maker gives the clip the same name as the source clip, which can mean two files with the same name in the Contents pane.

## ✔ Tips

- ■ To move a clip from one collection to another, it's probably easier simply to drag the clip from the Contents pane into the collection.

- ■ Use these same controls to delete, cut, copy, and paste still-image files.

# Relinking Lost Clips

If you move or change the name of an audio, video, or still-image clip after importing it into Movie Maker, the next time you open Movie Maker, you'll see a series of red Xs like those shown in **Figure 8.17**. Movie Maker hasn't declared your movies X-rated; rather, the program is telling you that Movie Maker has lost your clips.

Fortunately, you can easily relink your clips as described in the next task. In this example, I changed the name of the clip from *Video 1.avi* to *Clown scene.avi*. Let's see how to fix this.

### To relink a lost clip:

1. Select the X-rated clip.

2. Right-click and choose Browse for Missing File (**Figure 8.18**).

   Movie Maker opens the Browse for Video window (**Figure 8.19**).

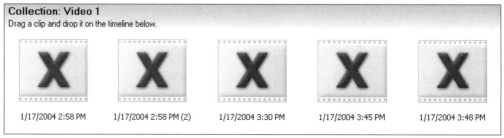

**Figure 8.17** Oops—somebody moved a file or changed the name.

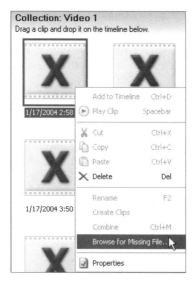

**Figure 8.18** No problem. Just choose Browse for Missing File.

**Figure 8.19** The Browse for Video window, where you can type the new name.

**3.** Do *one of the following:*

▲ If you *moved* the file, navigate to the new location and click the file.

▲ If you *changed the file name,* type the new name in the File Name text box.

**4.** Click Open.

Movie Maker repopulates the video icons (**Figure 8.20**).

**Figure 8.20** Order is restored.

# Part III: Editing

# TRIMMING AND ASSEMBLING YOUR MOVIE

Once you've captured your video, still image, and audio assets, you will have created a huge collection of files—usually far more than you'll want to include in your final production. The next steps are to cut out the fat and assemble the basic pieces of your project, all of which you do in the Storyboard/Timeline window.

You can and should do some of this cutting in the Contents pane, as discussed in "Working with Audio and Video in the Contents pane" in Chapter 8. In the Storyboard/Timeline window, you finalize this work, assembling all content into a cohesive production.

As you probably guessed from the name, there are two views to this window we're about to dive into: the Storyboard and the Timeline. This chapter discusses the strengths of each view and then teaches you how to customize and work efficiently within them. Considering how much time you'll spend working in these views—particularly the Timeline—spending a short time on the basics now will save you hours of work later.

# Looking at Storyboard / Timeline Views

The Storyboard/Timeline window offers two views: Storyboard and Timeline.

The Storyboard view uses a thumbnail image, or frame, to represent each asset in a project (**Figure 9.1**). This is a great view for sequencing your assets and inserting transitions between them, but little else, since you can't access tracks for titles, narration, or background music.

*Set audio levels*

*Narrate Timeline*

*Rewind Storyboard*

*Play Storyboard*

*Show Timeline*

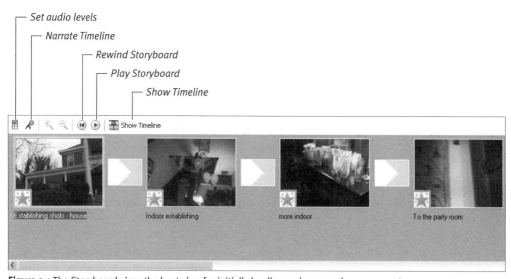

**Figure 9.1** The Storyboard view, the best view for initially loading and sequencing your assets.

The Timeline view is a graphical representation of an entire project, with the length of each clip on the Timeline representing the duration of that clip (**Figure 9.2**). Although Timeline view lets you recognize bits and pieces of clips, you won't be able to recognize most of the smaller clips, especially if you've zoomed out to get a bird's eye view. So it's best to sequence your videos in Storyboard view and then switch to Timeline view for serious editing tasks such as adding titles, background music and other elements.

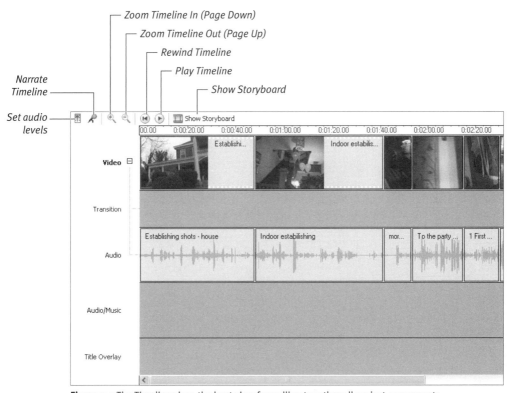

Figure 9.2 The Timeline view, the best view for pulling together all project components.

LOOKING AT STORYBOARD/TIMELINE VIEWS

## To switch from Storyboard to Timeline view:

◆ Do *one of the following*:

▲ At the upper right of the Storyboard window, click the Show Timeline button (Figure 9.1).

▲ On the Movie Maker main menu, choose View > Timeline (**Figure 9.3**).

▲ Press Ctrl+T.

## To switch from Timeline to Storyboard view:

◆ Do *one of the following*:

▲ At the upper right of the Timeline window, click the Show Storyboard button (Figure 9.2).

▲ In the Movie Maker menu, choose View > Storyboard (**Figure 9.4**).

▲ Press Ctrl+T.

**Figure 9.3** Switch to the Timeline view here, or press Ctrl+T.

**Figure 9.4** Switch to the Storyboard view here, or again press Ctrl+T.

Figure 9.5 Save your project as soon as you put assets in the Storyboard/Timeline window.

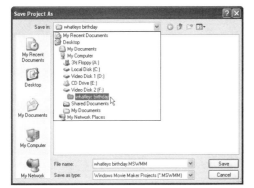

Figure 9.6 I like to save my project files with the project assets.

# Saving Your Projects

Collections are forever in Movie Maker, which means that you don't have to save a collection to ensure it will reappear next time you run the program. In contrast, once you drag an asset to the Storyboard/Timeline window, you've started a *project*, which you must save to retain your work.

While you're working, Windows Movie Maker periodically saves your project information so that it can restore your project automatically in the event of a crash or power loss. Initially, Movie Maker saves the project every 10 minutes, which is a default you can change as discussed in "Setting Project Defaults" in Chapter 3.

### To save your project:

1. From the main menu, choose File > Save Project (**Figure 9.5**).

   If this is the first time you've saved the file, Movie Maker opens the Save Project As dialog box. If you've previously named and saved the project, Movie Maker will simply save it again.

2. In the Save In list box, navigate to the desired storage location (**Figure 9.6**).

   Movie Maker defaults to Windows Desktop > My Documents Folder > My Videos. I generally store project files in the folder containing the project assets so that I can delete them all at once.

3. Type the project file name.

   It's always helpful to use descriptive project names so that you can more easily identify the project later.

4. Click Save.

   Movie Maker stores the file with the MSWMM extension, which stands for Microsoft Windows Movie Maker.

*continues on next page*

## ✔ Tips

■ As with most content creation applications, the project file contains pointers, or references to the content in the project, but not the original assets themselves. This makes project files fairly compact.

■ The Save Project option is different from the Save Movie File option (Figure 9.5). The latter actually produces the video file that you've been editing; whereas the former simply saves the project. We discuss how to use the Save Movie File option and produce your video files in Chapter 16.

■ Note the Save Project As option in Figure 9.5. It's useful to save a project under another name when creating derivative projects from another project. For example, to edit and output just the school portion of Whatley's birthday video, I would open whatleys birthday.mswmm, immediately save the new project as whatleys birthday–school only.mswmm, and then perform my edits. This preserves the original project file.

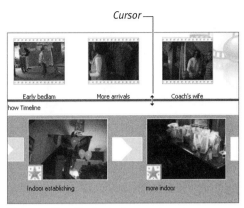

*Cursor*

**Figure 9.7** Drag the Contents pane down to see more frames.

# Working on the Storyboard

In traditional video productions, a storyboard is a large chart or series of charts with images representing the various clips of a project. It's a great tool for conceptualizing the content and flow of your movie, and it's even better in digital form, since you can easily rearrange your assets.

If you're at all unsure of the order of your clips, Movie Maker's Storyboard is a very convenient place for shuffling them around until you've decided. You can even add transitions and preview your project to quickly view the rough cut. However, when it's time to trim your videos and perform other more sophisticated editing, you'll need to use the superior tools available only in Timeline view.

By default, Movie Maker maintains audio and video synchronization in all Storyboard/Timeline window views by automatically tying the Audio track to the Video track through all edits. Accordingly, if you move, delete, split, or combine clips in the Video track, the Audio track automatically follows.

## To customize the Storyboard view:

1. Hover your pointer over the blue line between the Contents pane and the Timeline (**Figure 9.7**).

   The pointer converts to a two-headed pointer.

   *continues on next page*

**2.** Drag the pointer down toward the bottom of the Storyboard.

Movie Maker opens more frames (up to 15) in the Storyboard (**Figure 9.8**), though the images are smaller. Compare Figure 9.8 to Figure 9.1, which displays only six frames.

Use the bottom scroll bar to scroll to the right to see additional frames, or use the right and left arrow keys to move from frame to frame.

*— Scroll bar*

**Figure 9.8** More frames for sure, but they are tiny.

WORKING ON THE STORYBOARD

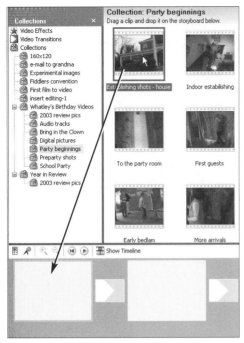

**Figure 9.9** Drag and drop the clip into the first frame.

## To drag a video clip to the Storyboard:

1. Select a clip in the Contents pane.

   The borders turn from white to blue, and Movie Maker highlights the text description.

2. Drag the clip toward the first empty frame at the upper left of the Storyboard (**Figure 9.9**).

   You'll see a faint image of the thumbnail attached to your pointer as you drag, and a small plus sign and box appear below the pointer (**Figure 9.10**). A small vertical line (the drop line) appears in front of the first open frame.

3. Release the mouse button.

   Movie Maker inserts the clip in the Storyboard frame (**Figure 9.11**).

   *continues on next page*

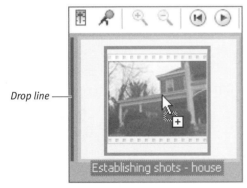

Drop line ——

**Figure 9.10** Note the drop line on the left, indicating that you can drop the image in this frame.

**Figure 9.11** The clip has been successfully inserted on the Storyboard.

**WORKING ON THE STORYBOARD**

## ✔ Tips

- To add multiple contiguous clips to the Storyboard, click the first clip, press the Shift key, click the last clip, and drag the clips to the Storyboard. For noncontiguous clips, press the Ctrl key, click each target clip, and drag the clips to the Storyboard.

- Movie Maker drops video and still image assets in the first available space at the beginning of a project. Although you can reorder assets at will once they're on the Timeline, you can't create gaps in the Video track of your projects in either the Storyboard or Timeline view.

- You have many options for getting clips to the Storyboard, including the Cut/Copy and Paste commands, main menu commands (Clip > Add to Storyboard), right-click controls (Add to Storyboard), and keyboard shortcuts (Ctrl+D). I find dragging and dropping the most intuitive.

### To insert a video clip between two clips in the Storyboard:

1. Select a clip in the Contents pane.

   The borders turn from white to blue.

2. Drag the clip to the desired location.

   You'll see a faint image of the thumbnail, and a small plus sign and box appears below the pointer (**Figure 9.12**). Note the drop line, which indicates where the new clip will appear.

3. Release the mouse button.

   Movie Maker inserts the clip between the existing clips (**Figure 9.13**).

### ✔ Tip

- Movie Maker inserts the new clip between the selected clips, pushing back all clips after the newly inserted clips. No clips are deleted or otherwise truncated.

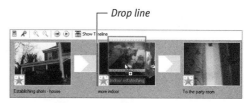

**Figure 9.12** To insert a clip between clips on the Storyboard, just drag and drop.

**Figure 9.13** The clip, successfully inserted.

*Selected clip*

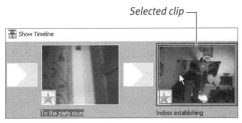

**Figure 9.14** Decided to reorder the clips? Select the clip you want to move, and Movie Maker highlights the clip.

*Drop line*

**Figure 9.15** There's that drop line again, telling you it's safe to drop the clip.

**Figure 9.16** Done. This ease of sequencing is why the Storyboard view is great for arranging your assets.

**Figure 9.17** Hover your mouse over the frame to see its name and duration.

## To arrange assets in Storyboard view:

1. On the Storyboard, select a clip.

   Movie Maker displays a blue frame around the selected clip (**Figure 9.14**).

2. Drag the clip to the desired location.

   A vertical drop line appears each time you cross an available space to drop the new clips, and a small box appears below the pointer (**Figure 9.15**).

3. Release the mouse button at the desired location.

   Movie Maker inserts the clip in the specified location (**Figure 9.16**).

## To see clip-related information on the Storyboard:

◆ On the Storyboard, hover the pointer over a clip for a moment.

   The clip name and duration appear in a yellow box beneath the pointer (**Figure 9.17**).

WORKING ON THE STORYBOARD

**161**

## To preview your video clip on the Storyboard:

1. Select the clip you want to preview. Movie Maker highlights the clip in blue.

2. Start playback by doing *one of the following*:

   ▲ At the top left of the Storyboard window, click the Play Storyboard button (Figure 9.1)

   ▲ In the Monitor, click Play (**Figure 9.18**). The Play key switches to Pause mode, which you can click to pause playback.

   ▲ Press the spacebar to start playback. Press the spacebar again to pause playback.

   ▲ Right-click and choose Play Storyboard (Ctrl+W).

   Playback automatically advances from clip to clip when multiple assets are present.

## ✔ Tips

■ Click the button on the bottom left of the Monitor to preview the video in full-screen mode (you can also press Alt-Enter on your keyboard). To exit full-screen mode and return to the main interface, press Esc on your keyboard or click anywhere on the screen.

■ The Monitor is your view of the *entire* project, and you can always use the Monitor Seek bar to reposition content in the Storyboard and Timeline.

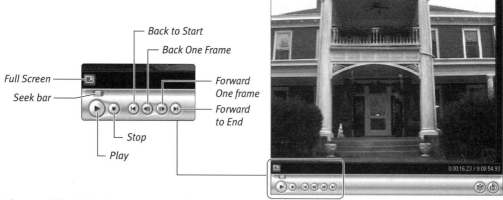

**Figure 9.18** The Monitor is your preview window.

# Getting Video Clips to the Timeline

Timeline view is where you'll spend the bulk of your editing time. Although it's not quite as straightforward as Storyboard view, the advantages of working in it quickly become apparent.

This section identifies the various Timeline tracks and explains how to get clips from the Contents pane to the Timeline. If your Timeline starts getting cramped or otherwise out of control, skip ahead one section to learn how to customize your Timeline view.

As mentioned earlier, Movie Maker automatically inserts the audio captured with the video file on the appropriate track when you transfer the video, so you don't have to worry about manually moving the Audio track yourself.

The critical components of the Timeline are summarized here (**Figure 9.19**).

◆ **Timescale:** Shows the absolute time of the assets displayed in Timeline view. You can modify the timescale to show more or less detail (see "Customizing Your Timeline View" later in this chapter).

*continues on next page*

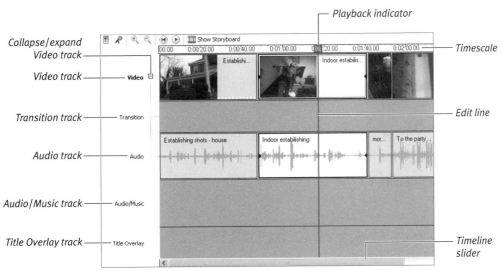

**Figure 9.19** The Timeline. Take a good look around; you'll be spending lots of time here.

GETTING VIDEO CLIPS TO THE TIMELINE

- **Video track:** The only track that can display video; it can also display still images. Note that the Video track originally appears in collapsed view, which doesn't show the Audio or Transition track. I always work in expanded view, which shows the Video, Transition, and Audio tracks. To get there, click the Expand Video Track button (**Figure 9.20**).

- **Audio track:** Contains the audio that was captured with the video clip.

- **Audio/Music track:** Movie Maker places all voice-over recordings on this track. You can also insert on this track audio from any source, such as background music tracks that you've ripped from CD, converted from analog sources or downloaded from a music service. In addition, to insert only the audio from a captured video file into the production, simply drag it to this track.

- **Title Overlay track:** Contains titles (for more information on creating titles, see Chapter 13).

- **Edit line:** The current editing position on the Timeline and the frame currently visible in the Monitor.

- **Playback indicator:** A tool used to drag the edit line to different positions on the Timeline.

- **Timeline slider:** A tool used to drag the visible area on the Timeline forward and backward through the project.

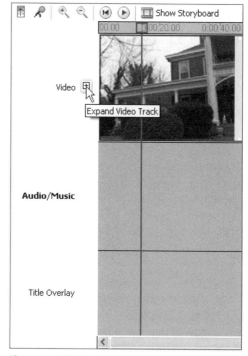

**Figure 9.20** Click here to expand the Video track to see transitions and audio.

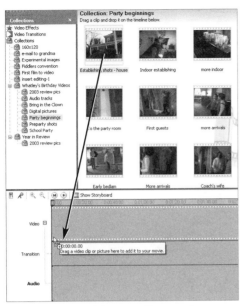

**Figure 9.21** Drag and drop your clips onto the Timeline.

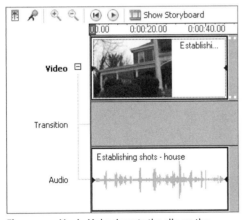

**Figure 9.22** Movie Maker inserts the clip on the Timeline.

■ You have many options for getting clips to the Timeline, including Cut/Copy and Paste commands, main menu commands (Clip > Add to Timeline), right-click controls (Add to Timeline), and keyboard shortcuts (Ctrl+D). I find dragging and dropping the most intuitive.

## To drag a video clip to the Timeline:

1. Select a clip in the Contents pane.

   The borders turn from white to blue, and Movie Maker highlights the text description.

2. Do *one of the following*:

   ▲ Drag the clip to the Video track.

   ▲ Drag the clip to the Audio/Music track.

   A small plus sign appears below the pointer, along with a box containing the start time for the new clip (**Figure 9.21**).

3. Release the mouse button.

   Movie Maker inserts the clip on the selected track (**Figure 9.22**).

## ✔ Tips

■ You add multiple contiguous and non-contiguous clips to the Timeline in the same way you add them to the Storyboard. For multiple contiguous clips, click the first clip, press the Shift key, click the last clip, and drag the clips to the Timeline. For noncontiguous clips, press the Ctrl key, click each target clip, and drag the clips to Timeline.

■ If you drop a video on the Video track, Movie Maker always inserts the associated audio on the Audio track.

■ If you drop a video file on the Audio/Music track, only the audio, not the video, is inserted on the track.

■ As with the Storyboard, Movie Maker always drops video and still image assets in the first available space at the beginning of a project. Although you can reorder assets at will once they're on the Timeline, you can't create gaps in the Video track of your projects in either the Storyboard or Timeline view.

## To insert a video clip between two clips on the Timeline

1. Select a clip in the Contents pane.

   The borders turn from white to blue.

2. Drag the clip to the desired location.

   A horizontal blue line appears between the two video clips, and a plus sign, small box, and data box containing the start time of the new clip and name and duration of the clip to be displaced appear next to the pointer (**Figure 9.23**).

3. Release the mouse button.

   Movie Maker inserts the clip between the existing clips (**Figure 9.24**).

### ✔ Tips

- Movie Maker inserts the new clip between the selected clips, pushing back all clips after the newly inserted clips (potentially out of your current view of the project). No clips are deleted or otherwise truncated.

- You can insert a clip only at the beginning or end of another clip, not in the middle of a clip. To insert a clip into the middle of another clip on the Timeline, you first have to *split* the clip on the Timeline, as described in "To split clips" later in this chapter.

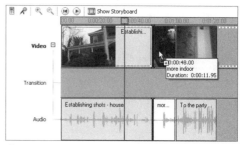

**Figure 9.23** To drag a clip between two clips, just drag and drop.

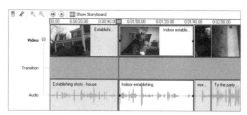

**Figure 9.24** There's the clip, safely inserted.

Selected clip —

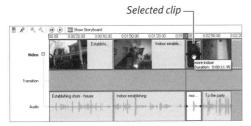

**Figure 9.25** You move clips on the Timeline the same way you do on the Storyboard, with slightly different cues. Start by selecting the clip.

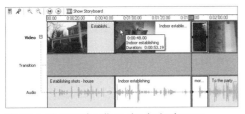

**Figure 9.26** Move the clip to the desired space, watching for the horizontal blue line, and then release the mouse button.

— Clip moved here

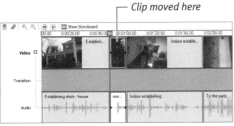

**Figure 9.27** Movie Maker inserts the clip and pushes all clips behind it to the back of the line.

## To arrange video clips on the Timeline:

1. Select a clip on the Video track.

   A small hand and a box containing the clip name and duration appear over the clip (**Figure 9.25**).

2. Drag the clip to the desired location.

   A horizontal blue line appears between the two selected video clips, and a plus sign, small box, and data box containing the start time of the new clip and name and duration of the clip to be displaced appear next to the pointer (**Figure 9.26**).

3. Release the mouse button.

   Movie Maker inserts the clip in the specified location (**Figure 9.27**).

GETTING VIDEO CLIPS TO THE TIMELINE

## To preview your video clip on the Timeline:

1. Do *one of the following:*

   ▲ Select the clip to preview.

   Movie Maker highlights the clip and positions the Playback indicator at the start of the scene.

   ▲ Drag the Playback indicator to the desired start location (**Figure 9.28**).

2. Start playback by doing *one of the following:*

   ▲ At the top left of the Timeline window, click the Play Timeline button (Figure 9.2)

   ▲ In the Monitor, click Play.

   The Play button switches to a Pause button, which you can click to pause playback.

   ▲ Press the spacebar to start playback. Press the spacebar again to pause playback.

   ▲ Right-click and choose Play Timeline (Ctrl+W).

   Playback advances automatically from clip to clip when multiple assets are present.

   During playback, the Playback indicator and Monitor Seek bar advance with the video.

## ✔ Tips

■ Click the button at the bottom left of the Monitor to preview the video in full-screen mode (you can also press Alt-Enter on your keyboard). To exit full-screen mode and return to the Movie Maker interface, press Esc on your keyboard or click anywhere on the screen.

■ The Monitor is your view of the *entire* project, and you can always use the Monitor Seek bar to reposition content in the Storyboard and Timeline.

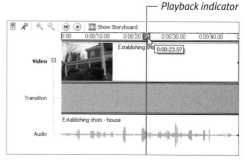

*— Playback indicator*

**Figure 9.28** Get familiar with the Playback indicator, which shifts the edit line and controls the frames viewed in the Monitor.

# Customizing Your Timeline View

You've probably already noticed that as you place additional videos on the Timeline, the big picture gets increasingly difficult to see. Fortunately, Movie Maker supplies several tools that help you control your Timeline environment.

First, Movie Maker provides a slider bar at the bottom of the Timeline that you can use to move easily through your production. In addition, you can stretch the Timeline so that it represents a longer period (and thus shows more video clips or longer stretches of a single video clip) to provide a high-level view. Or you can shrink down the Timeline

to a second-by-second view, which is helpful when you're synchronizing production elements such as audio and the main video.

### To move around the Timeline:

◆ Do *one of the following:*

▲ Drag the Timeline slider at the bottom of the Timeline to the right to reveal video clips inserted after the last visible track (**Figure 9.29**).

▲ At the upper left of the Timeline window, click Rewind Timeline to move to the start of the Timeline.

▲ Press the right arrow key to move forward to the next clip on the Timeline; press the left arrow key to move backward from clip to clip.

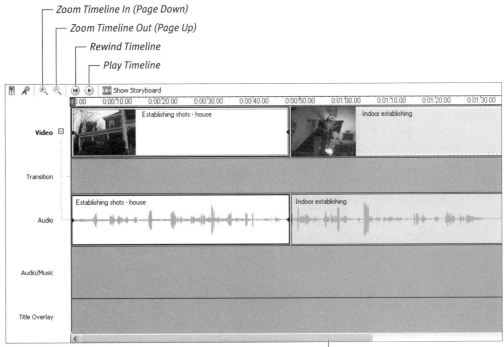

Figure 9.29 The Timeline slider moves you around your production.

## ✔ Tips

- The Timeline slider will shrink as the project gets longer, essentially representing the size of the video visible at that time on the Timeline relative to the entire project.

- You can also access right-click commands for navigating the Timeline by right-clicking the Timeline slider bar. The only command I find particularly helpful here is the Right Edge command that takes you to the end of the project (**Figure 9.30**). The rest perform their obvious namesake functions, except for Scroll Here, which I frankly couldn't figure out.

**Figure 9.30** Here are more controls for moving around the Timeline.

**Figure 9.31** Zoom to Fit places all project assets on the Timeline.

## To adjust the timescale of the Timeline:

- Do *one of the following*:
  - ▲ At the upper left of the Timeline, click Zoom Timeline In (Page Down) to zoom into the video on the Timeline, showing greater detail but less project duration.
  - ▲ At the upper left of the Timeline, click Zoom Timeline Out (Page Up) to zoom away from the video on the Timeline, showing less detail but more project duration.
  - ▲ In the main menu, choose View > Zoom to Fit (F9) to show the entire project in the Timeline (**Figure 9.31**).

Note that you can also access the Zoom In and Zoom Out controls from the View menu.

**Figure 9.32** One way to delete a clip in the Storyboard/Timeline window.

**Figure 9.33** Another way to delete, using the right-click command.

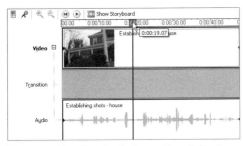

**Figure 9.34** To split a clip, first move the edit line to the desired location.

# Common Tasks

As you'd expect, Movie Maker has common commands for many housekeeping tasks you perform in the Storyboard and Timeline views. Here are the major ones, shown in the Timeline view for simplicity.

### To delete assets:

1. Select the asset to delete.

   Movie Maker highlights the clip.

2. Do *one of the following:*

   ▲ Press the Delete key.

   ▲ From the Movie Maker main menu, choose Edit > Delete (**Figure 9.32**).

   ▲ Right-click and choose Delete (**Figure 9.33**).

   Movie Maker deletes the clip from the Timeline, but not from the Contents pane or from your hard disk.

### ✔ Tips

- If you delete a video clip, all clips after the deleted clip automatically shift over to the left to close the gap.

- In addition to the options on the Edit menu and right-click menu, you can use keyboard commands to cut (Ctrl+X), copy (Ctrl+C), and paste (Ctrl+V) files.

### To split clips:

1. Use Monitor controls or drag the Playback indicator to move the edit line to the initial frame of the desired second clip (**Figure 9.34**).

   *continues on next page*

COMMON TASKS

**2.** Split the clip by doing *one of the following:*

▲ In the main menu, choose Clip > Split (Ctrl+L) (**Figure 9.35**).

▲ At the bottom right of the Monitor, click the Split the Clip button (Figure 9.18).

Movie Maker splits the clips at the edit line (**Figure 9.36**).

## ✔ Tip

■ If you apply special effects to a clip and later split the clip, Movie Maker will apply the effects to both components of the original clip. See Chapter 11 for details about working with special effects.

## To combine clips:

**1.** Select the clips to combine by doing *one of the following:*

▲ Hold down the Shift or Ctrl key and select two or more clips (**Figure 9.37**).

▲ From the Movie Maker main menu, choose Edit > Select All (Ctrl+A) to select all clips on the Storyboard or Timeline (**Figure 9.38**).

**Figure 9.35** Then choose clip > Split or press Ctrl+L.

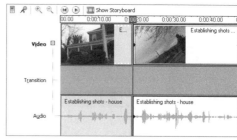

**Figure 9.36** You now have two clips.

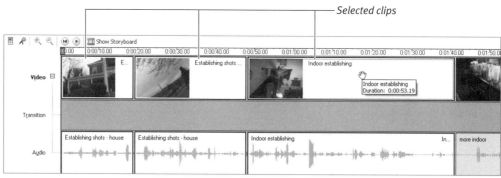

**Figure 9.37** To combine clips, hold down the Shift key while selecting two (or more) clips.

**Figure 9.38** Or select all the clips on the Timeline by choosing Edit > Select All (Ctrl+A).

**Figure 9.39** Then right-click and choose Combine (Ctrl+M).

**2.** From the main menu, choose Clip > Combine (Ctrl+M) (**Figure 9.39**).

Movie Maker combines all selected clips (**Figure 9.40**).

### ✔ Tips

- You can't combine two clips after you've inserted transitions between them, even if they are contiguous. To combine them, delete the transition.

- You can't combine clips after trimming frames from the beginning or end of either clip. To combine, restore each clip to its original length.

Combined clip

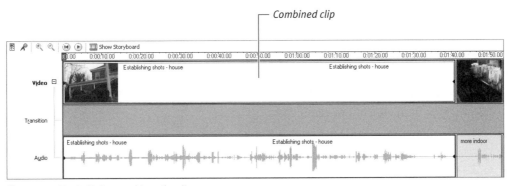

**Figure 9.40** Movie Maker combines the clips.

# Trimming Clips on the Timeline

Trimming video is the process of removing unwanted frames from the beginning and end of your clips. The start trim point is the first frame of the clip that will play in the final production, and the end trim point is the last frame.

In Movie Maker, trimming occurs exclusively on the Timeline, though there are two options. First, you can use trim handles to drag the start and end points to the desired location. In addition, you can use either menu commands or keyboard shortcuts to achieve the same result. Both approaches are covered here.

### To trim video using trim handles:

1. Select the clip.

   Movie Maker highlights the clip and places trim handles on both edges (**Figure 9.41**).

2. Hold the pointer over either edge.

   The pointer becomes a bidirectional arrow (**Figure 9.42**).

3. While holding down the mouse button and watching the video displayed in the Monitor, drag the arrow to the desired start or end frame.

4. Release the mouse button to set the trim.

   Movie Maker sets the start or end frame to the new location.

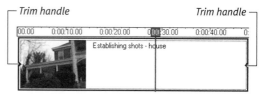

**Figure 9.41** The small triangles on both ends of the clip are trim handles you grab to trim the clip to a new duration.

**Figure 9.42** Grab the edge and drag to trim.

## ✔ Tips

- Although Movie Maker converts the pointer into a bidirectional arrow, which implies that you can drag the video in both directions, you can't drag the video to a point prior to the initial frame or beyond the final frame.

- Trimming with trim handles is generally easier when you're zoomed into the project and the Timescale covers a relatively short duration, since grabbing and moving the edge shifts only a few frames at a time. When long stretches of video are showing on the Timeline, grabbing and moving the edge may shift a few seconds at a time, making precise adjustments much more difficult to make.

## To trim video using menu commands:

1. Select the clip.

   Movie Maker highlights the clip and places trim handles on both edges (Figure 9.41).

2. Use the Monitor controls or drag the Playback indicator to move the edit line to the target start or end frame (**Figure 9.43**).

   Note that the Playback indicator is set at 40 seconds. In this example, we will set the end trim point to that location.

   *continues on next page*

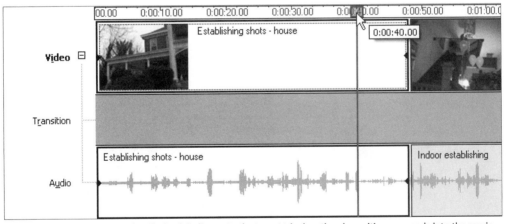

**Figure 9.43** Or you can move the Playback indicator to the target trim location; here, it's 40 seconds into the movie.

**3.** Trim the clip by doing *one of the following:*

▲ In the main menu, choose Clip > Set End Trim Point (Ctrl+Shift+O) to set the end trim point (**Figure 9.44**).

▲ In the main menu, choose Clip > Set Start Trim Point (Ctrl+Shift+I) to set the start trim point.

Movie Maker trims the clip as directed (**Figure 9.45**). Note that the clip now ends at 40 seconds.

**Figure 9.44** Then select either Set Start or Set End Trim Point to set the trim.

## ✔ Tips

■ Regardless which method you use, trimming in the Timeline doesn't affect the actual captured video file in any way. You're not really deleting any frames; you're just telling Movie Maker to use a different start frame and end frame when incorporating the clip into your production.

■ When trimming a video file, Movie Maker trims both the audio and video.

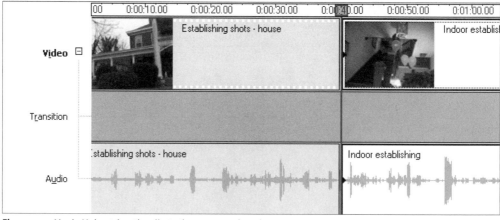

**Figure 9.45** Movie Maker trims the clip to the 40-second mark.

TRIMMING CLIPS ON THE TIMELINE

## Planning Your Trimming Activities

Before trimming your clips, consider whether you intend to fade into the first scene, fade out of the final scene, and/or use transitions between the clips. If you use any of these effects, you need to account for them in your trimming.

Briefly, transitions are animated effects inserted between clips to either smooth or emphasize the passage from one clip to the next (for details, see Chapter 10). The most commonly used transition is a cut, which is actually the absence of a transition: the video simply jumps from the last frame of the first clip to the first frame of the second clip. Other frequently used transitions are dissolves, wipes, and fades, which you implement using frames that overlap two clips.

If you were trimming two clips to be joined by a cut, the end frame for your first video clip would be the last frame you want to appear in the production. Similarly, the start frame for the second video clip would be the initial frame you want visible.

Video that I recently shot at the annual Fiddler's Convention here in Galax, Virginia, provides a great example of how you need to plan for your trimming activities. In this clip, my daughters are looking at some dodo-bird puppets (**Figure 9.46**). The visual is key because of the comment my eldest daughter made at the time: "Daddy, can we take these due-due birds home?" This brought a lot of chuckles from those around us.

**Figure 9.46** Two seconds can make a huge difference. If I cut into this clip at 7 seconds, 15 frames in, viewers see DODO BIRDS and get the joke. If I transition in using a 2-second transition, the first complete frame viewers see is DO BIRDS, and the context of the joke is lost.

If I cut from the previous clip into this scene, the frame shown on the left of Figure 9.46, which is located at 7 seconds and 15 frames into the scene, will be the first one shown, so the viewer will understand the visual context of the remark. In contrast, if I transition from the previous clip using a 2-second transition, the first completely visible frame will be 2 seconds later, shown on the right of Figure 9.46, located at 9 seconds and 15 frames into the clip. As you can see, "DODO BIRDS" is no longer visible (extinct, so to speak), and though the audio is still there, the visual context is lost.

*continues on next page*

## Planning Your Trimming Activities  *continued*

What this boils down to is that you need to leave sufficient frames at the front of the clip so that the target frame becomes the first visible frame after the transition. If you're using 2-second transitions or fades, then you should trim to 2 seconds before the target start frame.

Of course, the same approach applies at the end of the clip if you plan to fade out or transition into another scene. Specifically, if you're using a 2-second transition or fade, leave 2 seconds of video after the last frame you want completely visible before the transition or fade.

A similar approach is a good rule to use when shooting and capturing your video in general. Always start shooting 5 to 10 seconds before you think you actually want to start, and let the camera roll for a similar duration after the end of the shot. When capturing, always start the capture a few seconds before the target first frame, and continue a few seconds after the target last frame to provide the extra footage needed during editing.

## Trimming Precautions

When trimming on the Timeline, it's important to know how your work will affect content placed later in the Timeline, especially content placed in the Audio/Music or Title Overlay track. Here's why.

All trimming edits performed by Movie Maker are technically called ripple edits. Performing a ripple edit is very much like trimming a single clip on the Timeline—only that clip's duration is changed. However, the effect of the trimming *ripples* through the remainder of the video on the Video track (and associated Audio track) to close the gap created in the trimmed clip. For example, if you trim 2 seconds from a clip, you shorten the entire project by 2 seconds.

Sounds pretty logical, but here's what can happen if you're not on the lookout. As you can see in **Figure 9.47**, I've lined up a title (on the Title Overlay track) and a song (on the Audio/Music track) with the clip First Guests, at about 2:00 minutes into the video. As currently configured, when the video hits 2 minutes, the clip First Guests will start playing, the title "First Guest Arrives" will appear, and the joyful music of the Indigo Girls will well up, bringing happy tears to my spouse's eyes.

However, in **Figure 9.48**, I've trimmed the immediately preceding video, To the Party Room, by approximately 5 seconds, to the 1:55 mark. As you can see, the clip First Guests rippled back with the trim, but the music and title remained in their original positions. Basically, I've lost synchronization with the other elements in the project.

Here are the lessons. First, Movie Maker's ripple trims affect only the video and associated audio, not the other two tracks. So if you've added titles and background audio (or narration) to your production and later trim video or still images on the Video track, be prepared to resynchronize the titles and background audio.

*continues on next page*

## Trimming Precautions *continued*

Second, since Movie Maker doesn't ripple all the tracks, the most efficient approach generally is to trim and finalize all of your video components before you start adding background audio (music or narration) or titles to your video. Otherwise, any adjustments made to your video may necessitate the time-consuming resynchronization of other project components.

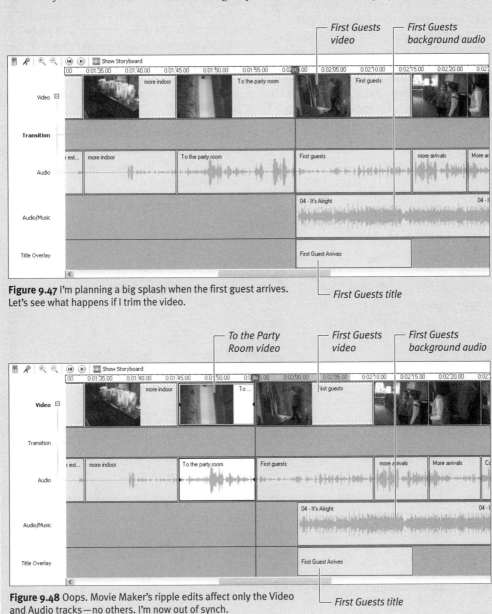

**Figure 9.47** I'm planning a big splash when the first guest arrives. Let's see what happens if I trim the video.

**Figure 9.48** Oops. Movie Maker's ripple edits affect only the Video and Audio tracks—no others. I'm now out of synch.

TRIMMING CLIPS ON THE TIMELINE

# Advanced Timeline Editing

Okay—you've worked through Timeline 101; now it's time for the advanced course. As previously mentioned, in its default state, Movie Maker maintains synchronization of the video file and the original audio file captured with the video and also uses global ripple edits to maintain the relative positions of assets on the Video track.

This approach works well in most instances, but sometimes you may want to use the audio from one Video track and the video from another. The following two examples—insert edits and split edits—show you what to do.

## Using insert edits

Briefly, an insert edit is a technique that lets you insert just the video portion of one clip into another larger clip, while using the background audio from the larger clip. In the birthday video, for example, I'll use insert edits to integrate cutaway shots of parents and kids watching the clown. This will introduce change into the video, which is always good, and show that the attendees were enjoying the show, which is probably the most important point of the entire video.

Another useful application of the insert edit is to seamlessly shorten the duration of some aspect of an event, such as the opening and closing processionals at a wedding, graduation, or other ceremony. In these instances, where background music is playing, cutting out segments where no one is on camera produces distracting audio breaks that draw attention to your editing.

Instead, by using insert editing to preserve the background audio track, you can shorten the sequence dramatically, yet still retain the highlights. And if you do your work well, no one will even notice.

### To create an insert edit:

1. Drag the clip containing the background audio onto the Video track.

2. Drag the same clip to the Audio/Music track (**Figure 9.49**).

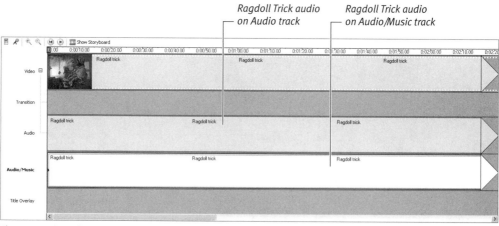

*Ragdoll Trick audio on Audio track*

*Ragdoll Trick audio on Audio/Music track*

**Figure 9.49** Start the insert edit by dragging the clip containing the background audio track down twice, once into the Video track, and once into the Audio/Music track.

**Figure 9.50** Then mute the Audio track, leaving all audio in the Audio/Music track.

**Figure 9.51** Locate the start of the insert edit. It's much easier when working with round numbers.

**3.** Right-click the file on the Audio track and choose Mute (**Figure 9.50**).

This mutes the audio from the Audio track, so the only remaining audio is from Audio/Music track.

**4.** Move the Playback indicator to the target starting frame for the cutaway clip that you want to insert (**Figure 9.51**).

As you'll see in a moment, operation is easier if you use a round number like the 30-second mark used in Figure 9.51. If you're having difficulty stopping on a round number, zoom into the Timeline or use the frame-by-frame controls on the Monitor to fine-tune your position (**Figure 9.52**).

**5.** At the bottom right of the Monitor, click Split the Clip.

Movie Maker splits the clip.

*continues on next page*

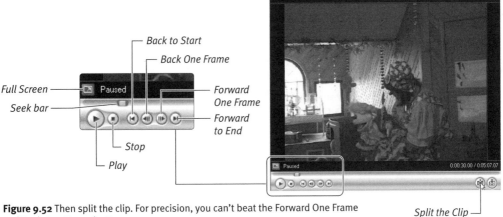

**Figure 9.52** Then split the clip. For precision, you can't beat the Forward One Frame and Back One Frame buttons.

ADVANCED TIMELINE EDITING

**181**

**6.** Move the Playback indicator to the target ending point for the inserted cutaway clip.

Choose an end point that will produce a duration slightly shorter than the cutaway clip. For example, I'll be inserting a cutaway approximately 7 seconds long, so I'll make a gap 6 seconds long. Once again, use a round number like the 36-second mark used in the **Figure 9.53**.

**7.** At the bottom right of the Monitor, click the Split the Clip button.

Movie Maker splits the clip, creating a clip exactly 6 seconds long.

**8.** Select the short clip, right-click, and choose Delete (**Figure 9.54**).

I've created a 6-second gap in the Video track that I must fill with a 6-second cutaway to maintain synchronization with the sound in the Audio/Music track.

**9.** Drag the cutaway clip into the split created by the deleted clip.

**10.** Grab the trim handles on the inserted cutaway clip and trim the clip to the same duration as the gap created by deleting the clip in Step 8 (in this example, 6 seconds) (**Figure 9.55**).

If you have trouble achieving the precise duration, zoom into the Timeline using the Zoom Timeline controls at the upper left of the Timeline (or press Page Down on your keyboard).

Your Timeline should now look like **Figure 9.56**, with a 6-second insert edit between the two segments.

**Figure 9.53** Move to the end location of the insert edit, again choosing a nice round number.

**Figure 9.54** Delete the clip you created with the two splits, creating a gap for the insert edit.

**Figure 9.55** Insert your cutaway clip and trim to the desired length.

**11.** Right-click the newly inserted file on the Audio track and choose Mute (Figure 9.50).

This mutes the audio from the cutaway clip.

### ✔ Tips

■ The art of insert editing is in finding cutaway clips that don't make it obvious that you're combining clips shot at different points in the event. For example, the cutaway clip inserted here was shot about 15 minutes after the Ragdoll Trick clip. I had to make sure that kids sitting in the cutaway weren't standing in the Ragdoll Trick clip, and that the sound tracks matched—for example, that the

kids weren't laughing or clapping in the cutaway to silence in the Audio/Music track. This is why you have to shoot tons of cutaways during filming to find multiple keepers during editing.

■ I also use this insert technique to hide bad camera moments, such as when I'm moving the camera from subject to subject or zooming in and out to frame a shot.

■ If you plan to do these type of edits, annotating your clips in the Contents pane speeds the process by helping you quickly identify the clips to insert (see "Customizing Your Collection Views" in Chapter 3).

*Inserted cutaway clip*

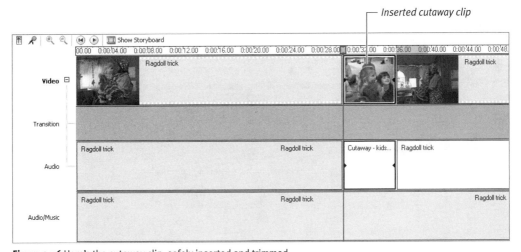

**Figure 9.56** Here's the cutaway clip, safely inserted and trimmed.

## To shorten a wedding processional:

1. Drag the clip containing the background audio onto the Video track.

2. Drag the same clip to the Audio/Music track (**Figure 9.57**).

   Note that the clip is just under 6:40 seconds in duration.

3. Right-click the file on the Audio track and choose Mute (Figure 9.50).

   This mutes the audio from the Audio track, so the only remaining audio is from the Audio/Music track.

4. Move the Playback indicator to the end of the first sequence.

   I'm condensing the opening processional at the beginning of the wedding. I started shooting as the first group started down the aisle and kept the camera rolling to ensure audio continuity. In this step, I'm moving the Playback indicator to the moment after the first group walked by the camera.

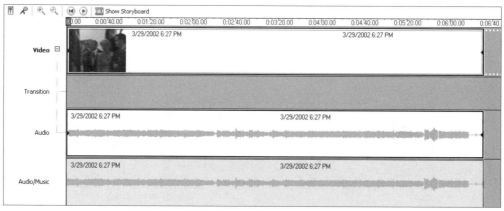

**Figure 9.57** Now let's shorten this wedding processional. It starts out 6:40 minutes long.

**Figure 9.58** The clip is split the moment after the first group walks by.

**Figure 9.59** Then the second clip is trimmed to where the second group is beginning to walk down the aisle.

**5.** At the bottom right of the Monitor, click the Split the Clip button.

Movie Maker splits the clip (**Figure 9.58**).

**6.** Grab the trim handle on the left edge of the second clip and trim to the start of the next group walking down the aisle (**Figure 9.59**).

**7.** Grab and move the Playback indicator to the end of this sequence.

**8.** At the bottom right of the Monitor, click the Split the Clip button.

Movie Maker splits the clip again.

**9.** Repeat Steps 6, 7, and 8 for each group in the processional.

With all the processional video adjusted, the Timeline looks like **Figure 9.60**. Note that the Audio/Music track is much longer than the Video track, since I haven't yet trimmed that track. The final duration of the Video track in this example is about 2:25, so that's what I'll trim the Audio/Music track to.

*continues on next page*

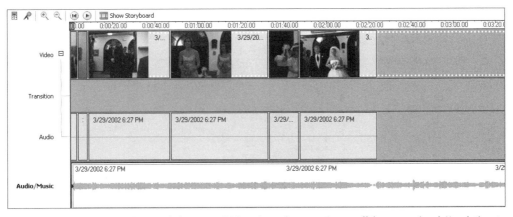

**Figure 9.60** Getting some serious work done now. We've trimmed over 4 minutes off the processional. Now let's get the audio right.

**10.** On the Audio/Music track, grab the trim handle on the left and pull to the right until the data box reports that your file is the same duration as the remaining video (**Figure 9.61**).

**11.** Drag the file on the Audio/Music track all the way to the left.

This last step matches the end of the Audio/Music file ("Here Comes the Bride") with the appearance of the bride

(**Figure 9.62**). This last adjustment in Steps 10 and 11 is necessary only if you have to match the audio to what's happening in the video. For example, in the closing processional, this type of edit wasn't necessary.

Overall, this process trimmed about 4 minutes from the processional (over 60 percent), but since the audio is continuous, most viewers won't even notice.

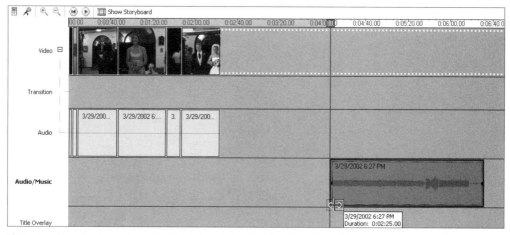

**Figure 9.61** Drag the clip in the Audio/Music track to the final duration of the video (2:25 in this example).

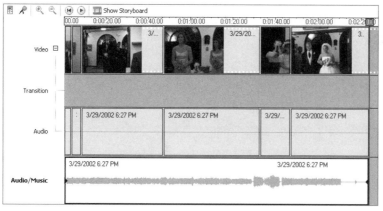

**Figure 9.62** Then drag the clip all the way to the left. Now "Here Comes the Bride" plays when the bride is coming—always a good thing.

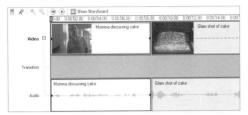

**Figure 9.63** Let's listen to my wife talk about the cake while we look at the cake.

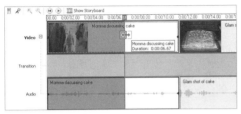

**Figure 9.64** Start by dragging the first clip back, essentially creating the audio to drag under the second clip.

# Using split edits

Split edits are transitions in which the audio and video start playing at different times. There are two basic types of split edits: L-cuts and J-cuts.

In an *L-cut*, the audio from the first video continues while the second video starts playing. The classic use is in newscasts, when the video switches from the anchor to a reporter on the scene. To make the transition feel seamless, the audio of the anchor asking a question continues to play while the video switches to a field reporter, usually nodding sagely to acknowledge the wisdom of the question.

In the task that follows, I've used an L-cut to transition from a sequence where Momma is describing how she baked the birthday cake to a view of the cake. Viewers hear Momma describing the ingredients for about 5 seconds while looking at the gorgeous result.

In a *J-cut*, the audio from the second video precedes the appearance of the actual frames. In the J-cut task that follows, the first video was shot while I was walking up the stairs to the playroom before the party; the second video was shot while the party was in full swing. I use the audio from the party to presage what viewers will see when I get to the top of the stairs. Though all this may sound complicated, Movie Maker makes short work of both kinds of edits.

## To create an L-cut:

1. Load two clips onto the Timeline and select the first clip (**Figure 9.63**).

2. Grab the trim handle and trim the first clip to the left until you reach the last frame to be displayed (**Figure 9.64**). Movie Maker trims the clip to the new duration.

*continues on next page*

**3.** Right-click the first clip and choose Copy.

**4.** Right-click the Audio/Music track and choose Paste.

Movie Maker pastes the audio from the first clip onto the Audio/Music track (**Figure 9.65**).

**5.** Grab the trim handle on the pasted audio file and drag it all the way to the right.

**6.** Drag the Playback indicator to the end of the audio file on the Audio/Music track (**Figure 9.66**).

**7.** At the bottom right of the Monitor, click the Split the Clip button to split the clip on the Video and Audio tracks.

**8.** Mute both files on the Audio track above the pasted file on the Audio/Music track by right-clicking and choosing Mute.

Movie Maker extends the audio from the first clip under the video to the second clip, forming the namesake *L* appearance (**Figure 9.67**).

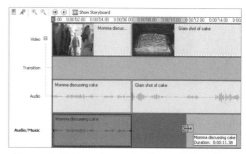

**Figure 9.65** Movie Maker pastes the audio from the first clip onto the Audio/Music track.

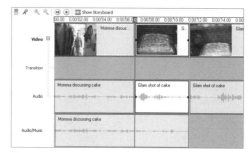

**Figure 9.66.** Looking good so far. Now mute the two tracks above the Audio/Music track.

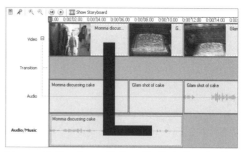

**Figure 9.67** Now the audio from the first clip extends beneath the second clip, completing the L-cut.

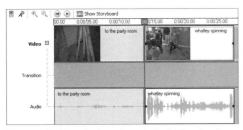

**Figure 9.68** Now the J-cut (no relation). The view here is of the stairs leading up to the playroom. Let's use the sound from the next clip to presage the action.

**Figure 9.69** Drag the second clip to the right to create the audio to drag under and create the J.

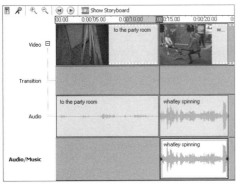

**Figure 9.70** Movie Maker pastes the audio from the second clip onto the Audio/Music track.

## To create a J-cut:

1. Load two clips onto the Timeline and select the second clip (**Figure 9.68**).

   It's a bit tough to see, but the image in the first clip shows the top of the stairs.

2. Grab the trim handle and trim the second clip to the right until you reach the first frame to be displayed after the cut (**Figure 9.69**).

   Movie Maker trims the clip to the new duration.

3. Right-click the second clip and choose Copy.

4. Right-click the Audio/Music track and choose Paste.

   Movie Maker pastes the audio from the second clip onto the Audio/Music track (**Figure 9.70**).

*continues on next page*

**5.** Grab the trim handle on the pasted audio file and drag it all the way to the left.

This extends the audio from the second video (the girls playing on the seesaw) so that it will also play during the first video (taken while walking up the stairs), presaging the fun that's going on in the play room.

**6.** Drag the Playback indicator to the beginning of the audio file on the Audio/Music track (**Figure 9.71**).

**7.** At the bottom right of the Monitor, click the Split the Clip button to split the clip on the Video and Audio tracks.

**8.** Mute both files on the Audio track above the pasted file on the Audio/Music track by right-clicking and choosing Mute.

Movie Maker extends the audio from the second clip to the desired position under the Video track of the first clip, forming the namesake *J* appearance (**Figure 9.72**).

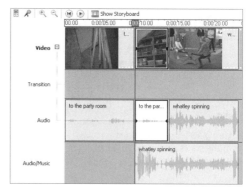

**Figure 9.71** Move the Playback indicator to the beginning of the audio file and split the video clip.

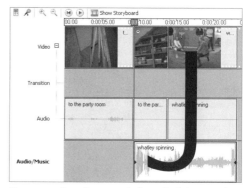

**Figure 9.72** Drag the second clip to the left, mute the two clips above it, and there's the "J".

# Editing Still Images

When you drop still images onto the Video track, Movie Maker treats the images almost the same way it treats video files, except that there are no duration limits or associated audio files. All the techniques described in the previous sections for getting videos into the Storyboard/Timeline window, moving them around, trimming them on the Timeline, and splitting and deleting them apply to still images as well.

You set the default duration for all images inserted into your projects in the Options dialog box using a process described in "Setting Project Defaults" in Chapter 3.

You can drag multiple images to the Timeline to create a slide show, and you can add audio, transitions, and special effects. If you're really psyched about slide shows, check out Appendix B, which describes how to create slide shows with Microsoft Plus! Photo Story, a component of Microsoft's $19.95 Plus! Digital Media Edition (DME).

## To create a slide show:

1. Start with the Storyboard/Timeline window in Storyboard view and the Contents pane open to a collection containing still images.

*continues on next page*

**2.** Do *one of the following:*

▲ Drag images one by one onto the Storyboard.

▲ To select all images on the Contents pane and drag them to the Storyboard, choose Edit > Select All from the Movie Maker main menu or press Ctrl+A.

▲ To select multiple sequential images and drag them to the Storyboard, click the first image, hold down the Shift key, and click the final image.

▲ To select multiple nonsequential images and drag them to the Storyboard, click the first image, hold down the Ctrl key, and click additional target images (**Figure 9.73**).

▲ To select groups of images and drag them to the Storyboard, click any white area in the album and drag over the target images.

Once your images are on the Storyboard, add, delete, and arrange them as desired via drag and drop (see "To arrange assets in Storyboard view" earlier in this chapter).

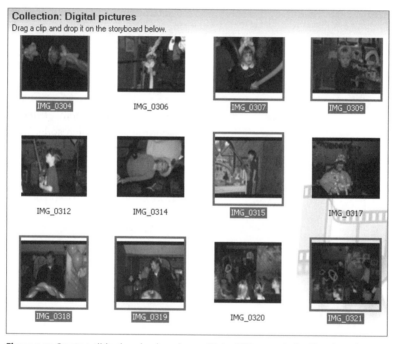

**Figure 9.73** Create a slide show by dragging multiple still images to the Storyboard.

## Slide Show Duration: How Much is Too Much?

I've been building digital slide shows since a trip to Egypt in 1998, where I brought a flash-less, clunky Kodak that grabbed 640x480 images and required nearly direct sunlight to produce legible images (a lesson I learned the hard way in the tombs of the Valley of the Kings).

Three observations: First, the slide show duration has to match the background beat of the selected music. For example, the slide show for the trip to Egypt was set to the Bangles' "Walk Like an Egyptian," and if I didn't change slides every second or two, the video segment looked like it was dragging.

Second, remember your intended audience when setting slide show duration. I do a lot of work just for my daughters, and their attention spans call for really short durations, definitely in the 1- to 2-second range. On the other hand, many folks beyond adolescence like to study the pictures (especially family shots), so you can go a bit longer.

Finally, even with the most lugubrious beat and mature audience, slides get really old after 5 seconds or so, and positively painful after 10 seconds. Doesn't sound like a long time, but preview your own slide shows and you'll see what I mean. Unless you have your audience chained to their chairs, I wouldn't extend beyond 5 seconds.

Movie Maker's default image duration is 5 seconds and is applied to all images inserted into the Storyboard or Timeline. Although you can change the duration for each image manually to match your background music, that obviously gets time consuming.

What I typically do is experiment with the first five or ten images to find the best duration. Then I change the default duration accordingly and import the rest of my images.

# Working with Audio Files

As we've seen, when you drag a video file into the Storyboard/Timeline window, Movie Maker drags the audio as well, placing it on the Audio track beneath the Transition track. You can also add audio alone to a Movie Maker project, using either of two approaches; in both cases, you drag the file onto the Audio/Music track.

Once you've imported an audio file into a collection, you can add it to a project by dragging it onto the Audio/Music track. Similarly, you can add just the audio from a video file in a collection by dragging the file onto the Audio/Music track.

Virtually all the techniques I described earlier for getting videos into the Storyboard/Timeline window, moving them around, trimming them on the Timeline, and splitting and deleting them apply to audio files as well. The only exception is that Movie Maker lets you place audio files anywhere in a production, even if doing so creates a gap in the playback audio. Be careful to avoid these unintended gaps when you place your files.

## To add audio to the Storyboard/ Timeline window:

1. Do *one of the following:*

   ▲ In the Collection window, click an Audio track.

   ▲ In the Collection window, click a Video track containing audio.

2. Drag the clip to the target location on the Audio/Music track (**Figure 9.74**).

   Movie Maker inserts the audio file at the selected location (**Figure 9.75**).

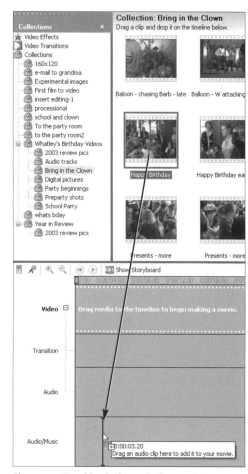

**Figure 9.74** To add only the audio from a clip to the project, drag and drop the clip onto the Audio/Music track.

## ✔ Tip

■ If you insert an audio file into the Audio/ Music track, you can't insert narration at that same location. If you want to add background music and narration in the same location, first add the background music and then render your project (see Chapter 16). When you are finished, import the video file into the Timeline, add the narration, and render again.

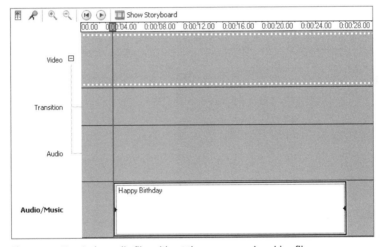

**Figure 9.75** Here's the audio file, without the accompanying video file.

# 10

# USING TRANSITIONS

Transitions are effects placed between video clips to help smooth the movement from one scene to another. We've all seen transitions, even if we don't recognize them by that name. In movies, for example, when the screen fades to black at the end of a dramatic scene and then fades back in from black to the next scene, the filmmaker is using a *fade* transition. When two scenes blend together for a moment before the second scene appears clearly, the filmmaker is using a *dissolve* transition.

On *Monday Night Football*, when the halftime stats swing back, down, and under, revealing Al and John, that's a transition, too. However, in most film and television productions, the most frequent transition is a *cut*, which is actually the absence of a transition, or the instantaneous jump from the last frame of the first clip to the first frame of the second clip.

Your ability to apply and customize transitions in Movie Maker depends upon whether you're displaying the Storyboard or Timeline window. This chapter begins with an overview of how transitions work in each and then describes both the transitions included in Movie Maker and those available from third-party vendors. Along the way, it includes information on when to use transitions and how to apply and customize them.

# Understanding Transitions

As you'll see, using and customizing transitions is easy. Using them effectively is also easy, if you keep several simple concepts in mind.

Let's examine these concepts with reference to the birthday party video I've been working on. To recap, here are the major project components.

- **Setting the scene:** Includes exterior shots of the house and interior shots as establishing shots.

- **Arrival:** People arriving, meeting and greeting, and getting set for the party.

- **Entertainment:** The longest segment of the video (about 15 minutes), with video of the clown and crowd reactions to the magic act.

- **Transition to cake scene:** Children having fun and then walking to the dining room.

- **Cake scene:** Shots of "Happy Birthday" and blowing out the candles.

- **Opening the presents:** The best part of the event, according to my daughter.

- **Parting is such sweet sorrow:** Hugs, kisses, and goodbyes.

- **Still picture slide show:** Pictures taken during the event.

- **Year in review pictures:** Pictures of my daughter taken since her last birthday.

## A little goes a long way

Recognize that you don't have to insert a transition between every two clips on the Timeline. Rather, use a transition only when it highlights a change in place or time that you want the viewer to perceive. Even then, use a transition only if you don't have footage that better shows the change in place or time.

For example, I probably won't use a transition *within* any of the first seven segments (all composed of video rather than still images), with one exception, which I'll discuss in a moment. I'll use cuts between each clip within each section because they took place at or near the same time.

When moving *between* sections, I probably will use both a title and a fade transition, to let the viewer know something is changing. The only exception is when I move from component 4 (the transition to the cake scene) to component 5 (the cake scene), where I have some great footage of the kids walking down the stairs from the playroom and into the dining room. Since this footage clues the viewer into the change in locale and activity, I don't need the title and transition.

The only time I'll use a transition *within* a scene is when I'm shortening a sequence and the start of a clip is so visually similar to the previous clip that the viewer will have difficulty understanding what's happening without a transition.

For example, in **Figure 10.1**, I'm shortening one of the magic acts by trimming out segments where little is going on. Each frame in the figure represents the start of a newly shortened sequence. As you can see, the scene doesn't change much between the segments, so without some transitions, the viewer may think the video skipped or some other kind of error occurred. This problem occurs frequently during interviews or other shots involving a static camera on a tripod, because the picture doesn't change significantly from shot to shot.

To avoid confusing the viewer, I'll insert a transition within this scene to signify that it's not the DVD skipping or some other error. However, I won't insert just any transition; I'll use a *motivated* transition, which is the type of transition you should be aiming to use most of the time. Read on for details on this very important concept.

**Figure 10.1** These three scenes are so close that using a cut between them would confuse the audience. This is one of the key scenarios for using a transition within a scene.

## Keep it motivated

*Motivated* transitions are transitions that relate to the content of the video. For example, the classic motivated transition for the problem shown in Figure 10.1 would be the clock wipe, where the hand of a clock reveals the second video while hiding the first. The transition is said to be motivated because showing a clock suggests that time has passed, which is exactly the impression we're trying to create.

Unfortunately, the closest Movie Maker comes to a clock wipe is the pinwheel transition, shown on the left in **Figure 10.2**. In fact, you'll likely find Movie Maker's library of motivated transitions very slim, especially compared to more comprehensive programs like Pinnacle Studio.

This limitation is no big deal, however, if you're willing to spend a little time and money to acquire several libraries of transitions that are available to significantly enhance Movie Maker's capabilities.

If it's winter, you can pick up the free Winter Fun Pack 2003 for Windows Movie Maker 2, which includes both Snow Wipe and Snow

Burst transitions, which will look great in your winter movies. Download the Winter Fun Pack at `http://www.microsoft.com/windowsxp/moviemaker/downloads/winterfun.asp`

Also consider the Microsoft Plus! Digital Media Edition, which costs $19.95 and can be downloaded at `http://www.microsoft.com/windows/plus/PlusHome.asp`

The Plus! pack includes the Analog Recorder, discussed in "Converting Analog Audio to Digital" in Chapter 7, as well as Photo Story 2, a tool for creating movies from digital images, detailed in Appendix B. It also includes the organic clock wipe transition shown on the right of Figure 10.2, plus a range of other useful transitions.

If you're serious about your transitions, however, surf over to `www.pixelan.com`, which includes both transitions and effects that extend Movie Maker's capabilities immensely (I'll cover the effects in Chapter 11). Among the motivated transitions, I just adore the $19 Spice Rack Pack of 25 PipFX transitions, especially in combination with some of the fun editing effects discussed in Chapter 9.

Pinwheel      Clock wipe

**Figure 10.2** Using either the pinwheel transition or clock wipe clues the viewer that I've cut some footage, eliminating any confusion.

UNDERSTANDING TRANSITIONS

Picture in picture

**Figure 10.3** Pixelan's way-cool picture-in-picture transition—looks just like the evening news!

For example, in "Using split edits" in Chapter 9, I discussed an L-cut that played the audio of my wife discussing the birthday cake she had baked with the video showing the birthday cake. Using a picture-in-picture transition from the Pixelan collection, I combined a shot of my wife talking about the cake with the video of the cake itself, producing a segment that looks just like the video on the evening news (**Figure 10.3**).

If you acquire all the collections mentioned here, you'll have lots of motivated transitions to enhance your video footage. For example, the heart transition is perfect for Valentine's Day, the evaporate transition is great for those hot summer days on the beach, two page-curl transitions look wonderful with image slide shows, and several fire transitions work well for barbeques or camping trips.

In my view, if you can't find the visual tie to your footage that makes a transition motivated, it's best to just keep it simple. When in doubt, a simple dissolve or fade is usually the best choice.

## Like meets like

The final rule is that your transitions should match the extent of change in place and time. For example, when you move from the dining room to the living room, the change is pretty minor. Here you might use a simple dissolve from the old scene to the new scene.

But you shouldn't fade to black and then fade back in to the living room scene because a fade to black suggests a very significant change in place and time. However, if the entire birthday party sequence, from start to finish, were part of a longer video, you might fade to black at the end of the party and then fade in from black at the next major scene: Thanksgiving or that trip to Disneyland.

## Fade? Dissolve? Cross-Fade?

Since I'm throwing these terms around so frequently, it makes sense to define them.

When applied to video, a *fade* is a transition that smoothly fades from video to video, showing elements of both during the transition, as shown on the left of **Figure 10.4**. Some programs refer to a fade between clips as a cross-fade, but I'll stick with Movie Maker's designation to avoid confusion.

Fade to black, of course, is when a video clip fades slowly to black. Clips can also fade to white or fade from black or white (or any color you choose).

In contrast, a *dissolve* is an effect that's like a fade, but includes some graininess or pixilation, making it slightly more obvious than a fade (on the right of Figure 10.4). Use a dissolve instead of a fade when you want to make it slightly more obvious that time, location, or both are changing.

Applied to audio, a fade is the slow transition from full volume to zero volume. A cross-fade involves two clips: one fading out (from 100 percent volume to 0 percent) and one fading in (from 0 percent to 100 percent).

**Figure 10.4** That's a fade transition on the left and a dissolve on the right.

*To open Video Transitions collection*

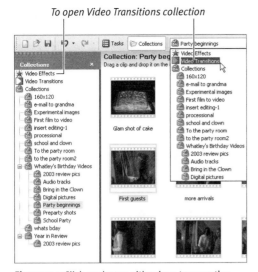

**Figure 10.5** Click or choose either icon to open the Video Transitions collection.

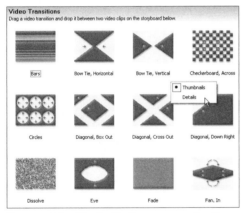

**Figure 10.6** As with all collections, you can view the transitions in both Thumbnails and Details modes.

# How Transitions Work in Movie Maker

Movie Maker stores all transitions in the Video Transitions collection, including those that ship with the program and those provided by third parties. You access them by clicking the collection in the Collections pane or choosing Video Transitions from the Collections list (**Figure 10.5**).

Note that Video Transitions is a bit of a misnomer, given that Movie Maker can apply these transitions to both video and still images. For this reason, I'll generically refer to Video Transitions simply as transitions.

Once opened, the Video Transitions collection looks like **Figure 10.6**, displayed in Thumbnail view. Right-click and choose Details to display the transitions in Details view, which is often helpful when you're trying to find a specific transition by name.

## Transitions in the Storyboard

Applying transitions in the Storyboard view gives you access to one great feature and presents you with one major limitation.

The great feature is the ability to apply transitions to multiple still images or video clips simultaneously, as detailed in "To insert a transition between slide show images" later in this chapter. This is a wonderful time saver if you're creating a slide show or similar production. Note that in the Timeline view, you can't apply multiple transitions; you can only apply one transition per application.

The major limitation of working in Storyboard view is that you can't customize the transition duration. Recall that you set the default transition duration on the Advanced tab of the Options window (**Figure 10.7**), which is accessed by choosing Tools > Options from the main menu (as described fully in "Setting Project Defaults" in Chapter 3).

When you insert a transition in the Storyboard view, Movie Maker applies this duration, but doesn't let you modify it. No sweat; you can modify the duration as described in "To modify the transition duration" later in this chapter, but you'll have to switch to Timeline view.

## Transitions in Timeline view

In Timeline view, you can apply a transition two ways. The first method is to drag a transition from the Video Transitions collection between two clips. However, this works only on the Video track.

On all other tracks, the only transition you can apply is a fade transition. Briefly, a fade is a transition where the first content slowly fades out while the second content slowly fades in. On tracks other than the Video track, you apply the fade transition between clips by dragging the second clip back toward the first. Movie Maker assists your efforts by displaying a fade indicator as you drag the clip (**Figure 10.8**).

Being able to insert a fade on other tracks provides significant creative opportunities. For example, when applying background music, you can fade between any two songs. When applying titles, you can have two titles on screen simultaneously, each driven by its own animation scheme, which can be very compelling. We'll explore these capabilities in detail in Chapters 12 and 13. For now, keep in mind that Movie Maker's transition capabilities extend to all tracks, but only in the Timeline view. In Storyboard view, you can insert transitions only between video clips or still images on the Video track.

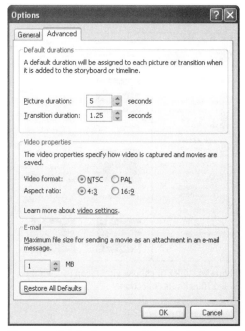

**Figure 10.7** Here's where you set the standard transition duration.

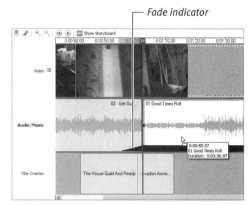

**Figure 10.8** Movie Maker can insert a fade transition on all tracks; just drag the second clip back into the first.

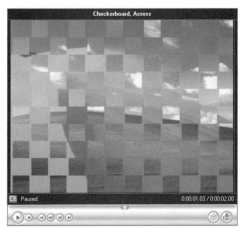

**Figure 10.9** Previewing the checkerboard transition with the Microsoft supplied images.

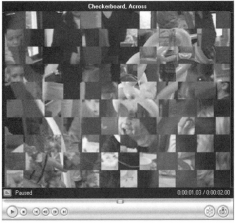

**Figure 10.10** You can easily substitute your own images for transition previews, which I've done here.

# Using Transitions

The next few pages cover the basics of working with transitions. Once you've mastered these, I'll describe how to customize transitions, how to use an image matte and fade transition to create long fade-in and fade-out effects, and how to insert multiple transitions into a slide show.

### To preview a transition effect in the Contents pane:

1. If the Video Transitions collection is not showing, click Video Transitions in the Collections pane or choose Video Transitions from the Collections list (Figure 10.5).

2. If necessary, scroll down to reveal the transition you want to preview.

3. To preview the transition, do *one of the following*:

   ▲ Double-click the transition.

   ▲ Drag the transition into the Monitor.

   Movie Maker plays the transition in the Monitor (**Figure 10.9**). The hillside beneath the cloudy sky is the first clip, and the sand dune is the second.

### ✔ Tip

■ The preview images are JPEG files called sample1.jpg and sample2.jpg that are produced at 320x240 resolution and stored in C:\program files\movie maker\shared. If you replace these images with similarly prepared images (320x240 JPEG images) of the same name, you can choose your own preview images, as shown in **Figure 10.10**. Don't use images that are too similar, or you'll have problems seeing more subtle transitions. I'm switching back to the default images to avoid confusion during the rest of this chapter.

## To insert a transition between two clips in the Storyboard:

1. With at least two clips in the Storyboard, drag any transition into the box between two clips.

   Movie Maker highlights the transition and transition box, and a small plus sign and box appear below the pointer (**Figure 10.11**).

2. Release the mouse button.

   Movie Maker inserts the transition.

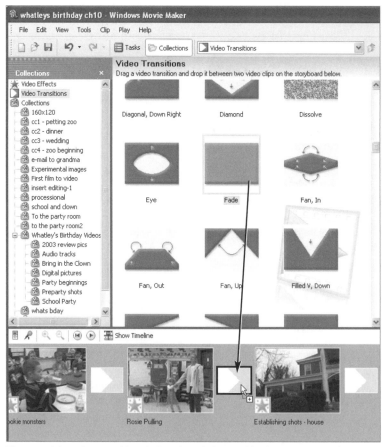

**Figure 10.11** Inserting transitions in Storyboard view couldn't be easier—just drag and drop.

## To insert a transition from the Video Transitions collection between two clips in the Timeline:

1. With at least two clips in the Timeline, drag any transition to the connecting line between two clips.

A horizontal blue line appears between the two video clips, and a plus sign, small box, and data box containing the insert time of the transition and the name and duration of the second clip appear next to the pointer (**Figure 10.12**).

*continues on next page*

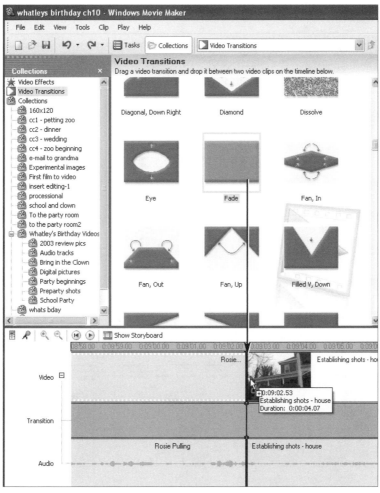

**Figure 10.12** Not too bad in Timeline mode either—just drag and drop between the two clips.

**2.** Release the mouse button.

Movie Maker inserts the transition (**Figure 10.13**).

### ✔ Tips

■ When Movie Maker inserts a transition between two clips, it also inserts a cross-fade between the two audio clips, simultaneously reducing the volume on the first clip from 100 percent to 0 percent and boosting the volume on the second clip from 0 percent to 100 percent.

■ If you drag a transition into the Timeline and the Video track isn't already expanded to show the Transition and Audio tracks, Movie Maker will expand it automatically.

### To insert a fade transition between clips on any track:

**1.** Place the Playback indicator between the two clips (**Figure 10.14**).

To produce a transition of a specific target length, note the location on the timescale—in this example, 9:02.53.

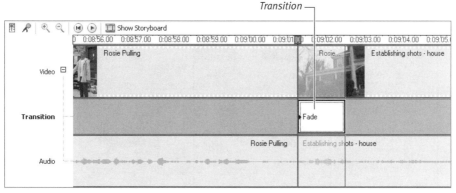

**Figure 10.13** There it is: fade transition safely inserted.

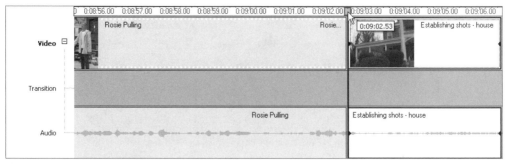

**Figure 10.14** To insert a fade transition with a custom duration, note the time on the Playback indicator between the two clips (9:02.53 here).

USING TRANSITIONS

**2.** Drag the second clip to the target position on the left.

A plus sign, small box, and data box containing the start time of the transition (9:00.53) and the name and duration of the first clip appear next to the pointer (**Figure 10.15**).

**3.** Release the mouse button.

Movie Maker inserts the fade transition (**Figure 10.16**). Note that the transition is 2 seconds long—the duration between the Playback indicator in Figure 10.14 (9:02.53) and the drop location in Figure 10.15 (9:00.53). In this manner, by watching the starting location and drop points, you can accurately set transition duration.

✔ **Tip**

■ You use the same procedure to fade between titles on the Title Overlay track or to fade audio files on the Audio/Music track.

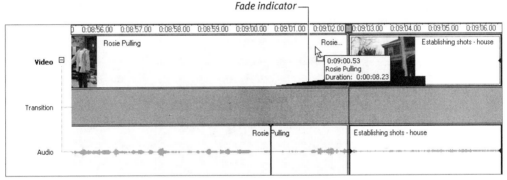

Fade indicator

**Figure 10.15** Then drag the second clip back, watching your timescale position (the top number minus 9:00.53), which is 2 seconds back.

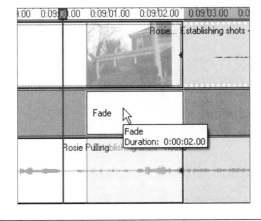

**Figure 10.16** Producing a 2-second transition.

USING TRANSITIONS

## To preview an inserted transition:

**1.** Click the transition in the Storyboard or Timeline to make it active (**Figure 10.17**).

**2.** To start the preview, click the Play button in the Monitor (or press the spacebar).

### ✔ Tip

■ This preview function works identically from either the Timeline or the Storyboard.

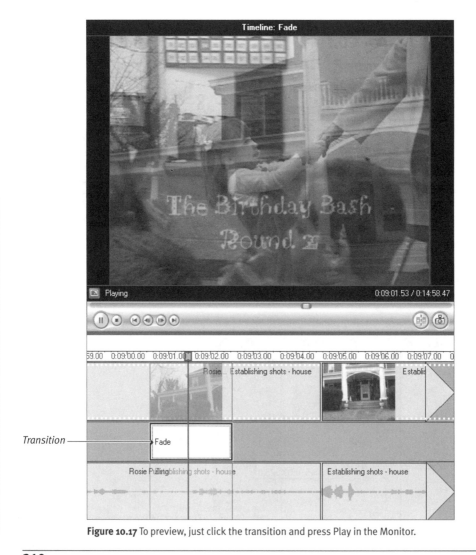

**Figure 10.17** To preview, just click the transition and press Play in the Monitor.

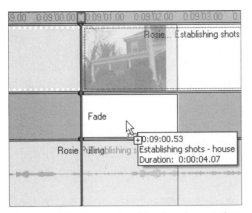

**Figure 10.18** To change a transition, just drop another on the first.

**Figure 10.19** Here's the new transition, a lovely sweep from Pixelan.

## To change transitions:

1. Drag another transition on top of the existing transition.

   A horizontal blue line appears between the two video clips, and next to the pointer appears a plus sign, a small box, and a data box that contains the insert time of the transition and the name and duration of the second clip (**Figure 10.18**).

2. Release the mouse button.

   Movie Maker replaces the previous effect, and you're ready to preview (**Figure 10.19**).

## To delete transitions:

1. Click the transition in the Storyboard or Timeline to make it active.

2. Do *one of the following:*

   ▲ Press the Delete key on your keyboard.

   ▲ Right-click and choose Delete.

   ▲ From the main menu, choose Edit > Delete.

# Transition Timing

Quick question: If you add a 2-second transition to a 12-second clip, what happens to the total duration? Does it increase by 2 seconds (we are *adding* a transition, after all), remain the same, or *decrease* by 2 seconds (how could *that* possibly be?).

Well, the answer is it decreases by 2 seconds. Let's see why.

**Figure 10.20** shows two clips, each 6 seconds long and totaling 12 seconds. Now let's add a 2-second dissolve between the two clips (**Figure 10.21**). Though the clips are still 6 inches each, overall the sequence is only 10 seconds long.

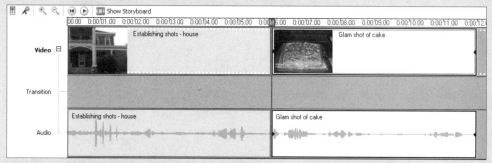

**Figure 10.20** Here's our starting point; two 6-second clips equal 12 seconds of total video.

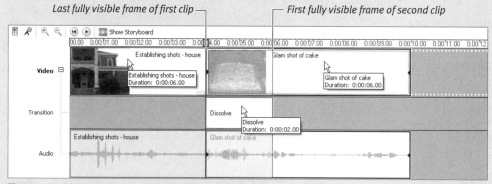

**Figure 10.21** Add a 2-second transition, and the video drops to 10 seconds.

*continues on next page*

## Transition Timing  *continued*

What happened? To show you, I loaded similar-length clips into an older version of Adobe Premiere, which offers what's called an A/B editing view that shows both the clips on the Timeline and the transition (**Figure 10.22**). (This transition works the same in Premiere as in Movie Maker; it's just presented differently in the Timeline.)

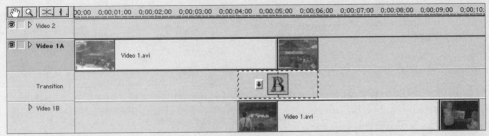

**Figure 10.22** A screen shot from Adobe Premiere tells the story. The 2-second dissolve transition overlaps 2 seconds in each video, which is why the video is shorter overall.

This figure reveals that to create the 2-second dissolve transition, Movie Maker uses the last 2 seconds of the first clip and the first 2 seconds of the second clip. Since segments from both clips are being used simultaneously, this shortens the video from 12 to 10 seconds.

Beyond the riddles, what are some practical ways to apply this information?

First, if you plan to use transitions other than cuts, be sure to trim your clips accordingly, leaving the planned durations of your transitions and fades at the beginning and end of each affected clip.

As you can see in Figure 10.20, the last completely visible frame in the first clip is 2 seconds from the end. Similarly, the first completely visible frame in the second clip is actually 2 seconds into the clip. Unless I planned accordingly while trimming, the transition could obscure valuable video content.

Second, if you're planning on a tight narration or music track, remember that two 6-second clips don't add up to 12 seconds of video if you have a 2-second dissolve between them. Though it's possible to do the math and compute the duration and precise starting points of each clip, it's generally easier to get the video lined up exactly the way you want it and then produce your audio.

# Customizing Transitions

Customizing transitions in Movie Maker is exceeding easy, primarily because the only thing you can customize is duration. Of course, if you're really adventurous, Microsoft has provided documentation that allows you to create your own transitions, but programming is required. You can access the documentation at http://msdn.microsoft.com/library/default.asp?url=/library/en-us/dnwmt/html/moviemakersfx.asp

I've looked over the materials, and they seem more like a problem for a beginning class on programming than a practical way to extend Movie Maker's transition capabilities.

So for us nonprogrammers, duration changes will have to do. Let's get to it.

### To modify the transition duration:

1. Select the target transition.

   A trim handle appears on the left.

2. Do *one of the following*:

   ▲ Pull the trim handle to the right to *shorten* the transition.

   ▲ Pull the trim handle to the left to *lengthen* the transition (**Figure 10.23**).

3. Release the mouse button to set the new duration.

### ✔ Tip

■ If you're attempting to set the transition duration to a specific duration, note the duration shown in the box beneath the trim cursor.

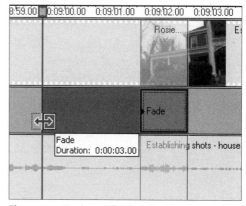

**Figure 10.23** To change the duration of a transition, grab the trim handle on the left and pull to the desired duration.

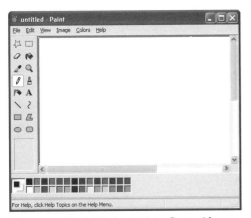

**Figure 10.24** Here's Windows Paint, a fine tool for making image mattes.

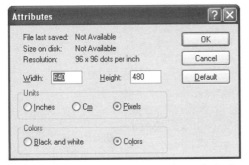

**Figure 10.25** Set your image to 640 x 480 resolution in this Attributes panel.

# Using Transitions to Create Customized Fades

Movie Maker has the ability to fade into and away from a clip in black and white, as you'll see in "Using Fade-In and Fade-Out Effects" in Chapter 11. However, each effect occurs in a relatively speedy 1 second, which may be too fast for some producers.

Fortunately, there's a relatively simple way to change the fade color and/or slow the fade. First you build an image in the desired color, typically called a matte. Then you import the matte into Movie Maker and onto your Timeline adjacent to the target clip. Then you insert a fade transition between the two clips and customize it to the target length of the fade.

Let's go through the process step by step, using Windows Paint, the simple paint program included with all copies of Windows, to build the matte.

## To build a matte:

1. Click Start > Programs > Accessories > Paint.

   Windows Paint opens (**Figure 10.24**).

2. From the Windows Paint main menu, choose Image > Attributes.

   The Attributes window opens (**Figure 10.25**).

*continues on next page*

**3.** Type 640 in the Width box and 480 in the Height box.

**4.** Click OK to close the Attributes window.

**5.** From the Windows Paint main menu, choose Colors > Edit Colors.

The Edit Colors window opens (**Figure 10.26**).

**6.** Click the target matte color in the Basic Colors grid.

I'm choosing black, which is the color at the bottom left. Paint highlights the color with a small black box.

**7.** Click OK to close the Edit Colors window.

**8.** At the upper left of the Paint toolbar, click the Fill icon (**Figure 10.27**).

Paint converts your pointer to a paint can.

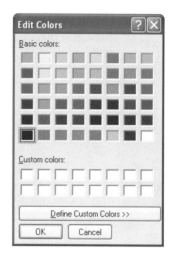

**Figure 10.26** Select the color of your matte; I'm going with basic black.

**Figure 10.27** Click here for the Fill tool.

**USING TRANSITIONS TO CREATE CUSTOMIZED FADES**

**Figure 10.28** Like Mick, I want it painted black! Click to make it so.

**Figure 10.29** Name the matte and save it where you can find it (I always choose the folder where I store other project assets).

**9.** Click anywhere on the image.

Paint fills your image with the selected color (**Figure 10.28**).

**10.** Click File > Save As.

Paint opens the Save As dialog box.

**11.** Navigate to the target storage folder and name the file (**Figure 10.29**).

**12.** Click Save to save the file.

## To create a customized fade:

**1.** Import the matte into a collection and drag in onto the Timeline adjacent to the file you want to fade out of (**Figure 10.30**).

If necessary, see "To import audio and still images into a Collection" in Chapter 3 and "Editing Still Images" in Chapter 9.

Drag the matte *before* a clip if you want to fade *into* the clip, and *after* the clip if you want to fade *away* from the clip. In the example, I'm fading away.

*continues on next page*

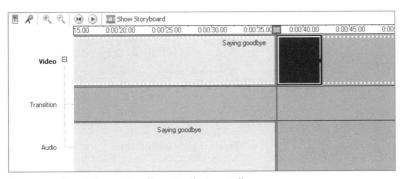

**Figure 10.30** Here's the matte, adjacent to the target clip.

**2.** Trim the matte to the target duration of the fade effect (**Figure 10.31**).

I'm using 4 seconds in the example.

**3.** Drag a fade transition between the matte and the clip.

Movie Maker inserts the fade transition (**Figure 10.32**).

**4.** Click the trim handle on the left of the fade transition and drag it all the way to the left (**Figure 10.33**).

Movie Maker creates the 4-second fade-to-black transition.

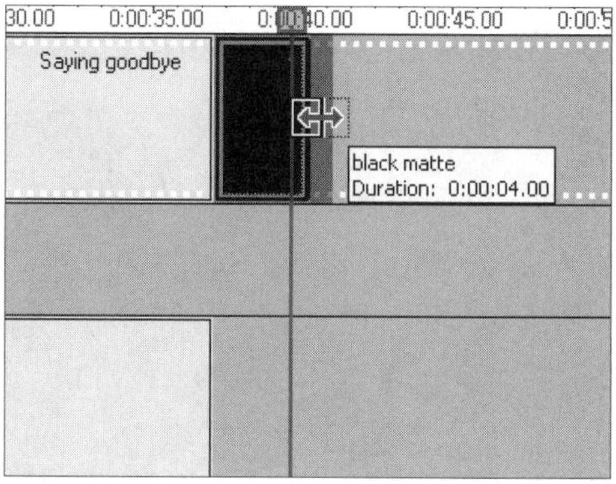

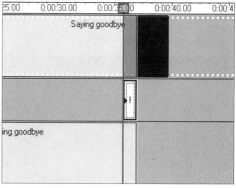

**Figure 10.31** The matte resized to the target transition duration.

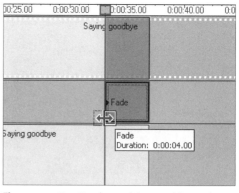

**Figure 10.32** I've inserted the fade transition.

**Figure 10.33** Now I've dragged the transition to the full duration of the matte, producing a 4-second fade to black. Très élégant (and very slimming).

# Inserting Multiple Transitions into a Slide Show

As discussed in "To create a slide show" in Chapter 9, you can create a slide show from still images by dragging multiple images to the Timeline. To spice up your slide shows, you can add transitions between images, a process that Movie Maker simplifies by enabling you to apply multiple transitions simultaneously.

Note, however, that you can apply multiple transitions only while in Storyboard view. Here's how to do it.

## To insert a transition between slide show images:

1. With your images in the Storyboard, do *one of the following* to select the target images:

    ▲ To insert the same transition between all images, choose Edit > Select All from the main menu (or press Ctrl+A) (**Figure 10.34**).

    ▲ To insert the same transition between multiple consecutive images, hold down the Shift key and select the first image and then the last image.

    ▲ To insert the same transition between multiple nonconsecutive images, hold down the Ctrl key and choose the target images with your pointer.

    *continues on next page*

**Figure 10.34** Select all slides using any of the three techniques discussed.

**2.** In the Video Transitions collection, right-click the target transition and choose Add to Storyboard (Ctrl+D) (**Figure 10.35**).

Movie Maker inserts the selected transition into the boxes between all selected clips (**Figure 10.36**).

### ✔ Tip

- After applying the transitions in Storyboard view, you can shift to the Timeline view to customize the transition duration.

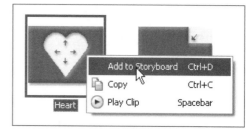

**Figure 10.35** Select your transition; then right-click and choose Add to Storyboard.

**Figure 10.36** Movie Maker inserts the transition into all selected slots.

# Applying Special Effects

Special effects are filters that change the appearance of video either to fix underlying problems (curative special effects) or enhance the video artistically (artistic special effects).

Microsoft's offerings for both purposes are fairly limited—about what you would expect from a free program. For example, Movie Maker has no real tools for correcting improper white balancing, a frequent problem for all videographers (and explained in detail in "The white balance issue" in Chapter 2). In addition, Microsoft's artistic special effects, though probably ideal for teenagers, are too flamboyant for my conservative tastes.

Fortunately, software developer Pixelan has two inexpensive effect packs that provide color correction, still image and video pan and zoom capabilities, and other useful effects. For this reason, I'll spend as much time discussing the Pixelan tools as those from Microsoft.

I start by describing the effects available from Microsoft and Pixelan and how to use these effects in Movie Maker. Then I address specific tasks such as how to fade clips in and out and how to correct underexposed video and incorrect white balancing.

Next I discuss how to change the playback speed of your video, an effect that I frequently use, and how to add motion to still images. If you like creating slide shows in Movie Maker, don't miss this last section.

# Movie Maker's Special Effects

Movie Maker ships with 28 effects, which Microsoft refers to as video effects. (This isn't the most accurate term, however, since you can apply them to both video clips and still images.) The video effects are stored in the Video Effects collection (**Figure 11.1**).

I've divided these effects into the following categories:

◆ **Curative effects:** Only two curative effects are included with Movie Maker: Brightness, Decrease, and Brightness, Increase, which perform their namesake functions to cure video that's either underexposed (the video is too dark) or overexposed (the video is too bright).

◆ **Fade effects:** Movie Maker has four effects that allow you to fade in from black or white and fade out to black or white. Unlike all other effects, which affect the entire clip to which you apply them, these effects alter only the beginning and/or ends of the clip.

◆ **Motion effects:** Movie Maker has two effects that add motion to a clip: Ease In, which slowly zooms into the clip, and Ease Out, which slowly zooms away from a clip. Both are valuable for adding motion to still images in a slide show and can be used quite effectively in a video clip as well. In **Figure 11.2**, I've used the Ease In effect to zoom in on my daughter while we were singing happy birthday, which worked quite well.

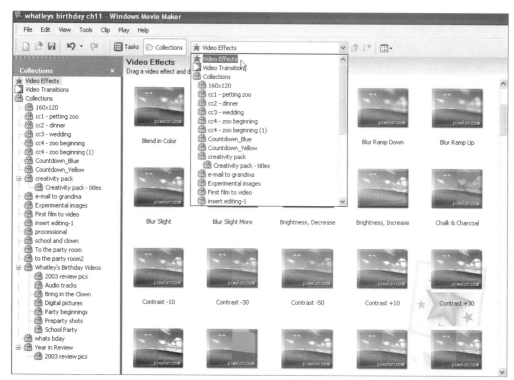

**Figure 11.1** Movie Maker's video effects are contained in a collection, accessible from the Collections pane or Collections list.

◆ **Film effects:** Movie Maker includes three Film Age effects: Film Age, Old; Film Age, Older; and Film Age, Oldest. Film Age, Old adds random noise and streaks to your image, but doesn't change the number of frames displayed each second, roughly simulating the look of an old VHS tape. Film Age, Older distorts the colors in the video, adds streaks, jumps individual frames up and down, and slows the frame rate to about 10 frames per second, simulating 8mm or 16mm film converted to video. Film Age, Oldest converts your video to black-and-white, blurs the video, and displays only 3 or 4 frames per second, simulating very old movies. In addition, an associated effect called Film Grain adds film-like graininess to your images, and the Grayscale effect simply converts your color videos to black-and-white.

◆ **Rotation effects:** These effects rotate the video by 90, 180, and 270 degrees. These may seem like they might be useful on still images shot in landscape mode, but when you try them, you'll find that Movie Maker squishes the rotated image to make it fit in the frame, which can distort the image (**Figure 11.3**). As a result, you'll want to use these rotation effects with care, checking to ensure that the effect produces the visual result you're looking for.

*continues on next page*

**Figure 11.2** Movie Maker's Ease In effect zooms you into the video or still image.

**Figure 11.3** Movie Maker's Rotation effects can scrunch your images, making your subjects look short and squat, so you're better off rotating your images in a photo editor.

MOVIE MAKER'S SPECIAL EFFECTS

- **Speed effects:** These effects either speed up or slow down the video clip and are useful for many types of productions.

- **Other artistic effects:** Movie Maker also includes a range of other artistic effects that blur, pixelate, convert to sepia, or otherwise change the appearance of your video.

### ✔ Tips

- To preview an effect, click on it. Movie Maker displays it in the monitor.

- Movie Maker can apply effects only to content on the Video track, which includes video, still images, and titles. Note that Movie Maker can also insert titles on the Title/Overlay track, but can't apply effects to titles inserted on that track. See Chapter 13 for more on working with titles.

## Add-on effects from Microsoft

Microsoft offers two opportunities to supplement Movie Maker's effects. You can download the free Winter Fun Pack 2003, which includes the Snowflake effect shown in **Figure 11.4** (www.microsoft.com/windowsxp/moviemaker/downloads/winterfun.asp). It has some other fun wintry theme components, including still images, animations, and sound effects, and the price is right, so it's a no-brainer download.

You can also get 25 additional effects by purchasing Microsoft Plus! Digital Media Edition version 1.1, which costs $19.95. It is available at www.microsoft.com/windows/plus/dme/dmehome.asp

**Figure 11.4** The Snowflake effect that ships with Microsoft's Winter Fun Pack 2003.

Most of the effects in the Plus! pack are artistic effects that I wouldn't typically use, so I wouldn't buy the Plus! pack *just* for the effects. However, the Plus! pack includes two great tools: Photo Story 2, which converts still images to slide shows, and the Analog Recorder, which converts analog audio to digital. (For more information on Photo Story 2, see Appendix B; for more information on the Analog Recorder, see "Converting Analog Audio to Digital" in Chapter 7.)

For producers who are interested in these two functions, the Plus! pack can be a worthwhile purchase, with the added, albeit minor, value of the effects and 25 additional transitions.

## Pixelan effects

As far as I'm aware, Pixelan is the only third-party developer with enhancement products for Movie Maker. The company offers two effect packs that any serious Movie Maker producer should strongly consider. Both are available at `www.pixelan.com/mm/intro.htm`.

The Color/Tint/Contrast/Blur Effects pack ($19) provides your only tools for correcting improper white balancing during shooting. (For more information on white balancing, see "The Art of Color Correction" later in this chapter.) The pack also includes contrast adjustments that significantly enhance your ability to correct underexposed video.

In addition, slide show aficionados should strongly consider Pixelan's Pan/Zoom effect pack, which includes 63 different pan and zoom combinations that you can apply to both still images and videos. These effects help bring slide shows to life and offer a great alternative to the capabilities of Photo Story 2, as discussed in Appendix B. I describe how to apply these effects in "Adding Motion to Still Images" later in this chapter.

### Pixelan or Photo Story?

The Pan and Zoom effects enabled by Pixelan are impressive, and they allow Movie Maker to create impressive-looking (and very entertaining) slide shows. Still, with features such as the ability to match slide duration to background music and automatically assign pan and zoom effects, Microsoft Photo Story, detailed in Appendix B, is a more complete package.

I tend to use the Pixelan effects when creating short slide shows that integrate into a larger production. However, if I'm producing a stand-alone slide show from images, I find Photo Story faster and easier to use.

# Using Movie Maker's Effects Interface

This section covers the basics of accessing and applying Movie Maker's special effects. Later sections explore some key special effects.

You should be aware of three fundamental rules before working with special effects:

◆ You can't configure any effects, whether they are supplied by Microsoft or Pixelan. For example, if you want to adjust the strength of an effect, you simply apply it multiple times to the target clip.

◆ You can apply up to six special effects (or one effect six times) to any clip.

◆ Movie Maker produces different results based on the order of the applied effects, so you may have to experiment with the effect to produce the desired result. (To get a sense of how this works, see "To fix underexposed video" later in this chapter.)

## To apply a video effect:

1. If the Video Effects collection is not displayed, click Video Effects in the Collections pane or choose Video Effects from the Collections list (Figure 11.1).

2. Locate the effect you want to use in the Video Effects collection.

   Use the scroll bar to the right of the collection to access effects that aren't visible.

3. Drag the effect you want to use onto the target clip (**Figure 11.5**).

   On the right of the pointer, you'll see a box with a plus sign and a data box containing the name, duration, and timeline location of the target clip.

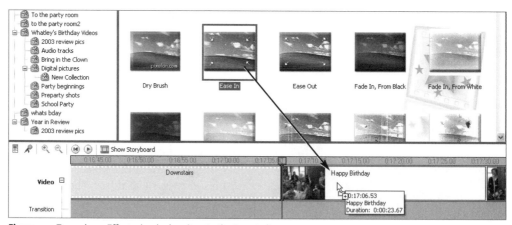

**Figure 11.5** To apply an Effect, simply drag it onto the target clip.

**4.** Release the mouse button.

Movie Maker applies the effect, in this case the Ease In effect shown in Figure 11.2 (**Figure 11.6**). Note the Star icon on the clip in the Timeline that indicates that Movie Maker has inserted an effect. This icon changes to the multiple stars shown in **Figure 11.7** if you insert multiple effects into the clip.

## ✔ Tips

■ As with all collections, you can display the Video Effects window in Detail mode, which I find useful when I need to find a particular effect. To toggle between Thumbnail and Detail modes, use the Views button (**Figure 11.8**).

■ To insert multiple effects, drag them to the target clip one after the other.

■ You can get around the six-effects limitation by applying the effects, rendering the clip, and then re-inputting the clip to apply additional effects. See "Rendering for Additional Production" in Chapter 16 for more details.

**USING MOVIE MAKER'S EFFECTS INTERFACE**

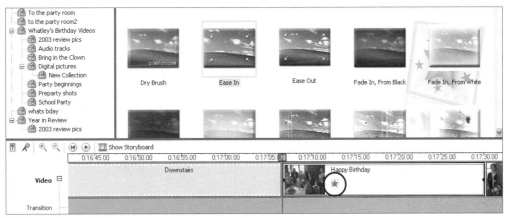

**Figure 11.6** The star on the Timeline lets you know that you've applied an effect to that clip.

**Figure 11.7** Multiple stars means multiple applied effects.

**Figure 11.8** Often I find locating effects easier in Details view.

### To reorder video effects:

1. Right-click the target clip and choose Video Effects (**Figure 11.9**).

   Movie Maker opens the Add or Remove Video Effects dialog box (**Figure 11.10**).

2. Click the effect you want to reposition.

3. Do *one of the following*:

   ▲ Click Move Up to move the effect up.

   ▲ Click Move Down to move the effect down.

4. Click OK to close the window.

### ✔ Tip

■ You can also add an effect in this window by clicking the effect in the Available Effects list on the left and clicking the Add button located in the middle of the window.

### To delete a video effect:

1. Right-click the target clip and choose Video Effects (Figure 11.9).

   Movie Maker opens the Add or Remove Video Effects dialog box (Figure 11.10).

2. Click the effect you want to use in the Displayed Effects list on the right (**Figure 11.11**).

3. Click the Remove button in the middle of the window.

   Movie Maker removes the effect (**Figure 11.12**).

4. Click OK to close the window.

**Figure 11.9** Here's how you access the Add or Remove Video Effects dialog box.

**Figure 11.10** This is where you add, remove, and reorder effects.

**Figure 11.11** To delete an effect, select it and click Remove.

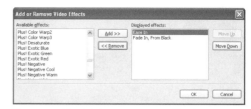

**Figure 11.12** The Brightness, Increase effect is now gone.

# Using Fade-In and Fade-Out Effects

A fade-in effect begins with a solid color (Movie Maker supports both black and white) and then fades into your video. A fade-out effect begins with the video and then fades into the solid color, again either black or white.

Fade-ins and fade-outs are among the most common effects used by video producers, because they're so effective at signaling the end of one scene and the start of another. Fortunately, they're also very easy to implement in Movie Maker. The only downside is that all Movie Maker fades last less than a second, a setting that you can't adjust. If this isn't long enough for you, or to fade into or out of a different color, check "Using Transitions to Create Customized Fades" in Chapter 10, which describes how to create fades of any duration and color.

## To fade a clip in or out:

1. Click the target clip on the Timeline.

2. Do *one of the following*:

   ▲ To fade in from black, drag the Fade In, From Black effect onto the target clip (**Figure 11.13**).

   ▲ To fade in from white, drag the Fade In, From White effect onto the target clip.

   ▲ To fade out to black, drag the Fade Out, To Black effect onto the target clip.

   ▲ To fade out to white, drag the Fade Out, To White effect onto the target clip.

3. Release the mouse button.

*continues on next page*

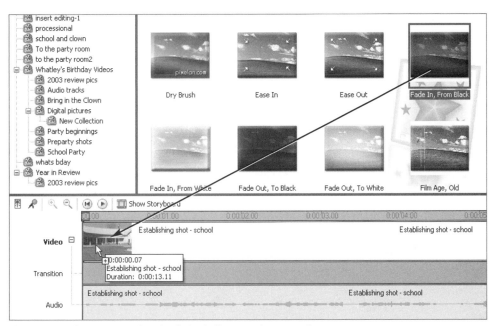

**Figure 11.13** To fade in or out, drag the desired effect onto the target clip.

## ✔ Tips

- You can also use the right-click commands shown in **Figure 11.14** to fade in from black or fade out to black.

- Usually when you fade into or out of a clip, you'll also apply a similar fade to the audio. An audio fade-in effect begins at zero volume and increases to 100 percent; an audio fade-out effect is the reverse, beginning at 100 percent and fading back to zero. Chapter 12 describes in detail how to fade audio in and out. The Cliff Notes version is that you can right-click any Audio track and choose either Fade In or Fade Out (**Figure 11.15**).

**Figure 11.14** You can fade in from black or fade out to black with these right-click commands.

**Figure 11.15** Typically, when you fade the video, you'll want to fade the audio as well. Movie Maker makes it simple with these commands that you can access by right-clicking the Audio track.

**USING FADE-IN AND FADE-OUT EFFECTS**

*Original*

*With Brightness, Increase applied five times*

*With Contrast +50 applied and the top effect*

*With Contrast +50 applied and the bottom effect*

**Figure 11.16** Here's how you rescue seriously underexposed video.

# Using Pixelan Effects to Fix Video Problems

Now let's jump in and address some problems that most producers experience at one time or another. If you haven't yet purchased Pixelan's Color/Tint/Contrast/Blur Effects pack, now would be a good time, because most of the fixes discussed here require Pixelan effects.

I'll start by fixing underexposed video, a very common problem, and then move on to two color correction examples. Since each exposure and color correction problem is unique, the solutions posed here probably won't work if applied verbatim to your footage, but you should get a feel for the types of adjustments necessary to address these common problems.

Since you can't see color correction in action in a book that uses black and white graphics, I'll post the two color correction screen shots to my Web site at www.doceo.com/ moviemaker.html.

### To fix underexposed video:

1. Place the target clip on the Timeline and select the clip.

   The starting point is shown at the upper left in **Figure 11.16**.

2. Drag the Brightness, Increase effect onto the clip up to five times to brighten the clip to normal levels.

   The result is shown in Figure 11.16 at the upper right. The image is brighter, but details are less clear, which frequently occurs when you brighten an underexposed video.

*continues on next page*

**3.** Drag the Contrast +50 effect onto the clip.

Note that this is a Pixelan effect not included in the base version of Movie Maker. The result shown at the bottom left of Figure 11.16 is actually worse than the original, but only because the Contrast +50 effect is the top effect (**Figure 11.17**).

**4.** Right-click the clip and choose Video Effects (Figure 11.9).

Movie Maker opens the Add or Remove Video Effects dialog box (Figure 11.17).

**5.** Click the Contrast +50 effect in the Displayed Effects list on the right.

**6.** Click Move Down five times to move the Contrast +50 effect to the bottom (**Figure 11.18**).

Movie Maker reapplies all effects, producing the optimal result shown at the bottom right of Figure 11.16.

**7.** Click OK to close the window.

## ✔ Tips

- No video editor can truly fix seriously underexposed video like that tackled in Figure 11.16. Typically, the best you can hope for is to improve the quality from unusable to mediocre.

- If you split a clip after applying special effects, Movie Maker applies all effects to both clips.

- If you combine two clips, Movie Maker will apply the effects used on the first clip to the combined clip.

**Figure 11.17** Effect order clearly matters. Here are the settings used for the image in the bottom-left corner of Figure 11.16.

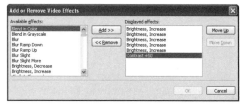

**Figure 11.18** Here are the settings used for the image at the bottom right of Figure 11.16. Same effects, different order, huge difference.

## The Art of Color Correction

When you color correct your video, you're typically correcting for improper white balancing during shooting. As discussed in "The white balance issue" in Chapter 2, white balance reflects what the camera perceives to be the color white. When white balancing is incorrect, all colors in the video are distorted, not just the white, in exactly the same way, which makes the problem fairly easy to fix.

One common example is described in Chapter 2, where footage shot in direct sunlight at Zoo Atlanta was tinged blue. When this occurs, you fix the problem by applying a color that, when combined with blue, produces white.

If you don't have the Pixelan Color/Tint/Contrast/ Blur Effects pack, you're totally out of luck, because Movie Maker has no subtle color adjustments; they're all wild, psychedelic, artistic special effects rather then the subtle curative effects that Pixelan supplies.

Specifically, the Color/Tint/Contrast/Blur Effects pack contains the 12 subtle colors shown in **Figure 11.19**. For example, to cure the blue tinge in my zoo video, I applied Tint Red Most, as shown in **Figure 11.20**. As you can see in the Add or Remove Video Effects dialog box, I also added brightness and contrast effects, two adjustments I almost always make when applying color correction.

*continues on next page*

|  |
| --- |
| ⭐ Tint Aqua |
| ⭐ Tint Blue |
| ⭐ Tint Blue More |
| ⭐ Tint Blue Most |
| ⭐ Tint Green |
| ⭐ Tint Green More |
| ⭐ Tint Green Most |
| ⭐ Tint Lime |
| ⭐ Tint Magenta |
| ⭐ Tint Red |
| ⭐ Tint Red More |
| ⭐ Tint Red Most |

**Figure 11.19** These Pixelan filters are the key to effective color correction with Movie Maker.

*Original*

*Corrected*

**Figure 11.20** You'll have a tough time telling in these grayscale images, but Movie Maker did a wonderful job of removing the blue from this video.

*Values*

## The Art of Color Correction *continued*

In **Figure 11.21**, correcting for an overly pinkish tinge, I applied the Tint Aqua effect with a slightly different order of brightness and contrast effects. Once again, the results you're seeing on the printed page are likely underwhelming, but surf over to www.doceo.com/moviemaker.html and check out the results in color.

*Original*

*Corrected*

**Figure 11.21** Movie Maker also removed the pinkish hue from this wedding video, restoring the dress to white.

*Values*

Note that color adjustment is a trial-and-error task that requires lots of back-and-forth checking between the adjusted and original videos. To facilitate this, I split the target clip into two segments of identical coloring (**Figure 11.22**). Then I apply the effects to the *first* clip and compare it to the second by clicking the Timeline above each clip, which displays the frame in the Monitor. Once I've identified the optimal combination and order of effects, I combine the clips and let Movie Maker apply the effects chosen for the first clip to the combined clip. See "Common Tasks" in Chapter 9 for details about splitting and combining clips on the Timeline.

Note that some producers prefer to apply effects in Storyboard mode because Movie Maker displays the names and order of all effects applied when you hover your cursor over the effect stars on the thumbnail (**Figure 11.23**).

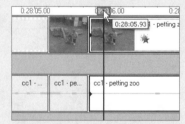

**Figure 11.22** Color correction requires frequent comparisons between the original and corrected versions. Splitting the clip on the Timeline makes this comparison easier.

**Figure 11.23** In Storyboard view, Movie Maker tells you which effects you've applied to each clip.

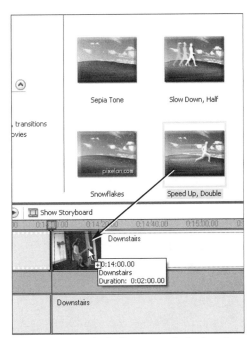

Figure 11.24 As with all effects, to apply the Speed Up, Double effect, drag it onto the target clip.

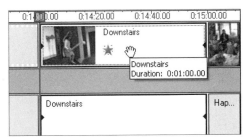

Figure 11.25 What was once 2 minutes is now 1 minute long. That's what happens when you double the speed.

# Using Playback Speed as an Effect

Video playback speed acceleration is one of my favorite effects because the faster motion adds a comic look and provides a nice break from the normal video. For example, in the birthday video, I might double the speed of the clip of the kids and parents walking down the stairs from the third-floor playroom to the downstairs dining room and match it with fast background party music, perhaps a salsa beat or some steel drum island music.

Note that changing the background audio isn't really optional. That's because when Movie Maker adjusts video playback speed, it also adjusts audio playback speed, usually distorting it beyond use. For this reason, you'll usually have to mute the Audio track and add your own background music to the Audio/Music track any time you change video speed. See "Working with Audio Files" in Chapter 9 and "Adjusting Volume" in Chapter 12 for details.

## To change playback speed:

1. Place the target clip on the Timeline and select the clip.

2. Do *one of the following:*
   ▲ To speed up the clip, drag the Speed Up, Double effect onto the target clip (**Figure 11.24**).
   ▲ To slow the clip down, drag the Slow Down, Half effect onto the target clip.

   Movie Maker applies the effect (**Figure 11.25**).

## ✔ Tip

■ When you change playback speed, Movie Maker automatically adjusts the position of all the content that is located after the affected clip backward (speed increase) or forward (slow motion) as necessary.

# Adding Motion to Still Images

Slide shows are a big part of most of my productions, and the birthday video will include two: one containing pictures taken at the party, and one containing pictures from the entire previous year. I like going whole hog with my slide shows, which means background music, interslide transitions, and motion effects that help maintain the viewer's interest.

Movie Maker includes two effects, Ease In and Ease Out, that can add motion to still images. If you're seriously into slide shows, however, you should supplement these with Pixelan's Pan/Zoom effects pack, which adds 63 pan and zoom effects.

You apply the effects as described earlier in "To apply a video effect"—that's the easy part. The hard part is deciphering Pixelan's text descriptions so that you can determine what each effect does and use it effectively. For more information on how to decode the text descriptions, see the sidebar "Identifying Pixelan's Effects."

## Identifying Pixelan's Effects

Probably the biggest hurdle for me when initially applying Pixelan's effects was figuring out what each one did. Sure, you can preview them easily enough, but that takes time. Surely, I thought, there was some rhyme or reason in the icons and text descriptions that I could use to identify each effect.

A quick visit to the help file that comes with the Pixelan pack provided some wisdom, and after experimenting a bit more, everything fell into place. As it turns out, both the text titles and the icons describe what the effect does. Look to **Figure 11.26** for some examples.

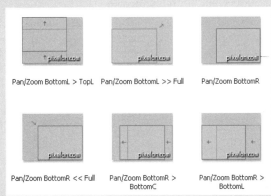

Pan/Zoom BottomL > TopL   Pan/Zoom BottomL >> Full   Pan/Zoom BottomR

Pan/Zoom BottomR << Full   Pan/Zoom BottomR > BottomC   Pan/Zoom BottomR > BottomL

**Figure 11.26** It took me awhile, but finally I started to understand which effect was which.

The rules for text titles are simple:

◆ Ignore the Pan/Zoom text phrase, which is in each text description.

◆ If the icon has no arrow marks, then there is no motion, and the effect starts and ends at the noted location. For example, the effect at the top right of Figure 11.26 is entitled Pan/Zoom BottomR. This tells you that the video window starts and stops in the bottom-right corner of the video.

◆ If the icon has one arrow, the effect pans (move sideways) or tilts (moves up and down) across the video, but stays at the same magnification level, which means no zoom in or out. For example, at the top left of Figure 11.26, the effect is labeled Pan/Zoom BottomL > TopL. This tells you that the effect starts zoomed into the bottom-left corner of the video and tilts up to the top left without any further change in magnification.

◆ If the icon has two arrows, the effect has a change in magnification as indicated by the direction of the arrows. For example the effect description in the middle of the top row, Pan/Zoom BottomL >> Full, tells you that the video window zooms from the bottom left to the full video window.

You can also identify the effect by analyzing the icon, though it's tough in the grayscale figure shown here. These are the rules:

◆ Boxes in the window indicate the effect's start and end points, with arrows showing the direction of the motion. If there are no arrows, there is no motion.

◆ Anytime the arrows point either directly up or down, or directly sideways, there is no change in magnification, just a pan or tilt.

◆ Anytime an arrow points toward a corner, the effect either zooms in or zooms out.

# The logic of inconsistency

When I add motion to still images, the one thing I consistently try to avoid is consistency. That is, I know that if I apply the same effect to multiple consecutive slides, it will quickly become boring to the viewer.

Here are some rules that I follow to avoid consistency and enhance the visual effect of the motion:

♦ **Zoom into or away from the focal point of the image.** Most images have a focal point such as the subject's face. To add motion, either zoom into that focal point, or start zoomed into the focal point and then zoom away. **Figure 11.27** shows the Pan/Zoom Center L >> Full effect, which *zoomed away* from a close-up of my daughter in the left center of the image to the full image. In **Figure 11.28**, I used the Pan/Zoom Center << Full effect to *zoom into* my daughter's face.

**Figure 11.27** In this still image, I zoomed away from the focal point.

**Figure 11.28**. Here I did the reverse, zooming into the close-up.

◆ **Pan across or tilt up and down as dictated by the slide content.** In **Figure 11.29**, my daughter is dressed for superhero day in kindergarten, as a long, tall traffic officer. I used the Pan/Zoom Bottom C > TopC effect to *tilt* from the bottom center to the top center. In **Figure 11.30**, with my elder daughter at the upper right, I used the Pan/Zoom TopL > TopR effect to *pan* across the top from left to right.

*continues on next page*

**Figure 11.29** In this image I tilted upward from the middle of the image to my daughter's face.

**Figure 11.30** Here I zoomed across the three girls to reveal my elder daughter on the right.

ADDING MOTION TO STILL IMAGES

◆ **Use multiple effects to customize even further. Figure 11.31** shows a combination of the Pan/Zoom Bottom R << Full effect with four Ease In effects to zoom closely into my daughter.

If you mix and match these four basic effects and throw in frequent customizations, you can present your still images in a visually exciting way that won't get repetitive.

If you're interested in seeing these effects in action, surf over to `www.doceo.com/moviemaker.html`. I produced the slide show with background music and transitions and posted the Windows Media file there.

## ✔ Tips

■ When you apply these filters in Movie Maker, the image in the Monitor will likely be noticeably blurry. When you actually produce the slide show, however, the images should be much sharper than what the Monitor shows.

■ You can apply Pixelan's Pan and Zoom effects to video as well as still images.

**Figure 11.31** This motion effect combines a pan and zoom into the bottom-right corner and four Ease In effects to get in tight.

# WORKING WITH AUDIO

The more you work with video, the more you realize that audio is at least as important as the visual presentation, and often more so, especially for Internet video, which is usually grainy and postage-stamp size. Whether the soundtrack is an informative or evocative narration or mood-establishing background music, audio is an extraordinarily powerful medium.

As you've probably noticed by now, Windows Movie Maker has only two audio tracks: one dedicated to the audio included with the captured or imported video, and one for all other audio. While this may sound limiting, there's a simple workaround, described in this chapter.

Also discussed in this chapter is how to connect for and produce a narration, how to set volume by clip or track, and where to access several free and inexpensive sources for background music and sound effects.

# About Audio Tracks and Workflow

Movie Maker has two audio tracks (**Figure 12.1**):

◆ The **Audio track** is reserved for audio that is part of the video file above it. If the video file contains no audio, Movie Maker still won't let you drag a different audio file onto this track. This means that all narrations, background music, and sound effects must be placed in the Audio/Music track.

◆ The **Audio/Music track** is the only audio track that accepts narrations, background music, and other audio files.

## Making tracks

The fact that Movie Maker has only two audio tracks may make you think that you can't insert background music and narration into the same video segment at the same time. But this isn't true.

You can work around this limitation by inserting an audio file into the Audio/Music track and then rendering the project to an intermediate file that you immediately input back into the project. All audio from that file will be contained in the Audio track, leaving the Audio/Music track open for additional audio. You can then add the desired audio and either render the final production or render another intermediate file that allows you to add another audio track.

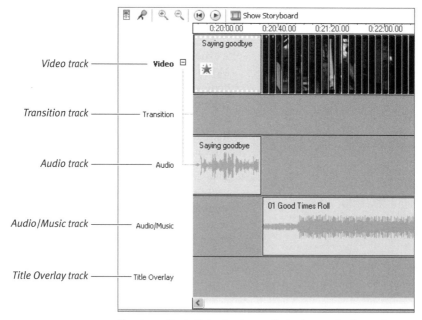

**Figure 12.1** Movie Maker has two audio tracks: one for the audio included in the video file and one for all other audio files.

You can use this technique multiple times until all audio is included. I recommend performing this procedure (creating the intermediate file and re-inputting) after completing all other work on the project and just before final rendering. That way, the timing and placement of all visual assets is set. For the settings you need to render this intermediate file, see "Rendering for Additional Production" in Chapter 16.

## Getting audio to the Timeline

As we've seen, Movie Maker populates the Audio track with audio associated with the video file. You can add only the audio from any video file by dragging the file from the collection to the Audio/Music track (for details, see "Working with Audio Files" in Chapter 9).

Movie Maker can import a range of audio formats, including Windows Media Audio (WMA), MP3, and WAV, as described in "To import audio and still images into a collection" in Chapter 3. Once a file is in a collection, you can add it to the production by dragging it onto the Audio/Music track.

### ✔ Tip

■ Create your audio tracks last, after all your video edits are finalized. That way, adjustments to the Video tracks won't throw off the synchronization of the Audio and Audio/Music tracks with the video.

# Recording Narration

Narrating your videos and slide shows is a great way to add context to the visual presentation, and Movie Maker makes narration simple to create and use. Even with an inexpensive microphone, you can create high-quality audio, but with the wrong gear or wrong setup, you'll be disappointed with the quality. For details, see the sidebar "Getting the Most from Your Narrations."

Movie Maker can accept narration only in Timeline view, and you must start narrating at a point in the project where the Audio/Music track is clear of other audio. From there, you can use either of the two available recording modes.

In default mode, you can record as long as you like, and Movie Maker inserts the complete narration into the Audio/Music track. If you've already inserted an audio file in the Audio/Music track later in the project, Movie Maker will push that track back as necessary to fit the narration.

You can also instead choose to limit the narration to the available time between the narration starting point and the downstream audio, in which case Movie Maker will stop recording the narration after filling the gap. I describe how to choose this option in "To record your narration," later in this chapter.

## Getting the Most from Your Narrations

To create a good-quality narration, you need to attend to both your narration's technical and artistic aspects.

From a technical perspective, you can achieve great results with an inexpensive microphone, but I recommend using a microphone that's part of a headset. Microphones and headsets are often sold together for use in Internet videoconferencing.

From an artistic standpoint, you'll get the best results by scripting your narration and taking the time for multiple takes until you get it right. Keep your comments short and to the point, or you'll complicate both the scripting and the performance.

If you're going to wing it without a script, adjust your expectations downward. While you may strive to emulate the baritone splendor of James Earl Jones, the fluidity of Bryant Gumble, or the mellifluous tones of yoga maven Tracey Rich, you'll never get finished if you insist on that level of perfection.

Finally, there are tools out there that can stretch or compress your narration to the duration of the corresponding video with minimal distortion and little or no change in pitch, which can save oodles of time compared to re-recording a 4-minute track to shave 15 seconds either way. Sony Pictures' CD Architect is a good place to start: www.mediasoftware.sonypictures.com

Recording Narration

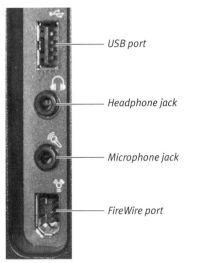

Figure 12.2 Plug your microphone into the microphone jack for best narration results.

Figure 12.3 Click this button to enter Timeline view.

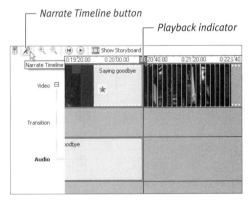

Figure 12.4 To start narrating, move the Playback indicator to a blank spot on the Audio/Music track and click the Narrate Timeline button.

## To connect for narration:

1. Connect your microphone to the microphone jack on your sound card or computer (**Figure 12.2**).

   Note that the internal settings for *line-in* are different from those for the microphone, so don't connect your microphone to the line-in connector.

2. Connect your headphones (if available) to the speaker port or headphones jack on your sound card or computer.

## ✔ Tips

- Many computers (like my Sony VAIO) designate the microphone connector with a red plug, which may match the plug on the microphone itself.

- If you have a microphone that connects via the computer's USB port, connect your microphone to that port.

## To set up for narration:

1. If you're in Storyboard view, click the Show Project Timeline button to switch to Timeline view (**Figure 12.3**).

2. Move the Playback indicator to the desired starting point for the narration, making sure there is no other audio file on the Audio/Music track at that location (**Figure 12.4**).

3. Click the Narrate Timeline button.

   Movie Maker opens the Narrate Timeline controls (see **Figure 12.5** on the following page).

*continues on next page*

RECORDING NARRATION

**4.** Click Show More Options.

Movie Maker displays all of the narration controls (**Figure 12.6**).

**5.** Click the arrow on the Audio Device list box and choose the audio device.

If your system has only one audio device, Movie Maker automatically selects that device.

**6.** Click the arrow on the Audio Input Source list box and choose the audio input source you'll be using (**Figure 12.7**).

**7.** If you're recording with a stand-alone microphone (as opposed to a headset), select the Mute Speakers check box.

This will mute your speakers during narration, preventing *feedback*—an annoying screeching sound that occurs when the microphone picks up output from the speakers.

**8.** If desired, select the Limit Narration to Available Free Space on Audio/Music check box.

This will limit your narration time to the time available between the starting point and the next audio track on the Audio/Music track.

If you leave the check box unchecked, you can record as long as desired, and Movie Maker will shift any subsequent files on the Audio/Music track as necessary to fit the complete narration onto the Audio/Music track.

**9.** Speak into the microphone in a normal voice, and adjust the volume slider so that the level displayed in the volume meter is at the top of the blue or into the yellow region, but never touches the red (**Figure 12.8**).

If the volume reaches the red zone, you may hear *clipping*, which often sounds like a mechanical click on the audio, or your voice may be distorted.

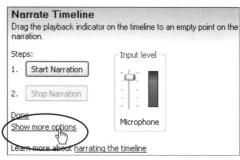

**Figure 12.5** Click here to show all narration options.

*Limit Narration*

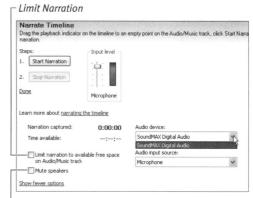

*Mute Speakers*

**Figure 12.6** Here's where you select your audio device. If you have only one audio device, Movie Maker will automatically select it.

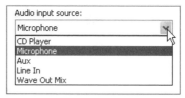

**Figure 12.7** Here's where you select your input source; generally, you'll use the microphone input for all narrations.

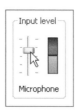

**Figure 12.8** Use this slider to adjust incoming narration volume, being careful to stay at the top of the green and out of the red.

**RECORDING NARRATION**

| | |
|---|---|
| Narration captured: | **0:00:51** |
| Time available: | **0:01:03** |

**Figure 12.9** Movie Maker lets you know how long you've been recording and, if you've limited narration duration, how much recording time you have left.

**Figure 12.10** When you're done, Movie Maker lets you name the file and choose where to save it.

Inserted narration ⎯

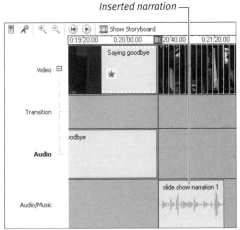

**Figure 12.11** Then Movie Maker inserts the narration into the Audio/Music track.

## To record your narration:

1. When you're ready to begin narrating, click the Start Narration button.

   If the Start Narration button is dimmed, the Playback indicator likely is positioned at a point where the Audio/Music track contains other audio. Move, edit, or delete the old audio, or change the location to a blank place in the track.

   While you're recording, Movie Maker moves the Playback indicator along the Timeline and displays the duration of the narration captured (**Figure 12.9**). If you checked the option to limit narration, Movie Maker also displays the remaining time available for the narration.

2. Click Stop Narration to stop recording.

   Movie Maker stops recording and opens the Save Windows Media File dialog box so you can name and change the location of the narration file (**Figure 12.10**).

3. If desired, change the location or file name and click Save.

   Movie Maker stores the file and inserts it into the Audio/Music track (**Figure 12.11**).

*continues on next page*

**RECORDING NARRATION**

**4.** In the Monitor, click Play to hear your recorded audio.

Since the proper levels haven't yet been set for the Audio/Music and Audio tracks, it may be difficult to hear the narration over the other tracks. To learn how to set the respective volumes, see "Adjusting Audio Volume" later in this chapter.

After you've finished recording, the narration track is just like any imported audio file, and you can trim, split, move, or delete it. For example, if you don't like the recorded track, simply select it and press Delete, and it's gone.

### ✔ Tip

■ If you need to locate your narrated files at some later point, the default location is My Documents\My Videos\Narration.

## Other Sources of Audio

I like adding sound effects and background music to my productions, and I find that more choices are better when it comes to locating just the right clip in either category. Although Movie Maker comes with no sound effects or background music, Microsoft offers two free sources of both.

The Creativity Fun Pack (www.microsoft.com/windowsxp/moviemaker/downloads/create.asp) comes with 53 sound effects in five varieties—animal, fun random, graduation, party, and sports—and three background music tracks. In addition, Microsoft's Windows Movie Maker 2 Winter Fun Pack 2003 (www.microsoft.com/windowsxp/moviemaker/downloads/winterfun.asp), also free, includes 92 sound effects and seven music tracks.

If you're seriously into background music, check out SmartSound Movie Maestro (www.smartsound.com/moviemaestro/index.html), a $49.95 program that can create custom background music tracks of any length. It's an amazing product; basically, you input your finished movie and select a theme and a few other parameters, and Movie Maestro creates the track. There's a great tutorial on the SmartSound site that you can consult for more information.

**Figure 12.12** To mute a track, right-click and choose Mute.

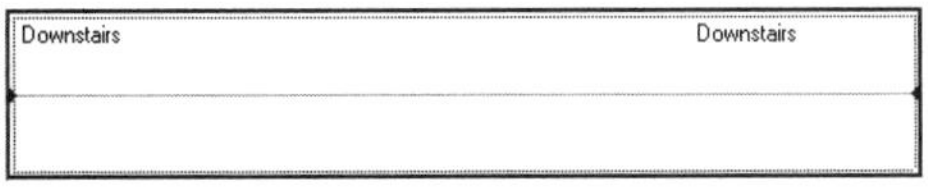

| Downstairs | Downstairs |
|---|---|

**Figure 12.13** Flat line! Here's what a muted clip looks like.

# Adjusting Audio Volume

Movie Maker offers two types of audio adjustments. The first are clip-specific adjustments that apply only to the selected clip. These include muting a clip, or turning the audio off completely, fading the audio in and fading it out, and adjusting the volume. Movie Maker also enables track-specific adjustments that apply to the Audio or Audio/Music track over the entire production.

To demonstrate clip-level adjustments, I'll refer to the clip I speeded up to double time in Chapter 11, which showed the party participants traveling from the third-floor playroom to the dining room to eat the cake (see "Using Playback Speed as an Effect" in Chapter 11). Because I increased the speed, I have to mute the Audio track because it now it sounds like Alvin and the Chipmunks. Then I'll fade in and out the music I've inserted into the Audio/Music track and boost the music clip's volume.

After demonstrating these clip-level adjustments, I'll make some track-level adjustments.

### To mute a clip:

1. Right-click the clip to open the menu (**Figure 12.12**).

2. Choose Mute.

    Movie Maker inserts a thin blue line in the middle of the clip, indicating that the volume has been set to zero (**Figure 12.13**).

## To fade a clip in or out:

1. Right-click the clip to open the menu (**Figure 12.14**).

2. Do *one of the following:*

   ▲ To fade the clip in, choose Fade In.

   ▲ To fade the clip out, Choose Fade Out.

   Note that Movie Maker provides no visual feedback on the Timeline to let you know that the clip has been faded in or out. The only way to verify your work is to right-click again and see if the desired effect is checked (**Figure 12.15**).

### ✔ Tips

■ Some video editors insert audio fades whenever a video transition is applied, automatically fading out the first clip and fading in the second. Consider inserting fades manually whenever you have a transition between two clips.

■ Most producers also fade audio in and out whenever they fade video in and out. If you're fading your video in or out, think audio fades as well.

**Figure 12.14** You also right-click to access fade-in, fade-out, and volume controls.

**Figure 12.15** The check mark confirms that you've inserted the Fade In effect.

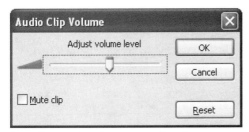

**Figure 12.16** Here's where you set clip volume, dragging left to decrease volume and right to increase volume.

## To adjust track volume:

1. Right-click the clip to open the menu (Figure 12.14).

2. Choose Volume.

   Movie Maker opens the Audio Clip Volume dialog box (**Figure 12.16**).

3. Do *one of the following:*

   ▲ To decrease clip volume, move the volume slider to the left.

   ▲ To increase clip volume, move the volume slider to the right.

4. Click OK to close the dialog box.

## ✔ Tips

■ You can't preview audio volume with the Audio Clip Volume dialog box open. You have to close it, test the volume, and then reopen it if necessary for further fine-tuning.

■ All clips start at 50 percent volume, a setting you can return to by clicking the Reset button.

■ The easiest way to fine-tune your volume adjustments is to use the arrow keys— press the left arrow to decrease volume and the right arrow to increase volume.

■ You can select the Mute Clip check box in the Audio Clip Volume dialog box (Figure 12.16) instead of using the right-click command described earlier in "To mute a clip."

## Deep Thoughts on Volume Adjustments

When adjusting audio, you should always keep two concepts in mind: the *absolute clip volume* and the *relative clip volume*.

Every clip has an optimal maximum volume, or *absolute clip volume*. Beyond this setting, boosting volume produces audio distortion. Finding the optimal setting is easy once you know what to look for.

For example, **Figure 12.17** shows an original clip and three adjustments. On the left is the *waveform* from Movie Maker's Audio/Music track. A waveform is a graphical representation of the audio file. The squiggly lines in the middle represent sound, and the length of the squiggles—specifically, how close they get to the top and bottom of the track—represent the volume.

*continues on next page*

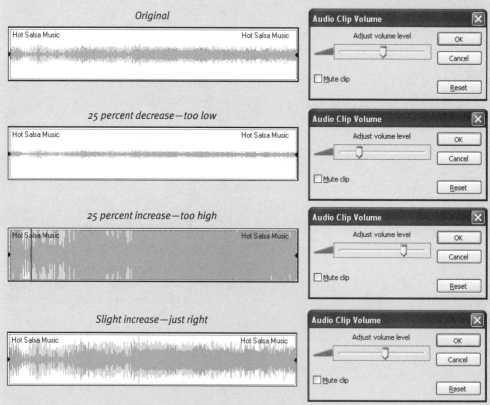

**Figure 12.17** The waveforms tell the story. Try to produce the look of the bottom track, where some of the highest peaks are barely brushing the top and bottom lines.

**ADJUSTING AUDIO VOLUME**

## Deep Thoughts on Volume Adjustments  *continued*

The original waveform shows lots of white space between the sound in the middle and the top and bottom of the track, indicating that you can increase volume significantly without introducing distortion. The second and third waveforms show the music file after the volume is decreased by about 25 percent and increased by about 25 percent.

Two points here: First, the volume control is very sensitive, with relatively minor adjustments having a huge impact. Second, in the track with the 25 percent increase, note how the waveform flattens against both the top and bottom of the track. This tells you instantly that the audio probably will sound very distorted.

The fourth clip shows the optimal volume setting, where one or two of the waveform peaks come close to, but don't flatten against, the top or bottom of the track, indicating that you've boosted volume as far as you can without producing distortion.

The other concept to keep in mind is the *relative clip volume*. Whenever you add audio from multiple sources to a production, volume will almost always vary from clip to clip. If the disparities are significant, they can be distracting during playback.

Some advanced video editors have a *normalize* tool that sets the volume from all audio sources at one level, eliminating the differences in volume. Movie Maker doesn't have such an automatic tool, making *you* the normalize tool.

I'm not suggesting an exhaustive, clip-by-clip comparison; life is way too short. Just be aware when you're setting the individual clip volumes that relative consistency is a goal. If any clip sounds way too loud or way too quiet, adjust the clip volume to bring the clip into line with the others.

ADJUSTING AUDIO VOLUME

## To adjust track volume:

1. At the top left of the Timeline, click the Set Audio Levels button (**Figure 12.18**). Movie Maker opens the Audio Levels dialog box (**Figure 12.19**).

2. Do *one of the following*:

   ▲ To give priority to the audio from the video, drag the slider to the left.

   ▲ To give priority to the audio from the Audio/Music track, drag the slider to the right.

## ✔ Tips

- If you drag the slider to either edge, you mute the other audio clip.

- I typically use this adjustment only for major changes, like muting the entire video track in favor of background music or narration. I make most of my adjustments with the clip-specific tools.

**Figure 12.18** Click here to set track levels.

**Figure 12.19** Drag to the left to give priority to the audio from the movie; drag to the right to give priority to the Audio/Music track.

# DESIGNING TITLES AND CREDITS

Titles and credits are text-based screens that appear solo on the Timeline or superimposed over video or still images. Although titles and credits are generally used differently—titles are used throughout a movie, while credits are employed at the end—you build both using the same tool in Windows Movie Maker. For the sake of simplicity, I focus primarily on titles in this chapter, but the process is identical for both.

Movie Maker titles have two basic components: the inserted text and the title animation scheme used to display the text. Title animations in Movie Maker not only animate the text, but also insert different backgrounds, banners, and special effects. This makes your choice of animation scheme a key creative option. To help in your selection, this chapter includes an extensive description of Movie Maker's animation schemes (see the sidebar "Title Animation Options" later in this chapter).

We'll begin the chapter by looking at the various options you have for inserting titles, which depend upon the track you use: either the Video or Title Overlay track. Then we'll look at how to insert, customize, and edit titles, as well as advanced topics, such as how to combine multiple titles simultaneously.

# Title Options and Track Type

Movie Maker can insert titles on two different tracks: the Video track and the Title Overlay track (**Figure 13.1**). How you work with the titles depends on the track you're using.

For example, titles inserted on the Video track appear against a configurable solid background color. When inserted, they push all other content on the Video and Audio tracks back by the duration of the title. If you've carefully synchronized background music or narration to your video or still images and then later insert titles on the Video track, you probably will lose the synchronization. This is why most producers insert background audio as the last possible production step.

This isn't true for the Title Overlay track, however—Movie Maker *doesn't* adjust content on it (the same is also true for the Audio/Music track).

Titles inserted into the Title Overlay track are superimposed over the video or still image that sits above it on the Video track. They don't affect the placement of other titles on the Title Overlay track and can span multiple clips on the Video track.

It's also important to know that while you can drag or copy and paste titles inserted on one track to the other, properties specific to titles on the source track don't carry over to the destination track. For example, you can apply special effects to titles inserted into the Video track, but you can't apply special effects to titles inserted in the Title Overlay track (see Chapter 11 for details on applying special effects). As a result, if you apply an effect to a title on the Video track and then drag the title to the Title Overlay track, Movie Maker will move the title but drop the special effect.

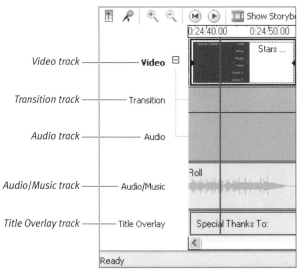

**Figure 13.1** You can insert titles on the Video and Title Overlay tracks.

**Figure 13.2** Click the Show Timeline button (if necessary) to switch to Timeline view.

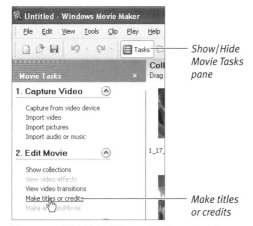

*Show/Hide Movie Tasks pane*

*Make titles or credits*

**Figure 13.3** Click Make Titles or Credits to start the Title wizard.

**Figure 13.4** Or choose this menu option to start the Title wizard.

## Where do you want to add a title?

Add title at the beginning of the movie.

Add title before the selected clip in the timeline.

Add title on the selected clip in the timeline.

Add title after the selected clip in the timeline.

Add credits at the end of the movie.

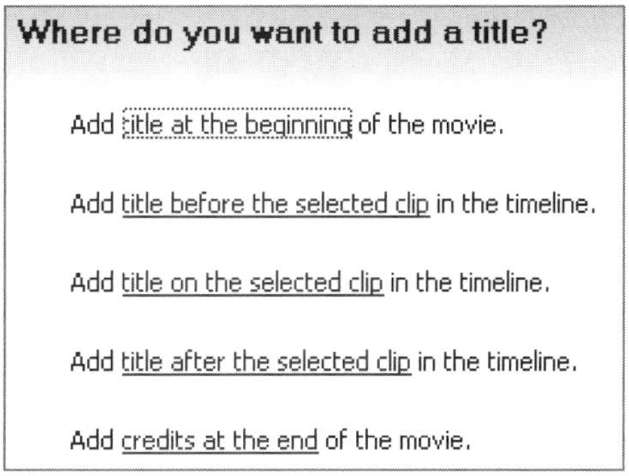

**Figure 13.5** Choose the target location for your title by clicking one of these options.

# Creating Titles

There are four steps to creating a title in Movie Maker: choosing the title location, inserting the text, customizing font and font characteristics, and choosing an animation scheme.

By now, you're probably working primarily in Timeline view, at least during these latter production stages. If not, note that if you attempt to insert a title into the Title Overlay track from Storyboard view, Movie Maker will automatically switch to Timeline view and then insert the title. For this reason, I recommend that you work in this view now.

## To insert a title:

1. If necessary, click the Show Timeline button to switch to Timeline view (**Figure 13.2**).

    Movie Maker switches to Timeline view.

2. Do *one of the following*:

    ▲ To create a title before, after, or on top of a clip, select the clip.

    ▲ To create a title at the beginning or end of the movie, go to Step 3.

3. To start the Title wizard, do *one of the following*:

    ▲ On the Movie Tasks pane, click Make Titles or Credits (**Figure 13.3**). (If the Movie Tasks pane isn't displayed, click the Show/Hide Movie Tasks Pane button on the toolbar.)

    ▲ From the main menu, choose Tools > Titles and Credits (**Figure 13.4**).

    Movie Maker opens the Title wizard (**Figure 13.5**).

*continues on next page*

CREATING TITLES

**4.** Do *one of the following:*

▲ Click Add Title at the Beginning of the Movie. Movie Maker will insert the title on the Video track at the start of the project

▲ Click Add Title Before the Selected Clip in the Timeline. Movie Maker will insert the title on the Video track immediately before the selected clip.

▲ Click Add Title on the Selected Clip in the Timeline. Movie Maker will insert the title on the Title Overlay track below the selected clip.

▲ Click Add Title After the Selected Clip in the Timeline. Movie Maker will insert the title on the Video track immediately after the selected clip.

▲ Click Add Credits at the End of the Movie. Movie Maker will insert credits on the Video track at the end of the movie.

After you choose a title location, Movie Maker opens the Enter Text for Title window (**Figure 13.6**).

**5.** Type the desired title text.

Each of the three classes of animation scheme has a different number of lines available for text entry. If the desired number of lines is not available at this step, change to the desired title animation scheme and then return to this window to enter the desired text. (See "To change the title animation scheme" later in this chapter for details.)

**6.** Do *one of the following:*

▲ Click Done to add the title to the project and continue editing.

▲ Click Change the Title Animation to change the title animation scheme (see "To change the title animation scheme" later in this chapter for more information).

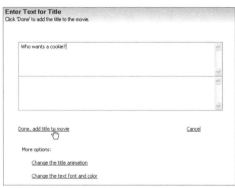

**Figure 13.6** Type your title text in this window.

CREATING TITLES

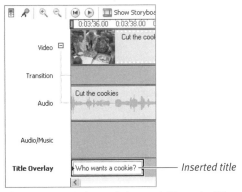

Figure 13.7 Here's the newly inserted title on the Title Overlay track.

Figure 13.8 Choose your title animation scheme here. Use the scroll bar to see all options.

▲ Click Change the Text Font and Color to customize the text font and other font characteristics (see "Customizing Text" later in this chapter for more information).

I inserted a title in the selected clip in the Timeline. **Figure 13.7** shows the inserted title.

### ✔ Tip

■ Movie Maker applies the last selected text characteristics and title animation scheme to the newly inserted title. Unless you need to change either variable, you should be finished at this point.

### To change the title animation scheme:

1. In the Enter Text for Title window, click Change the Title Animation (Figure 13.6). Movie Maker opens the Choose the Title Animation window (**Figure 13.8**). Use the scroll bar on the right to see all available animation schemes.

2. Click a title animation scheme. The animation will preview in the Monitor. See the sidebar "Title Animation Options" for more information on Movie Maker's title animation schemes.

3. Do *one of the following*:

   ▲ Click Done to add the title to the movie and return to editing.

   ▲ Click Edit the Title Text to change the title text (see "To insert a title" earlier in the chapter for more information).

   ▲ Click Change the Text Font and Color to customize the text font and other font characteristics (see "Customizing Text" later in this chapter for more information).

## Title Animation Options

Movie Maker includes three title animation categories:

◆ Titles, One Line—which contains 25 animation schemes

◆ Titles, Two Lines—which contains nine animation schemes (**Figure 13.9**)

◆ Credits—which contains nine animation schemes

| Name | Description | |
|------|-------------|---|
| **Titles, Two Lines** | | |
| Fade, In and Out | Fades in, pauses, fades out | |
| Fly In, Fades | Flies in from left, pauses, fades out | |
| Fly Out | Fades in, pauses, flies out right | |
| Fly In, Fly Out | Flies in from left, pauses, flies out right | |
| Moving Titles, Layered | Transparent overlapping titles | |
| Exploding Outline | Zooms in, outline explodes off screen | |

**Figure 13.9** These titles have two lines of text, each with a different font size.

**Figure 13.10** illustrates each of these categories. Notice that one-line titles have one line of text that Movie Maker will wrap into multiple lines if necessary to fit on screen, but all of the text uses only one font and font size. In contrast, two-line titles have two lines, and the top line uses a larger font. And credits, as seen on the far right, have multiple lines: one large, and the rest small and layered to look like production credits that appear at the end of a movie.

*continues on next page*

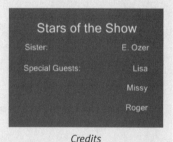

One-line title    Two-line title    Credits

**Figure 13.10** Movie Maker's three title types.

CREATING TITLES

## Title Animation Options *continued*

You can use any animation scheme anywhere in a movie. For example, you can apply a credit animation scheme to a title used in the middle of your production. In addition, you can use any two-line title with only one line of text, and Movie Maker will simply leave the other line blank.

To preview an animation, click it and Movie Maker plays it in the monitor, either using the text you've entered or the words "Windows Movie Maker" (for one-line titles) or "Microsoft" and "Windows Movie Maker" (for two-line titles and credits).

The titles I find most useful break into the following three general (albeit cryptic) categories:

**Conservative titles:** The two most conservative titles in this group, and the ones that I use most often are Basic Title and Fade, In and Out. Basic Title is a one-line title in which the text appears with no motion or fade. Fade, In and Out is a two-line title that fades in, pauses, and then fades out.

**Titles with banners (one- and two-line titles):** Banners are solid text regions that serve as background for the title text (**Figure 13.11**). I use banners when the background contains so many colors that it's hard to pick a font color that is easily readable throughout the entire frame.

**Subtitle (one-line title):** This places the text in a smallish font at the bottom of the video screen, which is useful when you don't want the title to obscure the background video (**Figure 13.12**).

*continues on next page*

**Figure 13.11** Banners make titles easy to read.

**Figure 13.12** Use the Subtitle animation scheme to place text at the bottom of the screen.

CREATING TITLES

## Title Animation Options *continued*

The following individual titles are ones I find particularly useful and worth noting:

**News Video, Inset (one-line title):** This is a professional-looking title for use in business or other serious projects or for a more polished look in family videos (**Figure 13.13**).

**Newspaper (two-line title):** This simulates the appearance of a newspaper with titles as headlines and the video above the title showing through the inset (**Figure 13.14**). This is a fun title for any family event with an "announcement" quality, such as birthdays, anniversaries, and graduations.

**Moving Titles, Layered (two-line title):** This is a dreamy, elegant look that I use for more artsy titles (**Figure 13.15**).

**Figure 13.13** This is the News Video, Inset title, which integrates the title with the video for a professional appearance.

**Figure 13.14** Animation schemes are more than just motion. This is another fun effect created with the Newspaper animation scheme.

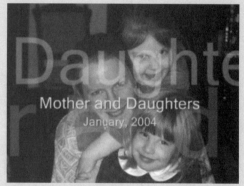

**Figure 13.15** Moving Titles, Layered—an elegant, dreamy look.

As you can see, some of Movie Maker's title animation schemes are quite elaborate and do much more than simply animate the text. Note that the names of the schemes tend to be a bit cryptic, however, so I encourage you to spend some time previewing the animation schemes to become familiar with them.

# Customizing Text

Movie Maker's text customization options are numerous but probably familiar to most readers who have used a word processor or presentation program. However, using text in a video production involves several additional considerations.

First, what's readable at full video resolution may not be readable after you've scaled the video down to its final output resolution. In addition, the lossy aspect of compression can degrade the clarity of the entire image, making the text harder to read, especially if you're producing for distribution at modem rates.

For this reason, most producers stick to clear fonts without serifs or other stylized elements that get mangled during compression. When you're experimenting with new title settings, it's good practice to produce a short clip at your final production parameters to make sure that the font and font parameters you've selected are readable.

### To change the text font:

1. In either the Enter Text for Title window (Figure 13.6) or the Choose the Title Animation window (Figure 13.8), click Change the Text Font and Color.

   Movie Maker opens the Select Title Font and Color window (**Figure 13.16**).

*continues on next page*

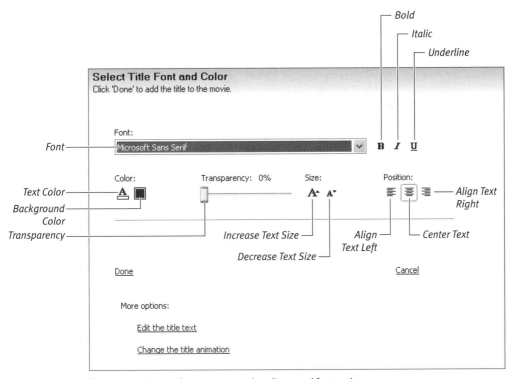

**Figure 13.16** Here's where you customize all text and font options.

**2.** Click the Font list box to display the available fonts (**Figure 13.17**).

**3.** Click the target font.

Movie Maker closes the Font list box and plays the title and new font once in the Monitor (**Figure 13.18**). To play the title again, click the Play button beneath the monitor.

**4.** If you want to change the text color, background color, text transparency, or any other aspect of the title, continue with the rest of the tasks in this section. If you are finished altering your title, do *one of the following*:

▲ Click Done to add the title to the movie and return to editing.

▲ Click Edit the Title Text to change the title text (and see "To insert a title" earlier in this chapter).

▲ Click Change the Title Animation to change the title animation scheme (and see "To change the title animation scheme" later in this chapter).

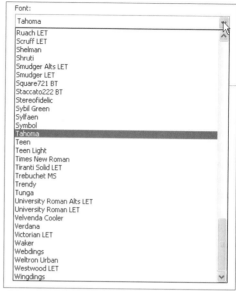

**Figure 13.17** Movie Maker lists the fonts available on your computer.

Play

**Figure 13.18** Click Play to preview your font selections.

CUSTOMIZING TEXT

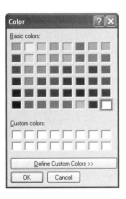

**Figure 13.19** You can choose any of the colors included in the Basic Colors palette.

Color picker —

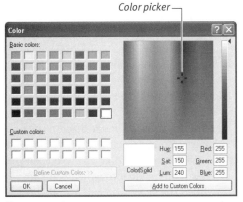

**Figure 13.20** Or you can create your own custom color.

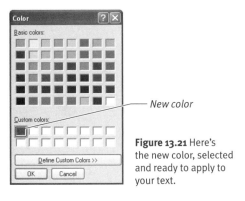

— New color

**Figure 13.21** Here's the new color, selected and ready to apply to your text.

## To change the font color:

1. If you don't already have the Select Title Font and Color window open (Figure 13.16), follow Step 1 of the previous task.

2. Click the Text Color button.
   Movie Maker opens the Color window (**Figure 13.19**).

3. Do *one of the following:*
   - ▲ Click one of the available colors in the Basic Colors palette and go to Step 7.
   - ▲ Click the Define Custom Colors button. Movie Maker expands the Color window to include custom color selection (**Figure 13.20**).

4. To define a custom color, do *one of the following:*
   - ▲ Select a color using the crosshairs in the color space.
   - ▲ In the Hue, Sat (saturation), and Lum (luminance) fields, enter new HSL values.
   - ▲ In the Red, Green, and Blue fields, enter new RGB values.

5. Click Add to Custom Colors to add the color to the Custom Colors palette.
   Movie Maker adds the color (**Figure 13.21**).

6. Click the desired custom color.

7. Click OK to close the Color window.
   Movie Maker changes the text to the new color.

8. If you want to change any other aspect of your title, continue with the rest of the tasks in this section. If you are finished altering your title, follow Step 4 of the previous task.

**CUSTOMIZING TEXT**

## To change the title background color:

1. In the Select Title Font and Color window (Figure 3.16), click the Background Color button.

   Movie Maker opens the Color window (Figure 13.19).

2. Do *one of the following:*

   ▲ Click one of the available colors in the Basic Colors palette and go to Step 6.

   ▲ Click the Define Custom Colors button.

   Movie Maker expands the Color window to include custom color selection (Figure 13.20).

3. To define a custom color, do *one of the following:*

   ▲ Select a color with the crosshairs in the color space.

   ▲ In the Hue, Sat (saturation), and Lum (luminance) fields, enter new HSL values.

   ▲ In the Red, Green, and Blue fields, enter new RGB values.

4. Click Add to Custom Colors to add the color to the Custom Colors palette. Movie Maker adds the color (Figure 13.21).

5. Click the desired custom color.

6. Click OK to close the Color window. Movie Maker changes the text to the new color.

7. If you want to change any other aspect of your title, continue with the rest of the tasks in this section. If you are finished altering your title, follow Step 4 of "To change the text font" earlier in this chapter.

### ✔ Tip

■ RGB and HSL values are two alternatives for precisely defining a color. In most instances, just eye-balling it with the crosshairs should provide an acceptable result. However, if you're attempting to match another color used with or around the video, such as text on a Web page or PowerPoint slide into which you plan to embed the video, you can use the RGB or HSL values to precisely match the colors.

CUSTOMIZING TEXT

**Figure 13.22** Drag this slider to the left to make the title as opaque as possible; drag to the right to increase transparency.

*0 percent transparent*

*80 percent transparent*

**Figure 13.23** On the top is text at 0 percent transparency; on the bottom text at 80 percent transparency.

## ✔ Tip

■ Note that Movie Maker applies all font settings to all text in the title, irrespective of whether you've selected and highlighted text in the Enter Text for Title window. While you can customize these characteristics for different titles, you can't customize different bits of text within a single title.

## To change the text transparency:

◆ In the Select Title Font and Color window (Figure 3.16), do *one of the following*:

▲ Drag the Transparency slider to the left to decrease transparency and make the text easier to read (**Figure 13.22**).

▲ Drag the slider to the right to increase the transparency and make the text fainter and harder to read.

## ✔ Tip

■ Zero percent transparency means the image is 100 percent opaque and highly viewable (**Figure 13.23**). In contrast, at 80 percent transparency, the image is very faint and difficult to read.

## To change font size, alignment, and text attributes:

1. If you don't already have the Select Title Font and Color window open (Figure 3.16), follow Step 1 of "To change the text font" earlier in this chapter.

2. To change the font size, do *one of the following*:

▲ Click the Increase Text Size button to make the text larger.

▲ Click the Decrease Text Size button to make the text smaller.

3. To change the alignment, select the desired alignment using the Align Text Left, Center Text, and Align Text Right buttons.

4. To change font attributes such as boldfacing, italics, and underlining, click the desired attributes, located to the right of the Font drop-down list.

5. If you are finished altering your title, follow Step 4 of "To change the text font" earlier in this chapter.

# Editing Titles

Once a title is inserted on the Timeline, you can modify its position and duration, or cut, copy, and paste it just like any other audio, video, or still-image content.

To change any title attribute other then text, animation, or font color and characteristics, see various sections in Chapter 9, including "To arrange video clips on the Timeline," "To delete assets," and "Trimming Clips on the Timeline."

### To edit title text, font characteristics, or title animation:

◆ Do *one of the following:*

 ▲ Double-click the title.

 ▲ Select the title and from the main menu, choose Edit > Edit Title (**Figure 13.24**).

Movie Maker opens the Edit Text for Title window (Figure 13.6). From there, you can edit the text directly, or you can click Change the Title Animation to choose another animation scheme or Change the Text Font and Color to modify the font and font characteristics.

**Figure 13.24** Choose Edit Title to modify text, animation scheme, or font characteristics.

# Advanced Title Topics

Now that we've covered the basics, let's explore some advanced title options. Let's begin with an overview of some of the free still-image and motion title backgrounds available from Microsoft, and then I'll describe how to integrate them into a project. Then I'll show you how to combine two titles to create an even more compelling presentation.

## Free Title Options

Microsoft's free Creativity Fun Pack, (www.microsoft.com/windowsxp/moviemaker/downloads/create.asp) provides three ways to enhance the visual appeal of your titles.

First, it comes with 14 still images that you can use as static backgrounds for your text titles. These include the image shown in the background on the center and left of Figure 13.10. Of course, you can use any still image as a title background, but the wide-open spaces available in these images allow text to show through very distinctly, a valuable feature for a title background.

Second, the pack includes two video backgrounds, one yellow and one blue, that you can also use as backgrounds for your titles. **Figure 13.25** shows the BlankBackground_Yellow video; you can just make out the filmstrip image in the background that scrolls while the video flashes slightly, simulating a projector.

*continues on next page*

**Figure 13.25** One of the video backgrounds Microsoft supplies free in the Creativity Fun Pack. It's tough to see from this shot, but it is an elegant background for your text titles.

## Free Title Options *continued*

Finally, the pack includes several videos designed for use at the beginning or end of your movie. For example, the Countdown_Blue video (**Figure 13.26**) counts down from five to zero and then flashes the word "Start." There are also several animations that display "The End," like TheEnd_Yellow shown in **Figure 13.27**. These videos are polished attention grabbers that start and end your video in style, so considering the price, you should definitely check them out.

**Figure 13.26** Another Microsoft animated title, counting down to the start of your movie.

**Figure 13.27** Another free title animation from Microsoft.

To use these elements, you treat them like other still image and video files, dragging them to the target points in the Timeline (see "Getting Video Clips to the Timeline" and "Editing Still Images" in Chapter 9 for more details).

After inserting the still image and video backgrounds, create your title *beneath* the new backgrounds on the Title Overlay track as described earlier in this chapter in "To insert a title." If you're using the starting and ending videos without additional titles, drag them to the beginning or end of your project, and you're done.

## Combining titles

There are two ways to combine titles. The first involves placing one title on the Video track and one on the Title Overlay track. This is shown in **Figure 13.28**, where I combined scrolling credits on top with the News Video, Inset title on the bottom, creating the combined title shown in **Figure 13.29**. This process is relatively straightforward; you simply follow the procedure outlined earlier in "To insert a title" for both titles.

You can also combine titles on the same track to fade one title into the next, which is useful when you need to combine titles that you want to display *over* the background video. Here's the procedure.

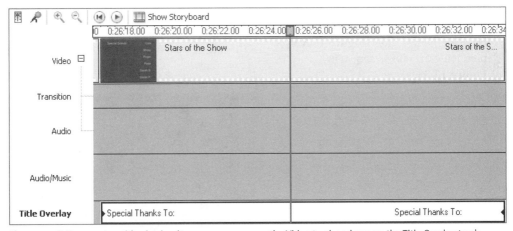

**Figure 13.28** Here are two titles in simultaneous use, one on the Video track and one on the Title Overlay track.

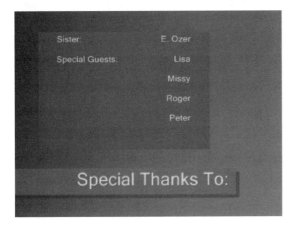

**Figure 13.29** Here's the combined title produced by the two titles in Figure 13.28.

## To insert two overlapping titles on the Title Overlay track:

1. Create the two titles and place them on the Title Overlay track (**Figure 13.30**).

   Here I'm combining two titles, the first using an animation scheme that places text on top of the screen (Typewriter animation), and the second using a scheme that places text on the bottom (Subtitle animation). This inserts text at the top and bottom of the screen simultaneously.

2. Drag the second title into the first (**Figure 13.31**).

   Movie Maker inserts a fade transition between the two titles (**Figure 13.32**), producing the effects shown in **Figure 13.33**.

**Figure 13.30** You can also merge two titles together on the same track. Start by producing them in sequence as shown here.

**Figure 13.31** Then drag the second onto the first.

**Figure 13.32** This introduces a fade transition between the titles.

**Figure 13.33** And produces this look, which I couldn't get from any single title.

# WORKING WITH AUTOMOVIE

As much as we like to think that video is about storytelling, sometimes there just isn't a story to tell. Maybe it's a day at the beach that's loaded with fun shots but no real story. How do you edit this into something watchable? Consider creating a music video with AutoMovie.

AutoMovie is a feature of Movie Maker that creates movies automatically. You select the clips to convert into a movie and, if desired, a background music track. Movie Maker analyzes the clip and background music, cuts the most relevant footage into scenes between four and six seconds long, inserts transitions and special effects, and synchronizes the clips to the background music, inserting the result on the Timeline for rendering or further editing.

Microsoft doesn't disclose much about the technology underlying AutoMovie, but it tends to accentuate shots of faces and heads. This makes it great for parties and sports activities, but it may not work very well for vacation videos of the Grand Canyon. I consider AutoMovie any time there's no real story to tell or when I want a nice filler for a scene or two in a longer project.

In this chapter, you'll learn about the types of projects in which you might want to use AutoMovie, how to prepare your projects to get the best results, and how to create AutoMovies from your video collections.

# AutoMovie Basics

AutoMovie is by no means hard to use, and in fact is wizard-driven, but a few minutes of introduction will enable you to use it more effectively without a lot of time-consuming trial and error.

AutoMovie has several characteristics you should consider before blindly diving in:

♦ It cuts all videos into segments of three to six seconds. This is great for MTV-style music videos, but not so great if you're trying to capture the wedding toast in its entirety.

♦ If you insert a background music track, Movie Maker produces a movie the length of the music track. If you don't, Movie Maker produces a movie three minutes long, or 3:13, if you consider the opening title and closing credits.

♦ Because you can enter only one song, if you want to create a longer AutoMovie you must combine two or more songs in an audio editor before inserting the result in the AutoMovie wizard.

♦ You can use AutoMovie only on a collection of clips with a combined duration of 30 seconds or more, and all inserted audio clips must be at least 30 seconds long. If you fail to comply, Movie Maker will ding you with the error message shown in **Figure 14.1**.

♦ AutoMovie decides which segments of the video to include in the AutoMovie, not you. This makes it not so great if you're trying to make sure that all attendees at an event appear in the final movie.

♦ AutoMovie decides which effects and transitions to use and when, not you.

You can edit an AutoMovie, of course, but remember that in creating an AutoMovie, Movie Maker synchronizes the video to the beat of the music. Edit too much, and you risk losing the precise synchronization to the music.

Figure 14.1 Start your AutoMovies with at least 30 seconds of video or you'll see this message.

## Practical applications

I consider using AutoMovie when I'm trying to provide a general sense of an experience. This could be kids playing, vacation pictures from Manhattan or the Rockies, or soccer practice. It can be a two-minute segment in a movie, or a complete five-minute video that's the only movie I produce with the video that I shot.

For example, at a wedding on Saint Simon's Island last April, my children spent a tantalizing 30 minutes running around the pool. Too cold to swim, just right for dipping their toes. The 10 minutes of video I shot turned into a 3-minute AutoMovie inserted as a segment within a much longer movie about the weekend.

I recently shot about 30 minutes of video of my wife and children going skating for the first time. I converted this into a 5-minute stand-alone AutoMovie.

I don't use AutoMovie when the audio in the movie—people talking or music playing in the background—is a critical element. That's because AutoMovie chops the audio and video into four-to-six-second discontinuous chunks, creating a result that works well visually, but sounds very choppy. I also don't use it when I'm trying to craft a visual story from my clips, because I obviously can't control which elements show up, or when, or for how long.

### AutoMovie and Still Images

You can use AutoMovie with collections of still images, but I find the results much less satisfying, primarily because slide shows are so easy to build manually. Note that if you create an AutoMovie with still images, Movie Maker displays each image for 6 seconds and stops the movie after using all slides one time. If you insert 10 images and a 3-minute song, your AutoMovie will be only 60 seconds long.

## AutoMovie and Movie Maker

AutoMovie is a completely separate function within Movie Maker. Here are some characteristics of the file produced, and their implications within a larger project, that you should consider before producing an AutoMovie.

The movie produced by AutoMovie is a series of clips on the Timeline with associated audio and transitions and an opening title and closing credits (**Figure 14.2**). You can edit these segments as desired, including dragging them to new locations. Basically, once inserted, movies created by AutoMovie are just like any other clips. However, if you have existing clips on the Timeline, Movie Maker inserts the AutoMovie as the last clips on the Timeline.

Note that Auto Movie doesn't assign any audio to the title and closing credits, starting the music with the first video sequence and concluding it with the last. This allows you to delete the title and closing credits without affecting synchronization—important if you're using the sequence in a longer production.

However, if you otherwise change the duration of any video within the sequence, say by adding another transition or a completely new clip, Movie Maker doesn't automatically maintain synchronization, so the video and audio will end at different times, and whatever efforts AutoMovie made to map cuts to the music will be lost from the point where you changed the video onward. You can fix this loss of synchronization, of course, but you'll have to do it manually.

When you select the background music track, you can prioritize the audio volume between the audio included with the video (the original audio) and the inserted background music. As you can see in Figure 14.2, the waveform for the original audio is completely flat, while the background music waveform is full. This is because I gave complete priority to the background music.

I generally give complete priority to the background music for most AutoMovies, the only exception being sporting events, where the shouts and grunts add to the effect. I always give complete priority to the background music when someone is talking in the video, since AutoMovie is likely to cut the speech short. Ditto if there's music in the background of the video, since AutoMovie will chop it up into discordant, discontinuous segments.

With this as prolog, let's jump in and create an AutoMovie.

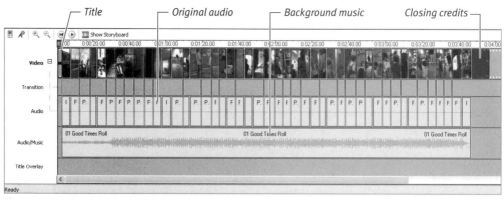

**Figure 14.2** Here's what a finished AutoMovie looks like.

## Choosing an Editing Style

When you apply AutoMovie, you must choose from one of five editing styles to apply to the video. The selected style controls the nature of the effects and transitions applied and the pace of the video (**Figure 14.3**). These are the five styles:

◆ **Flip and Slide:** Flip, slide, reveal, and page curl video transitions are applied between clips. (To get a sense of what these transitions look like, you can preview them in the Video Transitions collection as described in "How Transitions Work in Movie Maker" in Chapter 10.).

◆ **Highlights Movie:** Clean and simple editing with cuts and fades. This is the MovieMaker default.

◆ **Music Video:** Quick edits for fast beats, and longer edits for slow beats.

**Figure 14.3** Here are the styles you can choose to control the pace and effects applied to your movie.

◆ **Old Movie:** Film Age video effects applied to clips to simulate old black and white movies.

◆ **Sports Highlights:** Video clips with fast pans and zooms are selected to capture the action, and an exploding title (**Figure 14.4**) and credits are added at the beginning and end.

When creating an AutoMovie, I generally experiment with several styles before making my final selection. Usually, at least one sounds appropriate for my intended use, but it takes only a few minutes to try another. I always try the Old Movie Style, which I think is most unique, even if the footage is current.

**Figure 14.4** An exploding title in action.

In addition, note that each style produces a different result, depending upon the nature of the background music. For example, if you use a fast-paced song, Movie Maker will produce one result, and if you use slower song, it will produce a different result. My experiments with different songs produced unpredictable results, and again, Microsoft doesn't disclose much about the algorithms that drive AutoMovie operation. My best advice is to try a style and a song, and if you don't like the result, try a different song.

**AUTOMOVIE BASICS**

# Creating AutoMovies

For the purposes of this section, I'll assume that you've captured or imported video into a collection and, if desired, deleted the segments to be excluded in the AutoMovie (see the sidebar "Prepping Your Collection"). Note that you don't have to import the audio for an AutoMovie beforehand, since the wizard allows you to select audio from anywhere on your computer.

## To create an AutoMovie:

1. Do *one of the following:*

   ▲ In the Collections pane, choose the target collection (**Figure 14.5**).

   ▲ In the Contents pane, choose the target clips (**Figure 14.6**).

   As with all clip selections in the Contents pane, press the Ctrl key to select random clips, press the Shift key to select adjacent clips, or choose Edit > Select All to select all clips.

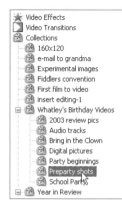

**Figure 14.5** Start by choosing a collection.

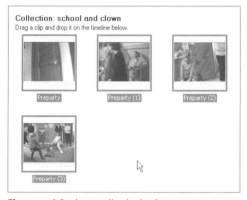

**Figure 14.6** Or choose clips in the Contents pane.

## Prepping Your Collection

You start the AutoMovie process by selecting clips in a collection or an entire collection. There is no way to tell AutoMovie to include certain segments within a clip or to exclude others.

For this reason, if you want certain scenes excluded, you can delete them from the collection before creating the AutoMovie as described in "Working with Audio and Video in the Contents Pane" in Chapter 8. I always eliminate any atrocious camera work and, perhaps, redundant scenes of individuals that I want only once in the final movie.

Note that AutoMovie doesn't change the order of the clips; it always works chronologically. This can be a bit of a pain if you shot certain footage out of order, but again, you can move scenes around after Movie Maker 2 generates the AutoMovie.

Figure 14.7 Click here to make an AutoMovie.

Figure 14.8 Or click here.

2. Do *one of the following:*

   ▲ In the Movie Tasks pane, choose Make an AutoMovie (**Figure 14.7**).

   ▲ From the main menu, choose Tools > AutoMovie (**Figure 14.8**).

   Movie Maker opens the AutoMovie wizard (**Figure 14.9**).

3. Select the target style.

   For help on choosing which editing style to use, see the sidebar "Choosing an Editing Style," earlier in this chapter.

4. If desired, click Enter a Title for the Movie.

   Movie Maker opens the Enter Text for Title screen (**Figure 14.10**).

5. Type the desired title text.

   Note that if you don't insert a title, Movie Maker will use the name of the first clip in the AutoMovie as the title.

   *continues on next page*

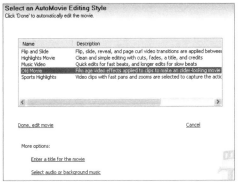

Figure 14.9 The AutoMovie wizard lets you choose among different editing styles.

Figure 14.10 If you don't enter a title, Movie Maker will use the name of the first video clip.

CREATING AUTOMOVIES

**6.** If desired, click Select Audio or Background Music.

Movie Maker opens the Add Audio or Background Music screen (**Figure 14.11**). Note that if you don't select a song, the AutoMovie will be three minutes long.

**7.** Click Browse.

The Open dialog appears (**Figure 14.12**).

**8.** Select the desired song and click Open.

**9.** Drag the Audio Levels slider to give priority to either Audio from Video or Audio/Music (**Figure 14.13**).

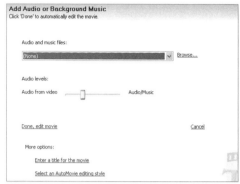

**Figure 14.11** Here's where you add audio and prioritize volume between the background music and original audio.

**Figure 14.12** Let the Good Times Roll!

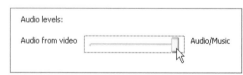

**Figure 14.13** Hmmm. Tough choice, The Cars or a bunch of screaming six-year-olds?

**Figure 14.14** Movie Maker analyzes the audio.

**Figure 14.15** Then it analyzes the video.

**10.** After selecting all audio options, click Done, edit movie (Figure 14.11).

Movie Maker analyzes the audio (**Figure 14.14**) and video (**Figure 14.15**).

When finished, Movie Maker places the segments and audio on the Timeline (**Figure 14.16**).

### ✔ Tip

- From here, you're free to edit the clips as desired, but recall that Movie Maker doesn't maintain the synchronization of the sequence. If you add a clip or transition, change the speed of any clip or otherwise change the duration of the video segments in the AutoMovie, the audio won't finish simultaneously with the video.

**Figure 14.16** And then it produces the AutoMovie.

CREATING AUTOMOVIES

# Part IV: Output

# WRITING TO TAPE

Writing projects back to tape, whether it's to analog formats like VHS or to DV tape, is useful for archiving your video editing efforts and distributing video to those who don't have DVD players or computers to play digital files. When writing back to DV tape using Windows Movie Maker, a wizard assists you using a two-step process.

First you set up your hardware, which is nearly identical to connecting for capture. Then you start the wizard, which checks your setup. If all the pieces are in place, it lets you know, and you can walk away and let Movie Maker finish the job. Once the video is safely on DV tape, you can dub copies to VHS or other analog formats.

Unfortunately, Movie Maker doesn't have a wizard for writing back to analog sources, probably because, unlike DV cards, which conform to strict standards, analog capture cards all work differently. I discuss how to send video back to VHS and other analog camcorders and decks in the sidebar "Writing Back to Analog Devices," at the end of this chapter.

## Distribution Options

For an overview of Movie Maker's output capabilities, see Chapter 3, particularly "So what can I do using Movie Maker?" and "What about producing DVDs?" Briefly, this chapter discusses writing back to DV and analog tape. Chapter 16 describes how to produce digital files for distribution or further production.

Movie Maker can't directly produce a DVD for viewing on a DVD player, though it can output files compatible with DVD authoring programs. See the sidebar "Rendering for Additional Production" in Chapter 16 for more information. Also see Appendix A for an introduction to Sonic Solutions' popular DVD authoring program, MyDVD.)

# Setting Up Your Hardware

Obviously, to write video from your computer to your DV camcorder, you have to get the two connected. I'll describe how to do that here, and then follow immediately with a discussion of the process of writing back to your DV camera.

## To set up your hardware:

1. Connect your camera or deck to the computer.

   For more information on connecting your DV camera, see Chapter 4; for more information on connecting your analog camera, see Chapter 5.

2. Make sure the camera or deck is in VTR, VCR, or Play mode.

3. If the camcorder has an LCD display, open the LCD and use the camcorder controls to display all tape location and recording/playback information (if available).

   Sony camcorders usually have a Display button that reveals this information.

4. If the camcorder or deck has an Input/ Output selector, select Input.

   I haven't seen this in a while, but my venerable Sony Hi-8 CCD-TR81 had an Input/Output switch that needed to be set before writing to tape.

5. If there is no LCD, or if you're writing to a stand-alone deck, connect a television or other analog monitor to the camcorder or deck.

   The only way to be sure you're actually writing to tape is to see the video in the camcorder or deck.

6. Check the time codes of the tape in the deck to make sure you have sufficient space for your production.

SETTING UP YOUR HARDWARE

**Figure 15.1** Movie Maker checks to make sure that you haven't copy protected your DV tapes.

**Figure 15.2** Writing back to DV tape takes lots of disk space, so be sure your temporary files are directed to your largest disk.

**7.** Check that any copy-protection features on the tape are disabled.

Most DV tapes have a copy-protection tab on the back panel, a great way to make sure you don't overwrite your valuable video.

Movie Maker checks to make sure that the tape is not copy protected; if it is, Movie Maker stops the process and displays an error message (**Figure 15.1**).

**8.** Close all extraneous programs on your computer and don't perform any other tasks on the computer while writing to tape.

## ✔ Tips

■ Like capturing, writing to tape is an extremely demanding process, and one slip can ruin the tape. Try not to touch the computer or camcorder over the course of this procedure.

■ As part of the writing-back-to-tape process, Movie Maker builds what can be an extremely large temporary file (about 13 GB per hour of video). Now would be a good time to make sure that your temporary storage location is set correctly, which you do in the Options window, accessed by choosing Tools > Options from the main menu (**Figure 15.2**). See "Setting Project Defaults" in Chapter 3 for more details.

**SETTING UP YOUR HARDWARE**

287

# Writing to Tape

Since you're reading this chapter, I will assume that your project is complete—all edits done (and redone and redone), background music in place, and titles fore, aft, and in the middle. In short, you're ready to push the proverbial big red button and get this project behind you.

I'm right with you on that one, but before recording a long segment to tape, try a one- or two-minute sequence, just to make sure everything is working. Writing back to tape is one of those "tough to get it right the first time" activities, at least for me, so test your setup with a shorter project to catch any errors.

### To write your project to tape:

1. In the Movie Tasks pane, click Send to DV Camera (**Figure 15.3**).

   ▲ If the Movie Tasks pane isn't showing, click the Show or Hide Movie Tasks Pane button on the Movie Maker task bar (**Figure 15.4**).

   ▲ If you have more than one DV device connected to your computer, Movie Maker displays the pane shown in **Figure 15.5**. Click the target device and then click Next.

   ▲ If your camera is not connected correctly, Movie Maker displays the pane shown in **Figure 15.6**. Connect your camera (or turn it off and on to restart it) and then click Next.

   ▲ If your camera is properly connected, Movie Maker displays the pane shown in **Figure 15.7**.

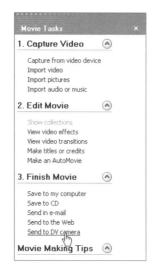

**Figure 15.3** Click here to start the process of writing back to DV tape.

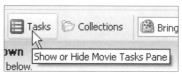

**Figure 15.4** Click here to display the Movie Tasks pane.

**Figure 15.5** Choose which camera you're writing back to and click Next.

**Figure 15.6** Oops. You need to connect your camera; make sure it's in VCR mode and turned on before starting.

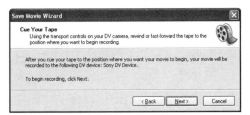

**Figure 15.7** Move your tape to the desired start position for the recording.

**Figure 15.8** Anything currently on the tape will be overwritten, so make sure you don't want to keep whatever is on your tape.

**Figure 15.9** The process is starting. Nothing to do but sit and wait.

**Figure 15.10** When this screen shows up, click Finish, and you can start your next project.

**2.** If necessary, use the controls on your camcorder to position the tape to the target starting point for the recording.

**3.** Click Next.

Movie Maker displays the dialog box shown in **Figure 15.8**.

**4.** Click Yes.

Movie Maker starts the rendering process, displaying the Recording Movie to Tape pane shown in **Figure 15.9**. Movie Maker first renders the video and then starts writing to tape, but the process is all automatic, so you don't need to intervene or even be around. When the process is complete, Movie Maker displays the message shown in **Figure 15.10**.

## ✔ Tips

- To stop Movie Maker during rendering, click Cancel in the Recording Movie to Tape pane (Figure 15.9).

- Some older DV cameras use nonstandard commands to start and stop recording and may not recognize Movie Maker's commands. If Movie Maker doesn't automatically start your DV recorder, wait until Movie Maker starts writing back to the DV camera and then manually start the record function.

## Troubleshooting

Writing back to DV tape is usually painless, but there can be some hurdles. Fortunately, Movie Maker tests for most potential issues and has very specific error messages to guide problem resolution.

First, understand that during rendering, Movie Maker builds the entire project into a DV file, which can be quite large. If you don't have sufficient disk space to store the file, Movie Maker will display the error message shown in **Figure 15.11.** Either choose another hard disk for your temporary file, free some disk space on the current drive by deleting other files, or shorten your project until it fits.

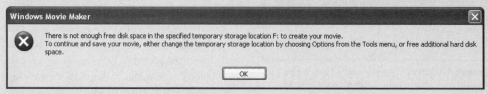

**Figure 15.11** You'll see this message if you don't have enough free space on your disk.

In addition, note that most DV tapes can record only 60 minutes of video in SP (Standard Play) mode. If your project is longer than 60 minutes, Movie Maker will advise you to switch into LP (Long Play) mode, which gives you up to 90 minutes of video (**Figure 15.12**). You can switch to LP mode or reduce the project size to under 60 minutes.

**Figure 15.12** Most tapes limit you to projects of about 60 minutes duration. You'll see this message if the project is longer than that.

Finally, some DV cameras react slowly when Movie Maker starts sending out the video and don't record the first few seconds of video. To compensate for this, add some nonessential video footage to the start of the project.

I like inserting a countdown video (as in 5, 4, 3, 2, 1) to the front of my projects, which you can download for free with the Creativity Fun Pack, discussed in "Free Title Options" in Chapter 13. Or you can create a black image matte and insert it at the beginning of the movie. See "To build a matte" in Chapter 10 for more details on creating a matte.

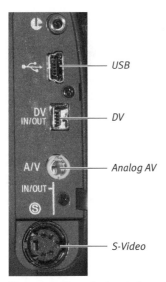

**Figure 15.13** The output ports from a DV camera, with one port, the analog AV port, outputting composite video and stereo audio.

**Figure 15.14** An S-Video cable, the preferred cable type, if both the camera and VHS deck support it.

# Dubbing from DV to VHS

Once the video is safely on DV tape, you can copy, or *dub,* the movie to VHS tape, so that you can send it to grandma and other viewers who don't have a DV camera, DVD player, or computer.

Here I describe how to set up your DV camera and VCR for dubbing and then how to execute the dub.

## ✔ Tip

■ Dubbing will overwrite any video currently on the VHS tape, so be sure the tape doesn't have video you want to keep.

### To connect for dubbing to VHS:

1. Plug in your DV camcorder to AC power.

2. Make sure the camcorder is in VCR, VTR, or Play mode.

3. Connect your video cables to the DV camera (**Figure 15.13**).

   If your DV camera and VHS deck both have S-Video connectors and you have the necessary cable (**Figure 15.14**), use the S-Video connector.

*continues on next page*

DUBBING FROM DV TO VHS

4. If S-Video is not available, use the composite video connectors by doing *one of the following*:

   ▲ If your DV camera has a specialty A/V port (the analog AV port in Figure 15.13), you should have received a specialty cable that looks like the one shown in **Figure 15.15**. Plug the single end into your DV camera. Most three-headed cables are coded yellow (composite video), red (right audio), and white (left audio and mono audio). Follow the color codes, and you'll speed up installation.

   ▲ If your DV camera has a separate composite video port (**Figure 15.16**), use a cable like the one shown in **Figure 15.17**.

5. Connect your audio cables to the DV camera by doing *one of the following*:

   ▲ If your DV camera has separate audio connectors (see Figure 15.15), connect a cable like that shown in Figure 15.17, being careful to match the colors of the connectors and output ports when applicable.

   ▲ If your DV camera has a specialty A/V port, you should have a specialty cable that looks like the one in Figure 15.15. Plug the single end into your camera.

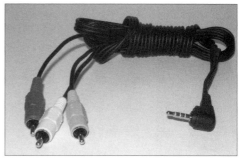

**Figure 15.15** Most DV cameras come with a specialty cable like this one that plugs into the analog AV port and outputs composite video and stereo audio.

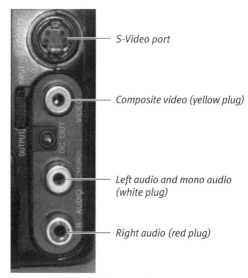

S-Video port

Composite video (yellow plug)

Left audio and mono audio (white plug)

Right audio (red plug)

**Figure 15.16** Some DV cameras have separate outputs for composite video and stereo audio.

**Figure 15.17** Cameras with separate ports for audio and video require a three-headed cable like this.

DUBBING FROM DV TO VHS

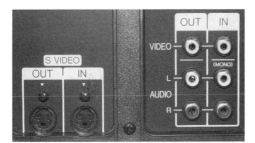

**Figure 15.18** The input/output ports of a VHS deck with S-Video input. Make sure you connect to the input ports.

6. Connect your video cable to the video input port of the VHS deck, using the S-Video connector if available or the composite if not.

 As shown in **Figure 15.18**, most VHS decks have input and output ports, so be certain you're choosing the input ports.

7. Connect your audio cables to the audio input ports of the VHS deck.

 Be sure to match the color-coded cables red to red and white to white. If the VHS deck only has one audio input port, use the *white* cable.

8. Use the controls on your VHS deck to select the connected port for video input. Typically, this is done through menu commands or by using the channel selector.

9. Insert a VHS tape into the VHS deck and use the deck's controls to cue the tape to the desired start location.

## ✔ Tips

■ You should always dub with a TV set connected to the VHS deck; otherwise, you won't be able to tell if video is actually being written to tape.

■ Once you have this setup in place, press Play on the DV camera, and the video should appear on the TV monitor. If not, something is wrong with your setup. Review Steps 1 through 8 in this task until you resolve the problem.

**DUBBING FROM DV TO VHS**

## To dub from DV to VHS:

1. Use controls on the DV camera to move to a position a few seconds before the video to dub to the VHS deck.

2. Press Record on the VHS deck.

   The deck begins recording.

3. Press Play on the DV camera.

   The DV camera starts to play. You should see video both on the LCD panel of the DV camera and on the television screen attached to the VHS deck. If you don't, stop recording and check your setup.

4. Once you've recorded the target video, stop both devices.

## Writing Back to Analog Devices

Movie Maker doesn't have a wizard for writing back to analog devices, probably because they are so nonstandard that one approach doesn't work for all analog devices. Of course, this lack of standardization makes it equally tough for a book to cover all alternatives, but I'll describe how the process *should* work and how it works with my ATI All-in-Wonder card.

To write back to an analog capture device, you need to send the audio and video signal out through the output ports of the capture device and back into the analog device. The first step, of course, is to connect your camcorder and computer as described earlier in this chapter in "To set up your hardware."

The next step is to actually play the video so that it is transmitted from your computer to the analog deck. With my ATI All-in-Wonder 9000 Pro card, this happens automatically when I preview the video by clicking Play in the Monitor. Specifically, to write back to my VHS deck, I position the Playback indicator at the start of the Timeline, press Record on the VHS deck, and then click Play on the Monitor, stopping the deck once the recording is complete.

This approach will probably also work for most devices similar to the All-in-Wonder, specifically graphics cards that have capture capabilities, as opposed to dedicated capture devices that only capture video. In any event, check your product's documentation for assistance.

If you're working with a dedicated capture device, check the product's documentation to see if it describes how to write files back to tape. If the process is not detailed there, check the company's Web site for FAQs or contact technical support for more information.

# OUTPUTTING DIGITAL FILES

# 16

Outputting your video project is like putting a cake in the oven; it's an obviously critical stage, but most of the hard work occurs beforehand. Similarly, most of the video production work occurs before final output, when you trim and arrange your clips and add transitions, effects, and titles. During output, your only decision is to choose a format and data rate and let Microsoft Windows Movie Maker bake the cake.

Fortunately, Movie Maker makes the format and data rate decisions quite simple, with wizards directing most activities. The only potential complexity lies in all the technical terms surrounding output, such as resolution, data rate, format, and compression. For definitions of these and other terms, as well as a good overview of the rendering process, return to the FAQ at the beginning of Chapter 3.

This chapter discusses how to create digital files for viewing on your computer, as well as how to burn them to a CD-R, send them via e-mail, and post them to a Web site. To upload video back to your camcorder, see Chapter 15. For an introduction to DVD authoring technologies, see Appendix A, which discusses MyDVD, a simple, consumer-oriented DVD authoring product.

# Supported Formats and Output Options

Movie Maker supports two formats (see Chapter 3 for the details). Here's a quick refresher.

One format is Audio/Video Interleave, or AVI. Specifically, Movie Maker produces an AVI file using the DV codec, which is the same compression technology used in DV camcorders. As discussed later in this chapter, in "Rendering for Additional Production," this format is primarily used to create high-quality files to re-input into Movie Maker for additional editing or to import into a DVD authoring program.

The other format Movie Maker produces is Windows Media Video, or WMV, which is useful for creating video for a wide range of purposes: everything from posting to a Web site and sending via e-mail to burning to CD and watching from your desktop. WMV is a flexible, robust format that should meet virtually all of your playback needs.

Movie Maker can't produce the MPEG-2 files necessary for DVD production and has no *DVD authoring* capabilities for producing DVDs with menus. Nor can it output MPEG-1 files or produce a Video CD or Super Video CD disc for playback on Video CD players and some DVD players. Rather, to produce a DVD, Super Video CD, or Video CD disc, you'll need a product like MyDVD that can accept files produced by Movie Maker (see Appendix A for an overview of MyDVD).

Similarly, Movie Maker cannot produce MPEG-4, DivX, or QuickTime files. Apple's QuickTime Pro, available at www.quicktime .com, is an inexpensive tool for MPEG-4 and QuickTime files. To find the latest, greatest DivX encoding tool, surf on over to www.divx.com.

## Who Can Play Your Videos?

The obvious purpose of most movie-making efforts is to create videos that others can watch. So when you're outputting your videos, the obvious first question is who can play them?

With the sole exception of DV-AVI files, which are too large to distribute for casual viewing, all other files produced by Movie Maker use Windows Media 9 compression technology. For other computers to play these files, they need a Windows Media 9 player, or an earlier version of Windows Media Player that can automatically download and play Windows Media 9 codecs (according to Microsoft, this includes all Windows–based players version 6.4 and later).

At the time of this writing, Microsoft has released Windows Media 9 players for Windows XP, Windows 2000, Windows 98 SE (Second Edition), and Windows Me (Millennium Edition). A Windows Media 9 player is also available for Mac OS X. All are available for free download at `www.microsoft.com/windows/windowsmedia/players.aspx`.

If your viewers are running any Macintosh version prior to OS X, they won't be able to play videos created by Movie Maker. In addition, computers running Linux or other UNIX flavors will not be able to play these files.

If you want to make your video available to viewers using any of these unsupported platforms, one approach is to output in DV-AVI format and then encode the file in MPEG-1 format, which is almost universally supported. There are a number of shareware and regular software programs that can produce MPEG-1 files. One popular free program is TMPGEnc, which is available at `www.tmpgenc.net`.

Alternatively, you could encode the file using a previous version of WMV as described in "Encoding with Windows Media Encoder" in Appendix C.

**SUPPORTED FORMATS AND OUTPUT OPTIONS**

Once you figure out what format you'll be using, you need to figure out how you want to output your files. Movie Maker's Save Movie wizard, accessible by choosing File > Save Movie File from the main menu, lists your choices (**Figure 16.1**):

**Figure 16.1** Movie Maker's Save Movie wizard: one starting point for all output efforts.

◆ **My Computer:** This is a catch-all category for all uses not specifically addressed by the next four options. Use this option to create AVI files for re-editing or DVD authoring and to create WMV files for posting to a Web site, playing back from your desktop, or other general uses.

◆ **Recordable CD:** Use this option to burn files directly to a CD recorder for playback on computers and consumer electronics devices that support Microsoft's HighMAT format (see "The Lowdown on HighMAT" later in this chapter). Note that CDs produced with this option are *not* Video CD compatible and *won't* play on the vast majority of stand-alone DVD players.

◆ **E-mail:** Use this option to create files to distribute via e-mail. This option includes convenient controls to limit output file size to comply with size restrictions common among Internet service providers (ISPs).

◆ **The Web:** Use this option if you have an account with a video-hosting provider that is compatible with Movie Maker. This option will produce and upload your video files to that hosting provider so they are available for viewing over the Web. To post to a Web site other than a Movie Maker– compatible video-hosting provider, use the first option (My Computer) to create the file and then manually upload the file.

◆ **DV Camera:** Use this option to write your movie back to your DV camera. This option is discussed in Chapter 15.

**Figure 16.2** I prefer using the Finish Movie commands on the Movie Tasks pane.

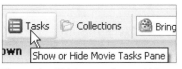

**Figure 16.3** Click here to show or hide the Movie Tasks pane.

**Figure 16.4** Enter the file name and target storage location.

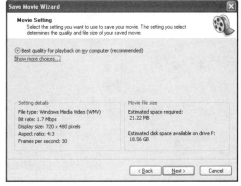

**Figure 16.5** The default settings are fine for most uses.

# Saving to My Computer

My Computer is the most general output category, used whenever the more specific categories don't apply. For example, if you're creating a file for posting to a Web site, but don't have an account with a Movie Maker–compatible video-hosting provider, use this option to produce the file.

As with all the output options, I assume that you've completed your project, and it's sitting on the Timeline ready for output. I'll start with the simplest case: saving a file for playback from your own hard disk using default settings. This is the simplest approach and should work for most users.

Then I'll tackle how to tinker with settings to produce files for playback on the Web, over a local area network, or from specialty devices such as a Pocket PC.

## To save a file using default settings:

1. In the Movie Tasks pane, click Save to My Computer (**Figure 16.2**). If you don't see the Movie Tasks pane, click the Show or Hide Movie Tasks Pane icon on the task bar (**Figure 16.3**) to display it.

   Movie Maker opens the Save Movie wizard to the Saved Movie File pane (**Figure 16.4**).

2. If desired, enter a file name for the saved movie.

3. If desired, change the location for the rendered file.

   The default location is the current location for temporary storage. (See "Setting Project Defaults" in Chapter 3 for details on how to change this setting.)

4. Click Next.

   Movie Maker opens the wizard's Movie Setting pane (**Figure 16.5**).

*continues on next page*

**5.** Click Next.

Movie Maker starts rendering your file, displaying the Saving Movie pane (**Figure 16.6**). To cancel rendering at this point, click the Cancel button.

As you would expect, rendering time is directly related to the length of the project and speed of your computer.

When Movie Maker is finished, it displays the Completing the Save Movie Wizard pane (**Figure 16.7**).

**6.** If desired, select the Play Movie When I Click Finish check box.

**7.** Click Finish.

The dialog box closes, and if you opted to play the rendered video, Microsoft's Windows Media Player opens and starts to play the file (**Figure 16.8**).

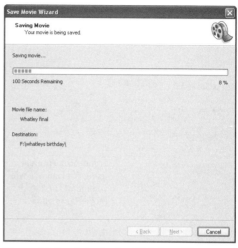

**Figure 16.6** Rendering begins. Click Cancel if you need to stop the process and make one last change.

**Figure 16.7** All done. Select the check box to play the movie.

**Figure 16.8** We're swinging now. I dig this compact skin for Windows Media Player.

SAVING TO MY COMPUTER

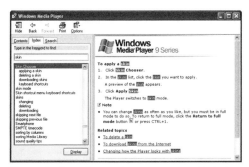

**Figure 16.9** Learn how to choose your own skin in the Windows Media Player help file.

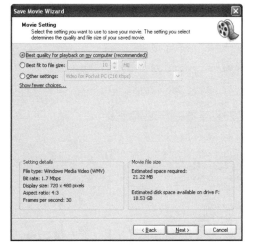

**Figure 16.10** Same Movie Setting pane as before, but now we're going to tinker with the settings.

## ✔ Tips

■ Your version of Windows Media Player may look different than mine because I've changed the *skin*, or user interface. To read more about skins, with Media Player running press F1 to access Media Player's Help file; then click the Index tab and type skin in the keyword search line (**Figure 16.9**).

■ You can start the output process by clicking File > Make Movie from the main menu, which will display the Save Movie wizard shown in Figure 16.1.

## To save a file applying custom settings:

1. In the Movie Tasks pane, click Save to My Computer (Figure 16.2). If the Movie Tasks pane isn't showing, click the Show or Hide Movie Tasks Pane icon on the Movie Maker task bar (Figure 16.3).

   Movie Maker opens the Save Movie wizard to the Saved Movie File pane (Figure 16.4).

2. If desired, enter a file name for the saved movie.

3. If desired, change the location for the rendered file.

   The default location is the current location for temporary storage. See "Setting Project Defaults" in Chapter 3 for details on how to change this setting.

4. Click Next.

   Movie Maker opens the Movie Setting pane of the wizard (Figure 16.5).

5. Click Show More Choices.

   Movie Maker displays additional output options (**Figure 16.10**).

   *continues on next page*

**6.** Do *one of the following*:

▲ To produce a file of a specific size, click Best Fit to File Size and enter the target size (**Figure 16.11**). Proceed to Step 8.

▲ To access other encoding options, click Other Settings and then click the arrow beside the list box to see all encoding options (**Figure 16.12**).

**Figure 16.11** Here's how you produce a file of a specific size.

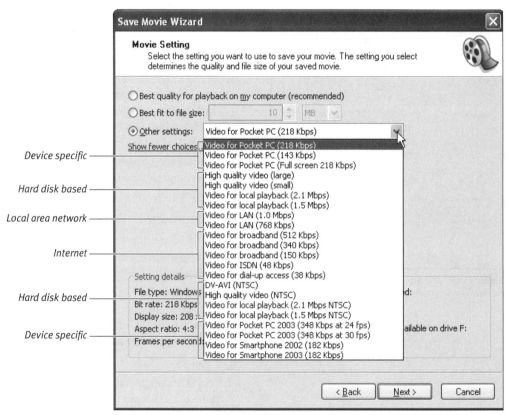

**Figure 16.12** Sometimes you can have too many choices.

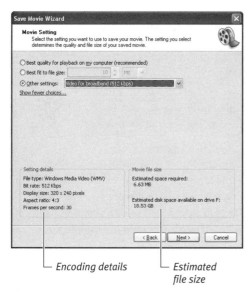

Encoding details — Estimated file size

**Figure 16.13** Once you choose a setting, the wizard displays encoding details and estimated file size.

7. Choose the setting you want to use (**Figure 16.13**). For help in selecting the right setting, see "Choosing Your Compression Settings" later in this chapter.

   Note the encoding details shown at the lower left of the Movie Setting window and the file size requirements and available disk space at the right.

8. Click Next.

   Movie Maker starts rendering your file, displaying the wizard's Saving Movie pane (Figure 16.6). To cancel rendering at this point, click the Cancel button.

   Rendering time relates to the project size, computer speed, and selected output setting, with files with higher-quality output settings taking longer to produce.

   When Movie Maker is finished, it displays the Completing the Save Movie Wizard pane shown in Figure 16.7.

9. If desired, select the Play Movie When I Click Finish check box.

10. Click Finish.

    The dialog box closes, and if you opted to play the rendered video, Microsoft's Windows Media Player opens and starts to play the file (Figure 16.8).

**SAVING TO MY COMPUTER**

## Choosing Your Compression Settings

Movie Maker offers an extensive range of output presets that are likely to be confusing to most users (Figure 16.12). Let's try to narrow them to make your selection easier.

Before we begin, notice that each preset has a number in parenthesis after it, which specifies the *bit rate* of the encoded file. I define bit rate in "The Jan-FAQs" in Chapter 3, but briefly, it's the amount of data associated with each second of video. For your reference, *Kbps* is kilobits per second, and *Mbps* is megabits per second.

Higher numbers mean bigger files and better quality, since Movie Maker applies less lossy compression when producing the files. However, there's always a trade-off, since larger files are much slower to access via the Internet and can clog a local area network and consume gobs of storage on your local hard disk. Basically, bigger is always better, unless you don't have the storage space, or if your viewers don't have high-speed Internet connections to quickly download and view the files.

With this as background, let's examine the choices available in Figure 16.12.

The DV-AVI (NTSC) option, which is located about halfway down the list, is used primarily to produce files for additional editing or authoring, not for casual playback (see the sidebar "Rendering for Additional Production" later in this chapter for more information). So, unless you're saving for additional production, you can forget about this option.

Next notice that there are a number of presets for specific devices, like the Pocket PC, Pocket PC 2003, and Smartphone 2002. If you're producing files for transfer to these devices, choose the preset that provides the best mix of quality and storage space.

If you're producing video for posting to a Web site, choose the best alternative presented in the options designated for the Internet.

For example, some producers like to match the selected bit rate to the connection speed used by their viewers, which speeds access to the video files. So if grandpa connects via a dial-up modem and gets cranky if he has to wait a moment or two to see the video, consider using 38 Kbps. On the other hand, if the video is short, most users don't mind waiting a few moments to see the file, especially if it looks good, and it certainly will look better when encoded at a higher bit rate. To achieve this additional quality, I produce most of my files destined for the Internet at either 340 Kbps or 512 Kbps.

*continues on next page*

## Choosing Your Compression Settings *continued*

That said, if you're posting to a Web site hosted by an ISP and anticipate high download volumes, high-bit-rate files mean high-bandwidth usage, which may translate into higher hosting fees. So balance these issues and choose the best rate among the Internet presets.

If you're posting video to a local area network other than in your home, check with the LAN administrator before posting any files. Most home LANs can comfortably transfer files of either 1 Mbps or 768 Kbps, so choose the format that best balances your storage capacity and quality needs.

Finally, there are seven options for local playback, with several featuring almost identical output parameters. Note that you can identify and compare the specific output parameters by selecting the preset and then looking in the Setting Details section of the wizard's Movie Setting pane (Figure 16.13).

Note that at the highest bit rate (2.1 Mbps), an hour of video consumes about 945 MB, a fraction of the capacity of most current hard drives. Unless you're absolutely starved for disk space, I would choose Video for Local Playback (2.1 Mbps) for most local playback.

## Rendering for Additional Production

Movie Maker has several limitations, such as only one general-purpose audio track, that make it useful to output a file and then re-input the same file for additional editing. Alternatively, you may want to use Movie Maker to produce files for input to a DVD authoring program. In both instances, you should output the file using the DV-AVI setting. Here's why.

Each time Movie Maker outputs a file, it compresses the file into the selected format. As you already know, all video compression techniques applied by Movie Maker are *lossy*, which means they degrade the quality of the video in the file. (See "The Jan-FAQs" in Chapter 3 for more information.)

So when you're producing files for additional production within Movie Maker, you should render at the highest possible quality, which is always the DV-AVI option (Figure 16.12). Then, when you're producing your final file, output it using the actual settings you want.

Similarly, you should output in DV-AVI format when producing a file for input to a DVD authoring program such as MyDVD. This maximizes quality and, since the DV-AVI format is almost universally supported, helps ensure that your authoring program can load the file.

**SAVING TO MY COMPUTER**

# Saving to CD

While DVD recorders are still a bit rare, most computers have CD recorders that can burn up to 700 MB of data on one disc, or about 55 minutes of video if you use Movie Maker's default setting. This Movie Maker option burns your output file directly to a recordable CD.

All Windows-based computers with a CD or DVD drive should be able to play the video, as well as any consumer electronics device that supports the HighMAT format. At the time of this writing, however, only one company—Panasonic—is producing devices that actually support the HighMAT spec (for more information, see `www.highmat.com/wheretogetit/`).

Note that discs produced by Movie Maker will *not* play on most stand-alone DVD players. To produce discs that play on these devices, you'll need a DVD authoring program like MyDVD. Of course, you can save to CD only if you have a recordable drive on your system and a recordable disc in the drive.

## To save to CD:

1. In the Movie Tasks pane, click Save to CD (**Figure 16.14**). If the Movie Tasks pane isn't showing, click the Show or Hide Movie Tasks Pane icon on the Movie Maker task bar (Figure 16.3).

   Movie Maker opens the Save Movie wizard to the Saved Movie File pane (**Figure 16.15**).

2. If desired, enter a file name for the saved movie.

3. If desired, enter a name for the CD.

**Figure 16.14** Click here to save your output files to CD.

**Figure 16.15** Name your file and the CD here.

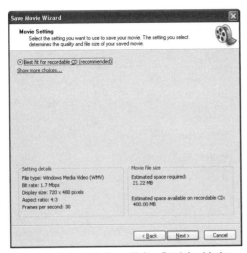

**Figure 16.16** Movie Maker will do a fine job with the default settings.

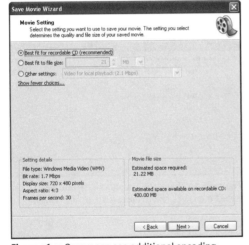

**Figure 16.17** Or you can see additional encoding options like these.

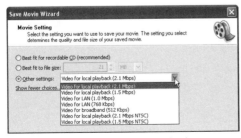

**Figure 16.18** Choose your custom setting here.

**4.** Click Next.

Movie Maker opens the wizard's Movie Setting pane (**Figure 16.16**).

**5.** Do *one of the following*:

▲ To produce your video using Movie Maker's default setting, click Next and proceed to Step 8.

▲ To access other encoding options, click Show More Choices. The Movie Setting pane displays additional output options (**Figure 16.17**).

**6.** Do *one of the following*:

▲ To produce a file of a specific size, click Best Fit to File Size and enter the size you want to use (Figure 16.11). Proceed to Step 8.

▲ To access other encoding options, click Other Settings and then click the arrow on the list box to see all encoding options (**Figure 16.18**).

**7.** Choose the setting you want to use. For help in choosing the right one, see "Choosing Your Compression Settings" earlier in this chapter.

Once you've made your selection, the encoding details will appear at the lower left and the file size requirements and available disk space at the lower right of the Movie Setting pane (Figure 16.13).

*continues on next page*

SAVING TO CD

**8.** Click Next.

Movie Maker starts rendering your file, displaying the dialog box shown in **Figure 16.19**. To cancel rendering at this point, click the Cancel button.

Rendering time relates to the project size, computer speed, and selected output setting, with files with higher-quality output settings taking longer to produce.

When Movie Maker is finished, the wizard displays the Completing the Save Movie Wizard pane (**Figure 16.20**).

**9.** If desired, select the check box to produce another recordable CD.

If you select this option, the Finish button on the bottom right of the Completing the Save Movie Wizard pane changes to a Next button. Insert another CD and click Next, and the wizard displays the Saved Movie File pane to restart the burning process (Figure 16.15).

If you elect this option, you can't change the encoding settings because Movie Maker simply burns the movie you just encoded onto another CD. To change encoding settings and burn another disc, click Finish and begin the process again.

**10.** Click Finish.

The dialog box closes, and if you opted to play the rendered video, Microsoft's Windows Media Player opens and starts to play the file (Figure 16.8).

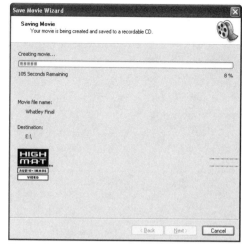

**Figure 16.19** Rendering begins. Click the Cancel button if you suddenly remember that you want to add one last flourish that your production can't live without.

**Figure 16.20** Thank you sir, may I have another? Select the check box to make it so, or click Finish.

## ✔ Tips

■ You can burn multiple times to a single recordable disc until the disc is full, and Movie Maker will warn you if there is insufficient space on the disc for the file you're attempting to write.

■ Since most DVD recorders also write to CD recordable media, you can also use this procedure if you have a DVD recorder, but only for writing to CD recordable media, not DVD recordable media.

## The Lowdown on HighMAT

You can download a HighMAT viewer (www.highmat.com/download/) that can play a HighMAT-formatted disc so you can see how it would appear on a HighMAT-compatible consumer electronics device (**Figure 16.21**).

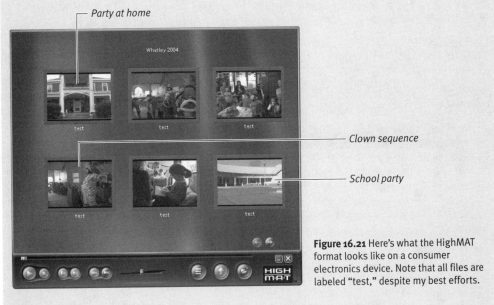

*Party at home*

*Clown sequence*

*School party*

**Figure 16.21** Here's what the HighMAT format looks like on a consumer electronics device. Note that all files are labeled "test," despite my best efforts.

However, in using the viewer, several issues become evident immediately.

First, notice that the initial frame of each movie is used as the thumbnail that you must select to play the video. This can be problematic. For instance, if you fade into a video segment from black, the first frame of your video will be black, which means the thumbnail image will also be black. Because a black thumbnail provides absolutely no guidance as to clip content, fading your clips in from black probably isn't the best option for HighMAT viewing.

*continues on next page*

## The Lowdown on HighMAT *continued*

Second, in producing the separate thumbnails, you have to create each segment separately and burn it to the CD before starting the next segment. This isn't necessarily bad, but it's different from the normal, start-to-finish, production workflow, where you build your movie as one complete whole, not a series of individual segments.

I also didn't like the lack of rhyme or reason to the order of video thumbnails displayed on the menu. For example, the first video I burned to the CD was the school party, at the lower right, and the next was the party at the house, at the upper left. Next was the clown sequence at the bottom left. The order presented on the menu is definitely not the way I wanted the story to unfold.

Also, despite my best efforts, Movie Maker gave each video segment the same name, "test," and I promise that I didn't make the same mistake six times. All this tells me that while HighMAT seems like a great idea, it probably needs a little more time in the oven.

Note, however, that the baby doesn't have to go out with the bathwater. Though I'm guessing that HighMAT won't play a big role in the short-term digital future, the Save to CD option is still a very convenient way to save WMV files to a recordable CD. Otherwise, if you choose not to use this option, you can always burn WMV files to disc with whatever software you normally use to burn files to your CD recorder.

For example, if you look at **Figure 16.22**, which is a view of the same disc in Windows Explorer, you'll notice that despite all the issues I just noted, Movie Maker's wizard otherwise worked as advertised when burning the disc, properly naming the disc and files and storing them neatly on the CD. So if you're sending files to viewers on recordable CDs, the Save to CD option is still a fast and easy way to burn the files.

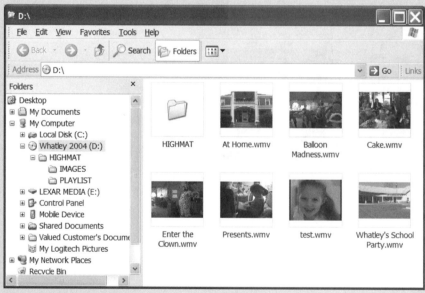

**Figure 16.22** The same disc in Windows Explorer, with files correctly named.

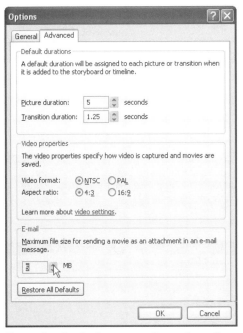

Figure 16.23 Here's where you set the maximum file attachment size.

Figure 16.24 Starting the process to send a Movie Maker file in e-mail.

Figure 16.25 You can also adjust the maximum attachment size on this screen.

# Sending Your Video in E-mail

Use the next procedure to produce a file for transmitting your video via e-mail. Note, however, that most ISPs limit the size of attachments you can send with e-mails. Send a file that's too large, and your ISP won't deliver it, usually also sending you an e-mail saying so, but not always.

For example, my Hotmail account won't send files larger than 1 MB, while my Earthlink account won't go beyond 5 MB. For this reason, when sending files via e-mail, think short and sweet, not *War and Peace*.

Note that you can set the maximum file size produced by Movie Maker for attachment to an e-mail message on the Advanced Options screen (**Figure 16.23**), accessed by choosing Tools > Options from the main menu. See "Setting Project Defaults" in Chapter 3 for details on setting these defaults.

### To send a file in an e-mail:

1. In the Movie Tasks pane, click Send in E-mail (**Figure 16.24**). If the Movie Tasks pane isn't showing, click the Show or Hide Movie Tasks Pane icon on the Movie Maker task bar (Figure 16.3).

   If the movie is too long for the configured attachment size, you'll see the dialog box in **Figure 16.25**. Either increase the attachment file size (assuming that your ISP allows a larger file) and click Next, or click Cancel and shorten the movie on the Timeline.

   *continues on next page*

If your movie length is acceptable, Movie Maker will start encoding the file and display the Saving Movie dialog box (**Figure 16.26**).

When encoding is complete, Movie Maker will display the Ready to Send by E-mail dialog (**Figure 16.27**).

2. If desired, click Play the Movie to play the video.

3. If desired, click Save a Copy of My Movie on My Computer to save a copy of the video on your computer.

Movie Maker opens the Save Movie dialog box to save the file (**Figure 16.28**).

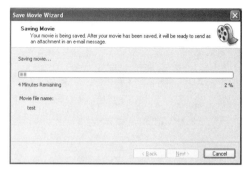

**Figure 16.26** Rendering begins. Click the Cancel button if you see a misspelling in one of your titles and want to correct it.

**Figure 16.27** Ready to send via e-mail.

**Figure 16.28** Or save the file if you want to send it from another computer.

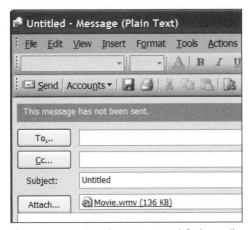

Figure 16.29 Movie Maker opens your default e-mail program, here Microsoft Outlook, with the video inserted.

Figure 16.30 If an error occurs, you get one last chance to save the file.

**4.** Click Next.

Movie Maker runs the default e-mail program installed on your computer and opens a new message with the encoded video file inserted as an attachment (**Figure 16.29**).

Insert an address and message and send the message as you normally would.

If you don't have an e-mail program on your encoding station, Movie Maker will display the message shown in **Figure 16.30**, giving you one last chance to save the file to e-mail from another computer.

## ✔ Tip

■ I don't send e-mail from my video workstations, so I use this procedure to create a file under the prescribed size limit, save the file to disk (Step 3), and then cancel out of the remaining steps of the procedure (Figure 16.27).

SENDING YOUR VIDEO IN E-MAIL

# Saving to a Video-Hosting Provider

Sharing video files over the Internet is one of the great dreams of modern-day video producers, but the reality is that posting files to a Web site can be technically complex. Every video-hosting provider has different rules for posting video files, which in most cases has to be done manually.

To make posting files to a Web site easier, Microsoft designed a seamless file upload capability into Movie Maker and to date has partnered with Web site Neptune Mediashare to host Movie Maker files. Note that after a free seven-day trial of the Neptune service, you have to pay $49 for a one-year subscription. However, I was pretty impressed—for $49 you get 150 MB of storage for pictures or movies and your own URL to send to potential viewers. This is definitely an easy-to-use, high-quality option for sharing your videos.

Follow the steps in the next task to produce and upload files to Neptune Mediashare (or another video-hosting provider that supports Movie Maker, should more providers get on board).

To post to a Web site other than a Movie Maker–compatible video-hosting provider, use the first option presented in this chapter (My Computer) to create the file and then manually upload the file to your Web site.

For the purposes of this section, I've assumed the machine on which you're running Movie Maker has an Internet connection and that you have already created a trial account with Neptune. (To set up a trial account, go to www.neptune.com.)

**Figure 16.31** Click here to send the file to a video-hosting provider that supports Movie Maker files.

**Figure 16.32** Name the file here.

## To save your video to a video-hosting provider:

1. In the Movie Tasks pane, click Send to the Web (**Figure 16.31**).

   If the Movie Tasks pane isn't showing, click the Show or Hide Movie Tasks Pane icon on the Movie Maker task bar (Figure 16.3).

   Movie Maker opens the Save Movie wizard to the Saved Movie File pane.

2. If desired, enter a file name for the saved movie (**Figure 16.32**).

3. Click Next.

   The wizard's Movie Setting pane opens (**Figure 16.33**).

4. Do *one of the following*:

   ▲ To produce your video using one of Movie Maker's default settings, click the desired setting and proceed to Step 8.

   ▲ To access other encoding options, click Show More Choices. The Movie Setting pane displays additional output options (**Figure 16.34**).

   *continues on next page*

**Figure 16.33** Here's the familiar Movie Setting dialog box where you choose your encoding parameters.

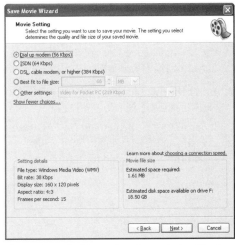

**Figure 16.34** All of the options for producing files for the Web.

**5.** Do *one of the following*:

   ▲ To produce a file of a specific size, click Best Fit to File Size and enter the size you want to use (Figure 16.11). Proceed to Step 8.

   ▲ To access other encoding options, click Other Settings and then click the arrow on the Other Settings list box (**Figure 16.35**).

**6.** Choose the setting you want to use. For help in choosing the right one, see "Choosing Your Compression Settings" earlier in this chapter.

   Once you choose your setting, the encoding details will be displayed at the lower left and the file size requirements and available disk space will be displayed at the lower right of the Movie Setting pane (Figure 16.13).

**7.** Click Next.

   Movie Maker starts rendering your file, displaying the Saving Movie pane (**Figure 16.36**). To cancel rendering at this point, click the Cancel button.

   Rendering time relates to the project size, computer speed, and selected output setting, with files with higher-quality output settings taking longer to produce.

   When the wizard is finished, it displays the Select a Video Hosting Provider and Sign In pane (**Figure 16.37**).

**8.** Enter the information required to sign into your video-hosting provider.

   If desired, select Remember My Password, and Movie Maker will automatically retain this information for future uploads.

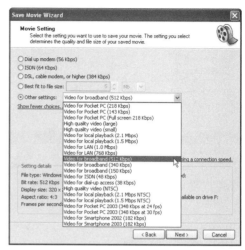

**Figure 16.35** Choose your target setting here.

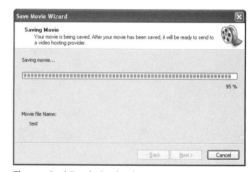

**Figure 16.36** Rendering begins.

**Figure 16.37** Enter your login information here.

**SAVING TO A VIDEO-HOSTING PROVIDER**

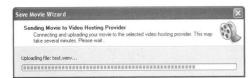

**Figure 16.38** Movie Maker will upload the file to the video-hosting provider.

**Figure 16.39** All done. Select the check box to play the file.

**9.** Click Next.

Movie Maker starts uploading the file (**Figure 16.38**). When uploading is complete, Movie Maker displays the Completing the Save Movie Wizard dialog box (**Figure 16.39**).

**10.** If desired, select Watch My Movie on the Web After I Click Finish.

After you click Finish, Movie Maker will automatically launch your browser and play the file (**Figure 16.40**).

**11.** If desired, click Save a Copy of My Movie on My Computer.

Movie Maker opens the Save Movie dialog box to save the file (Figure 16.28). Save the file in the usual way.

**12.** Click Finish.

## ✔ Tip

- At the time of this writing, Neptune Mediashare did not support Macintosh playback. It may now, but if any of your viewers are running Mac OS X, check to make sure that Neptune supports the Mac before sending them to watch your videos.

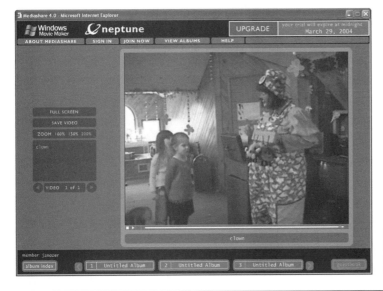

**Figure 16.40** Yippee! I'm on the 'Net, baby! (Actually, that's *not* me in the clown outfit; I was speaking metaphorically.)

SAVING TO A VIDEO-HOSTING PROVIDER

# SONIC SOLUTIONS MYDVD

I like recording my videos to DVD for many reasons. First, the video is much more accessible than linear formats like VHS or even DV tape, so viewers can get to the footage they want to see more quickly. Second, DVDs don't degrade like analog tape, so if you play the videos frequently, you don't lose quality. Finally, DVD is a much more stable format than analog tape, which can start to decay in as few as 10 years.

Though videos produced with Movie Maker can be integrated into DVD projects, Movie Maker itself can't produce a DVD playable on DVD players. For that, you need a DVD authoring program like Sonic MyDVD.

MyDVD matches up well with Movie Maker for several reasons. First, it costs as little as $49.99 direct from Sonic at www.mydvd.com. Second, MyDVD is one of the few authoring programs that can accept Windows Media files as input. Though I prefer using DV-AVI files (as discussed in the sidebar "Rendering for Additional Production" in Chapter 16), MyDVD can accept Windows Media files as input if you choose to go that route. Third, MyDVD is the DVD authoring program recommended by Microsoft for burning DVDs from Movie Maker output (see www.microsoft.com/windowsxp/moviemaker/learnmore/dvdburn.asp). And finally (he said humbly), there's a great guide to working with MyDVD called *MyDVD 5 for Windows: Visual QuickStart Guide*, written by yours truly.

So here's a 50,000-foot view of the MyDVD production workflow. This should give you a feel for how easily MyDVD can produce a DVD with content produced in Movie Maker.

# The MyDVD Workflow

When you first run MyDVD, you immediately find yourself in a project menu that looks identical to what the viewer sees when playing your DVD. When creating your DVD, you import videos and slide shows (collectively called content) directly into the menu, and MyDVD creates a titled button that viewers click to play the content. **Figure A.1** shows the default MyDVD menu with one video already inserted.

Each MyDVD menu can contain up to six buttons, and there are three techniques to add more menus. The first involves simply importing more than six movies into your menu; MyDVD will then create an additional menu to house the seventh.

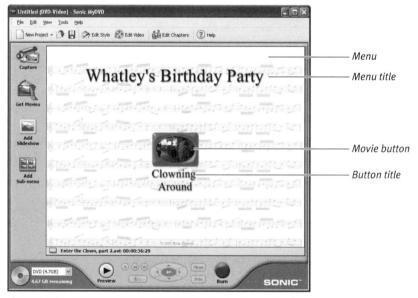

**Figure A.1** The starting point for most MyDVD projects: drag a video into the menu to produce a button for accessing the video and a button file.

Fortunately, MyDVD also automatically creates all links necessary to navigate back and forth between the first menu in the project, also called the main or title menu, and any subsequent menus.

The second method for creating multiple-menu projects involves the use of chapter points, or links in the video that the viewer can directly jump to via a chapter selection menu. Chapter points are the links in your Hollywood DVDs that allow you to jump from scene to scene or to select a scene by number from a chapter menu, and MyDVD supports them as well. You use the Chapter Points window to create chapter points for your movies (**Figure A.2**).

**Figure A.2** Here I'm creating chapter points in the video, so the viewer can jump directly to specific segments of the movie.

Once you add chapter points, you can opt to have the button that previously linked directly to the imported movie instead link to the chapter selection menu (**Figure A.3**). During design and playback, you and your viewers click the top button to access the chapter selection menu, and you click the buttons therein to access video at the various chapter points.

The third way to create multiple menu projects is to use submenus, or buttons that link directly to other menu pages. Submenus add tremendous flexibility to MyDVD because they allow much greater navigation control than either of the other two methods of creating additional menu stages.

**Figure A.3** After you create the chapter points, the video button converts to a chapter button (top) that links to a chapter menu (bottom).

**Figure A.4** The Party at Home button on the top menu is a submenu that links to other menus. Submenus are the best means of creating a logical navigational structure in large projects.

Specifically, submenus let me divide my video into much more accessible chunks: one for the party at school, one for the party at home, and so on. As you can see in **Figure A.4**, I used submenus to create separate menus for each chunk, so that viewers can easily find the desired video.

All three techniques for creating multiple menus have their strengths and weaknesses, and you'll probably end up using all three methods, sometimes even in the same project. Understanding and leveraging these strengths and weakness is key to producing a video that's intuitive and easy for your audience to view. These alternatives are covered in detail in Chapter 3 of *MyDVD 5 for Windows: Visual QuickStart Guide*.

## Capturing and editing

While MyDVD can capture video and perform some basic editing tasks, Movie Maker's capabilities are much more powerful and flexible, so you're better off capturing and editing in Movie Maker and importing the video into MyDVD.

The same applies to creating slide shows. Although MyDVD has a dedicated slide show tool, Movie Maker and Photo Story (see Appendix B) are both superior production alternatives.

## Styling

Each menu in MyDVD has a style: essentially, a customized collection of background image or video file, fonts, and button frames. Using the Edit Style window (**Figure A.5**), you can customize your menus significantly, changing fonts, button frames, and background images, and adding audio and video that plays when the menu loads, much like Hollywood DVDs.

For me, customizing menus is one of the most fun aspects of DVD production (**Figure A.6**), and MyDVD provides an excellent palette for my creative urges.

**Figure A.5** The Edit Style window is where you trick out your menus with different styles, customize your background images, and add audio and video backgrounds.

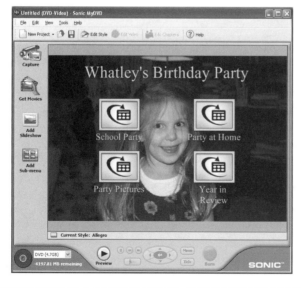

**Figure A.6** Here's a menu with a custom background image, button frames, and text font. Pretty sweet, eh?

## Previewing and burning

Once you've designed your menu structure, added your content, and customized your menu, it's time to preview and burn your DVD. Since most mastering decisions are made during capture or editing, these two activities are relatively straightforward.

## Other tasks

MyDVD is an exceptional tool for automating the conversion of analog or DV tape to DVD. In particular, if you have libraries of home movies in VHS or other analog formats that are quickly reaching the ends of their useful lives, MyDVD's efficient conversion process can preserve your memories on DVD.

# Other Alternatives

There are a number of alternatives to MyDVD, including Ulead MovieFactory, Pinnacle Studio, and Roxio Easy Media Creator. These products all cost around $100 because in addition to DVD authoring capabilities, they include full-featured video editors and tools for data backup and other functions you may not need.

In my view, at $49.99, the base version of MyDVD is the best alternative for burning DVDs with movies produced in Movie Maker. If you're considering moving on from Movie Maker to a more fully featured editor, I would recommend considering MovieFactory, Studio, or Easy Media Creator. However, if you're happy with Movie Maker, I would recommend using MyDVD to produce your DVDs.

# CREATING MOVIES IN PHOTO STORY

As described in "Editing Still Images" in Chapter 9, Movie Maker can create slide shows from your digital images, complete with narration and background music. What Movie Maker can't do is add pans and zooms to the images, like those popularized by Ken Burns in his *Baseball* and *Civil War* documentaries (and often called Ken Burns' effects). For this, you need a product like Microsoft Plus! Photo Story, a component of Microsoft's $19.95 Plus! Digital Media Edition (DME).

Photo Story is designed solely for creating slide shows, or *stories,* as Microsoft likes to call them, from digital images. With it, you can publish your slide shows as stand-alone movies, convert them to Video CDs you can play on a DVD player, or import the finished movies into a Movie Maker project.

# The 50,000-Foot View

Before we get started, let's make sure we're on the same page. What I call a slide show, Photo Story calls a *story*. Similarly, what I call a digital image, Photo Story calls a *picture*. To avoid any confusion between my description and terms in the Photo Story interface, I'll use Photo Story's terminology for this appendix.

Photo Story is a wizard-driven tool that logically walks you through the production workflow. You start by adding and sequencing picture slides to the production; the slides can be in a number of formats, including JPG, BMP, GIF, and TIF.

You can output the finished story at a resolution of 320x240 or 640x480, or even larger if you download some custom profiles. For optimal picture quality, you should use pictures with a resolution higher than the output resolution and prepare your pictures as discussed in "Editing Pictures" in Chapter 6.

Once you've input your pictures, you can set the duration each picture remains on the screen in three ways. You can narrate a description of the picture for up to 4 minutes and 10 seconds per picture—a great way to add context to the visual presentation. Or you can set a custom duration for each picture, or you can set one default duration for all pictures.

You also have great control over the pans and zooms applied to each picture. If you record a narration for a picture, you can use your mouse to suggest picture regions that Photo Story should highlight with the pan and zoom effects. Or you can let Photo Story select the pan and zoom parameters, or customize the parameters picture by picture.

Other creative opportunities include the ability to create a title page and to select a background audio track, music or otherwise, for the entire story. Music files must be in Windows Media Audio, MP3, or WAV format.

Photo Story can save your project file so you can later tweak your results, and you can import the finished story into Movie Maker, produce a Video CD, or just enjoy the standalone file. Overall, if you're digital camera fanatic like I am, Photo Story is an excellent tool for sharing your pictures.

## ✔ Tips

- A *pan* occurs when the camera moves across a picture; a zoom occurs when the camera moves closer to or farther away from the picture.

- Photo Story displays all previews at 320x240 resolution. Note that you can render the final story at 640x480 resolution if desired.

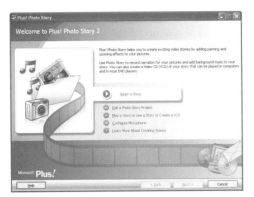

**Figure B.1**. Photo Story's opening screen.

**Figure B.2** The Import and Arrange Your Pictures screen, where you import your pictures.

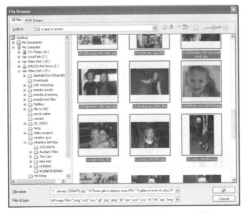

**Figure B.3** I'll take this one and that one and this one.

# Creating a Photo Story

With the 50,000-foot view as prolog, let's jump in and create a Photo Story. I'll assume that you have the program purchased, loaded, and ready to go.

I'll also assume that you have your microphone connected and working. If not, check "To connect for narration" in Chapter 12 for details.

## To import and arrange pictures in Photo Story:

1. Click Start > Microsoft Plus! Digital Media Edition > Plus! Photo Story.

   The welcome screen for Plus! Photo Story appears (**Figure B.1**).

2. Click Begin a Story.

   Plus! Photo Story opens to the Import and Arrange Your Pictures screen (**Figure B.2**).

3. Click Import Pictures.

   Plus! Photo Story opens the File Browser screen (**Figure B.3**).

*continues on next page*

**4.** Navigate to the folder containing the pictures and do *one or more of the following*:

▲ Expand the Browser window by grabbing the bottom-right corner with your mouse and dragging the window to a larger size.

▲ Adjust the size of the thumbnail pictures by dragging the slider at the upper right.

▲ Select sequential pictures by clicking a picture, holding down the Shift key, and clicking another picture. Photo Story will highlight all pictures between the two selected pictures.

▲ Select multiple individual pictures by holding down the Ctrl key and clicking them.

Note that a story can contain a maximum of 150 pictures.

**5.** When you've finished selecting the pictures, click OK.

Photo Story imports the pictures into the filmstrip (**Figure B.4**).

**Figure B.4** Here's where you arrange the pictures into the proper order.

**6.** To arrange the order of the pictures in the filmstrip, do *one of the following*:

▲ Select a picture and move it forward and backward using the buttons to the right of the filmstrip.

▲ Select the picture and drag it to the desired location, using the slider beneath the filmstrip to navigate to unexposed portions of the filmstrip. When you release a picture over another picture, Photo Story shifts that picture and all subsequent pictures to the right.

▲ To delete a picture, select the picture and click the Delete button or press the Delete key on your keyboard.

**7.** Click Next.

The Record Your Story window appears (**Figure B.5**).

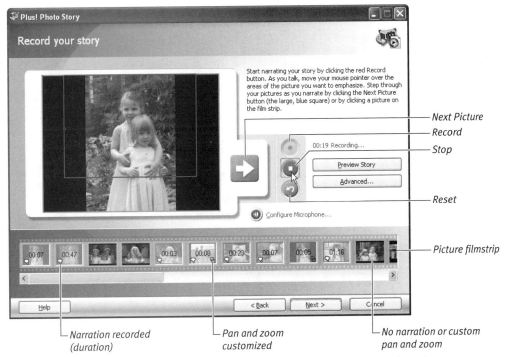

Figure B.5 Here's where you record your narration. Note the legends on the pictures in the filmstrip.

## To narrate a recording and select advanced settings for your pictures:

**1.** In the Record Your Story window (Figure B.5), do *one or more of the following*:

▲ Select the picture.

▲ Click the Record button to start recording. While recording, hold your mouse over the most important regions in the picture, and Photo Story will "take this into account" when generating the pan and zoom effects (**Figure B.6**).

▲ Click the Stop button to stop recording.

▲ Click the Reset button to delete the recording.

▲ Click the Preview Story button to preview the narration and pan and zoom effects. Use the playback controls to move through the story (**Figure B.7**).

▲ Click the Next Picture button or another slide to store the narration and to create a narration for another picture.

*Pointer*

**Figure B.6** Use your cursor to tell Photo Story which image regions to emphasize.

Plus! Photo Story Preview

*Slider*
*Next Picture*
*Previous Picture*
*Stop*
*Play/Pause*

**Figure B.7** Here's the preview screen, which is always at 320x240 resolution.

CREATING A PHOTO STORY

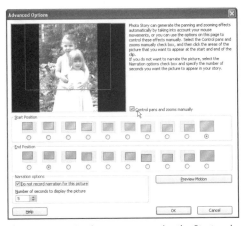

**Figure B.8** Here's where you customize the Start and End positions and set picture duration.

**Figure B.9** Preview the results of your pan and zoom settings here.

2. To manually control the pan and zoom effects, do the following:

▲ In the Record Your Story window, click the Advanced button (Figure B.5).

▲ In the Advanced Options window that appears, select the Control Pans and Zooms Manually check box (**Figure B.8**).

▲ Select the radio button below your desired start and end positions. While rendering, Photo Story will move from start to end positions, creating the necessary pan and zoom effect. To eliminate any motion, click the same start and end positions.

▲ If you want to preview the effect, click the Preview Motion button. The Preview window appears, showing you the pan and zoom effects you just created (**Figure B.9**).

▲ Click OK to return to the Record Your Story window.

3. To specify a duration for a picture, do the following:

▲ In the Record Your Story window, click Advanced (Figure B.5).

▲ At the bottom left of the Advanced Options window (Figure B.8), select the Do Not Record Narration for This Picture check box.

▲ If desired, change the display duration by typing a new number or adjusting the duration with the arrows to the right of the number box. The default duration is five seconds.

*continues on next page*

**CREATING A PHOTO STORY**

▲ If desired, click the Preview Motion button to preview the pan and zoom effects (Figure B.9).

▲ Click OK to return to the Record Your Story window.

Note the legends that Photo Story applies to pictures in the Record Your Story film-strip. If you record narration, Photo Story dims the picture, places a small text balloon at the bottom left of the picture, and displays the narration duration (Figure B.5). If you customize the pan and zoom settings, Photo Story displays interlocking rectangles at the bottom right of the picture.

4. After narrating and selecting advanced settings for all target pictures, click Next.

If you haven't narrated or selected advanced settings for all pictures, Photo Story will display the dialog box shown in **Figure B.10**. Click yes to continue to the Add a Title Page window (**Figure B.11**), or no to return to the Record a Story window.

**Figure B.10** Photo Story warns you if you haven't customized all pictures.

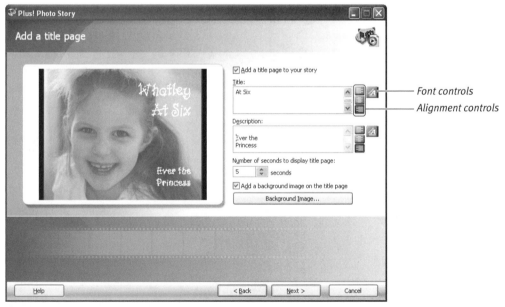

Font controls

Alignment controls

**Figure B.11** A dressy title page is a must!

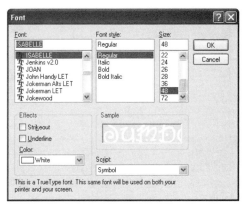

**Figure B.12** The typical Font dialog box.

**Figure B.13** Choosing the background image for the title.

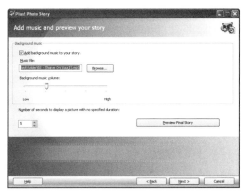

**Figure B.14** Adding background music.

## To add a title:

1. In the Add a Title Page window (Figure B.11), select the Add a Title Page to Your Story check box.

2. To customize the title page, do *one or more of the following*:

   ▲ Type a title and description.

   ▲ To move the title text *up* on the screen, press Enter one or more times *after* the text.

   ▲ To move the description *down* on the screen, press Enter one or more times *at the beginning* of the text.

   ▲ Use the font controls to select the font, font size, font style, and other attributes (**Figure B.12**).

   ▲ Use the alignment controls to set text alignment.

   ▲ Change the display duration of the title by typing a new number or adjusting the duration with the arrows to the right of the number box.

   ▲ To add a picture, select the Add a Background Image on the Title Page check box. To open the File Browser and select a picture, click the Background Image button. The File Browser window opens (**Figure B.13**). Photo Story can import a variety of formats, including BMP, JPEG, GIF, TIF, and TGA.

3. After customizing the title, click Next. Photo Story opens the Add Music and Preview Your Story window (**Figure B.14**).

## To add background music:

1. In the Add Music and Preview Your Story window (Figure B.14), do *one or more of the following*:

   ▲ Select the Add Background Music to Your Story check box.

   ▲ Click the Browse button. The Open dialog appears, where you can select a file. Click OK to return to the Add Music and Preview Your Story window.

   ▲ Use the Background Music Volume slider to adjust the music volume.

   If you've narrated any of the pictures, keep the volume on the background music track fairly low, and preview your final story to ensure that the music doesn't drown out the narration.

2. To change the number of seconds a picture with no specified duration is displayed, type a new number or adjust the duration using the arrows to the right of the number box.

3. To preview, click the Preview Final Story button. Use the preview controls shown in Figure B.7 to move through the story.

4. When you're finished previewing, click Next.

   Photo Story opens the Select Quality Settings for Your Story window (**Figure B.15**).

**Figure B.15** Selecting the project output settings.

**Figure B.16** Here's where you insert a custom output profile.

**Figure B.17** You can download custom output profiles from Microsoft's Web site.

**Figure B.18** Getting close now—select the story file and project names.

## To select the project output settings:

1. In the Select Quality Settings for Your Story window (Figure B.15), choose the video output settings, using the following recommendations:

   ▲ For stories created for input to a Movie Maker project, choose High Quality video and audio. This will produce a movie with a resolution of 640x480, which plays at 30 frames per second with CD-quality audio.

   ▲ For stories created for playback on a computer hard disk, choose High Quality video and audio.

   ▲ For stories created for conversion to a Video CD disk, choose High Quality video and audio.

   ▲ For stories created for playback on a Pocket PC or similar device, choose Medium Quality video and audio. This will produce a movie with a resolution of 320x240, which plays at 20 frames per second, with FM-quality audio.

   ▲ For stories created for posting to a Web site or for e-mail, choose Medium Quality video and audio.

   ▲ Select a custom encoding profile by clicking the Advanced button (**Figure B.16**).

   Note that you can download custom profiles from Microsoft's Web site (**Figure B.17**) by clicking the Check the Availability of Custom Encoding Profiles link in the Select Custom Encoding Profile window.

2. Once you've selected your encoding parameters, click Next.

   Photo Story opens the Save Your Story and Project window (**Figure B.18**).

## To save your story and project:

1. In the Save Your Story and Project window (Figure B.18), customize the story file name and location.

2. Click the Save Project check box to save the story, and customize the project file name and location if desired.

3. Click Next when you're ready to render. Photo Story displays the Building Your Story dialog box (**Figure B.19**). When the story building is complete, Photo Story displays the screen shown in **Figure B.20**.

4. Do *one of the following*:

   ▲ Click View Your Story to play the story in Media Player.

   ▲ Click Create a Video CD of Your Story to create a Video CD. The Create a Video CD screen appears (**Figure B.21**). See the next task to proceed.

   ▲ Click Create Another Story to start another project.

   ▲ Click Exit to exit the program.

**Figure B.19** Photo Story is producing the file.

**Figure B.20** You're done unless you want to create a Video CD.

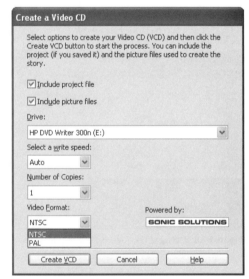

**Figure B.21** Your Video CD production options.

### To create a Video CD:

1. In the Create a Video CD window (Figure B.21), do *one or more of the following*:

   ▲ Click Include Project File to include the project file on the CD. This archives the project file, but it won't enable recipients to re-create the story because they won't have either the narration or background music track.

   ▲ Click Include Picture Files to include the picture files on the Video CD. This allows the recipient of the disk to access the original pictures in the story.

   ▲ If necessary, choose another drive.

   ▲ If necessary, select a different write speed.

   ▲ If desired, specify the number of desired copies. After producing the first Video CD disc, Photo Story will prompt you to insert additional discs until it completes the requested number of copies.

   ▲ Choose the proper video format. Use NTSC for the United States and PAL for most European countries. If you're unsure of which format to use, Photo Story has a complete listing in the help file, which you can find by choosing Plus! Photo Story > Creating a VCD > Choosing a Video Format for Your Story.

   *continues on next page*

**2.** After choosing all the options, click Create VCD.

Photo Story produces the Video CD, displaying the dialog box shown in **Figure B.22** when the task is complete.

### ✔ Tip

■ Theoretically, Photo Story can produce stories over 10 hours in length, but the maximum Video CD duration is about 60 minutes—and less if you store the original images and project file on the CD. If your story is too long to store on Video CD, Photo Story will display an error message.

**Figure B.22** Your Video CD is done!

---

## About Video CDs

Video CD is a format that uses CD-Recordable media to produce discs playable by most DVD players. If you have a CD recorder, blank CD-R media, and Photo Story, you can produce a disc grandma can play in her living room on her new DVD player.

Note, however, that Video CD uses MPEG-1 video encoded at 352x240, a comparatively low resolution. This means that the story that looks so lovely on your computer may look blocky and distorted when grandma plays it, especially if she splurged on a big-screen TV.

You'll get the best visual results producing your story at a 640x480 resolution in Windows Media Video format, but unfortunately, these files will play only on a computer or on those few DVD players that support the Windows Media format. Video CD may be your only option for displaying your stories in Grandma's living room, but be prepared for less than optimal quality.

# WINDOWS MEDIA ENCODER AND TOOLS

As discussed throughout this book, Windows Movie Maker is part of an extensive suite of tools and accessories developed by Microsoft for producing or compressing digital video. This appendix discusses two components of another such tool suite: the Windows Media Encoder 9 Series.

First up is Windows Media File Editor, which can trim videos encoded in the Windows Media Video (WMV) format *without* re-encoding. In contrast, though Movie Maker can certainly trim video files, it *always* re-encodes them, which takes longer and potentially degrades the quality of the output file. File Editor can also insert markers into the video stream, enhancing interactivity, and can change the file's attributes, or the title, author, and copyright information shown by Windows Media Player when playing back the file.

Next, this appendix looks at Windows Media Encoder itself, which is useful if you need to encode a file to parameters not offered by Movie Maker. For example, Macs running pre-OS X versions can't play back files encoded in WMV version 9, the only version Movie Maker 2 can output. Using Windows Media Encoder, you can produce files in WMV 7, which Macs running Mac OS 8.1 and higher can play.

Finally, this appendix looks at the Windows Media Encoder screen capture facility, which can capture a video of an application on your Windows desktop, which can be very helpful when training someone to use a Windows-based program. For example, you can build short movies that show users how to format a document in their word processor or add or edit data in a database.

All these tools are available as part of the free Windows Media Encoder 9 Series, which is available for download at www.microsoft.com/windows/windowsmedia/9series/encoder/default.aspx. The discussion that follows assumes that you've downloaded and installed the series and are ready to go.

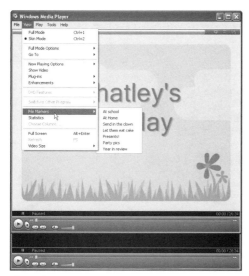

**Figure C.1** Annotations like these, inserted using Windows Media File Editor, make your video file very accessible to viewers.

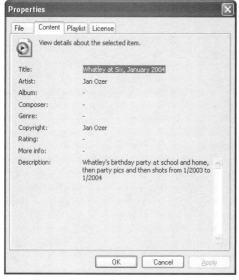

**Figure C.2** Windows Media File Editor also lets you customize the information in some of these fields.

# Working with Windows Media File Editor

Windows Media File Editor performs four basic functions. First, it can trim frames from the start and end of a video, which is useful when you want to shorten a WMV file for, say, sending via e-mail.

Second, File Editor can insert markers (**Figure C.1**) noting selected scene changes in the video. Using the Windows Media Player menu, viewers can jump directly to the listed scenes, allowing much faster access to the content.

Third, File Editor can add script commands that can insert text messages during playback in Windows Media Player and open the viewer's browser to a specific Web page.

Fourth, File Editor can insert author, copyright, and general description information into your WMV file (**Figure C.2**). This information is useful when you're concerned about protecting your copyright in the video. In addition, others who view your video can scan the Description field to quickly see what's in the file.

## To trim a video file:

**1.** Click Start > Programs > Windows Media > Utilities > Windows Media File Editor.

File Editor opens (**Figure C.3**).

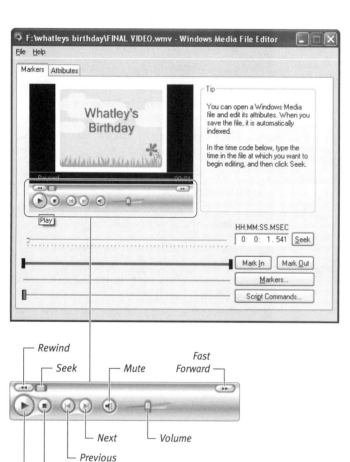

**Figure C.3** Here's Windows Media File Editor.

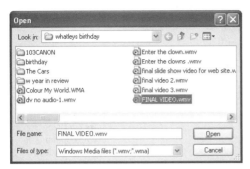

**Figure C.4** Let's trim this file.

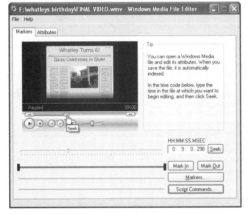

**Figure C.5** You can select In and Out points by dragging the Seek bar to the desired location or entering the time code directly and clicking Seek.

**Figure C.6** The slider next to the Mark In and Mark Out buttons shows the truncated duration.

**2.** Click File > Open.

The Open dialog box appears (**Figure C.4**).

**3.** Navigate to the target file and click Open.

File Editor loads the file.

**4.** Do *one of the following*:

▲ Drag the Seek control to the desired start location for the trimmed clip (**Figure C.5**).

▲ Enter the desired start time in the counter box next to the Seek button and click Seek.

Note that File Editor doesn't update the video display after you move the Seek bar until you click Play. This makes finding the target start location difficult; I find it easier to watch the video in Windows Media Player, find the target start and stop locations, and then simply enter them directly (option 2).

**5.** Click Mark In.

**6.** Do *one of the following*:

▲ Drag the Seek control to the desired end location for the trimmed clip.

▲ Enter the desired end time in the counter box next to the Seek button and Click Seek.

**7.** Click Mark Out.

File Editor adjusts the trim bar to reflect the new start and end positions (**Figure C.6**).

*continues on next page*

WORKING WITH WINDOWS MEDIA FILE EDITOR

8. Do *one of the following*:

   ▲ To save the changes to the *same* file (and truncate the original input file), choose File > Save and Index (**Figure C.7**). File Editor saves the file.

   ▲ To save the edited file as a *new* file, choose File > Save As and Index. File Editor opens the Save As dialog box (**Figure C.8**).

9. Enter the target name and location and click Save.

### ✔ Tip

■ Indexing is a file storage technique that enables Windows Media Player to move quickly and smoothly forward and backward through the file, with no negative consequences.

### To add markers:

1. Click Start > Programs > Windows Media > Utilities > Windows Media File Editor.
   File Editor opens (Figure C.3).

2. Click File > Open.
   The Open dialog box appears (Figure C.4).

3. Navigate to the target file and click Open.
   File Editor loads the file.

4. Do *one of the following*:

   ▲ Drag the Seek control to the desired location for the marker (Figure C.5).

   ▲ Enter the desired start time for the marker in the counter box next to the Seek button and Click Seek.

5. Click Markers.
   File Editor opens the Markers dialog box (**Figure C.9**).

**Figure C.7** Using the Save As command to save to a new file.

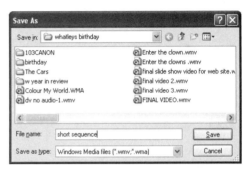

**Figure C.8** You know the drill. Use the controls to choose a location for the new file and type a new name.

**Figure C.9** Here's where you add markers to the video file.

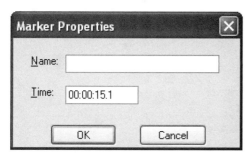

Figure C.10 Enter the name of the marker and the time (if it's not already filled in) and click OK.

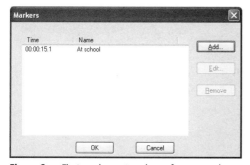

Figure C.11. First marker entered—so far, so good.

Figure C.12 Here are all the markers, which allow the viewer to directly access each section as shown in Figure C.1.

6. Click Add.

   File Editor opens the Marker Properties dialog box (**Figure C.10**). The time you selected in Step 4 will appear in the Time counter.

7. Enter the name for the marker in the Name field.

8. Click OK.

   File Editor adds the marker (**Figure C.11**).

9. Repeat Steps 4 through 8 until all markers are inserted (**Figure C.12**).

10. Click OK.

11. Do *one of the following*:

    ▲ To save the changes to the *same* file, click Save and Index (Figure C.7). File Editor saves the file.

    ▲ To save the file as a *new* file, click Save As and Index. File Editor opens the Save As dialog box (Figure C.8).

12. Enter the target name and location and click Save.

## ✔ Tips

■ You can speed this process by browsing through the file in Windows Media Player beforehand and noting the desired time for all markers. That way, you can skip Steps 4 and 5 and enter the marker time manually each time you open the Marker Properties dialog box.

■ The results of this exercise are the markers shown in shown in Figure C.1. As you can see, viewers can jump directly to each marker by choosing View > File Makers > and the desired marker from within Windows Media Player.

WORKING WITH WINDOWS MEDIA FILE EDITOR

## To add script commands:

1. Click Start > Programs > Windows Media > Utilities > Windows Media File Editor.

   File Editor opens (Figure C.3).

2. Click File > Open.

   The Open dialog box appears (Figure C.4).

3. Navigate to the target file and click Open.

   File Editor loads the file.

4. Do *one of the following*:

   ▲ Drag the Seek control to the desired location for the script command (Figure C.5).

   ▲ Enter the desired start time for the script command in the counter box next to the Seek button and click Seek.

5. Click Script Commands.

   File Editor opens the Script Commands dialog box (**Figure C.13**).

6. Click Add.

   File Editor opens the Script Command Properties dialog box (**Figure C.14**). The time you selected in Step 4 will appear in the Time counter.

7. Click the Type list box and choose the target effect.

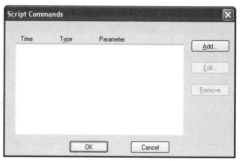

**Figure C.13** Here's where you add script commands to the file.

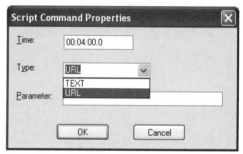

**Figure C.14** A URL script opens the viewer's browser to the designated page, while a text script inserts a subtitle into the file.

**Figure C.15** During playback, when the viewer gets to the 4-minute mark, the browser will open and take the viewer to www.doceo.com.

**Figure C.16** During playback, when the viewer gets to the 4-minute, 4-second mark, the message shown in the parameter field will appear.

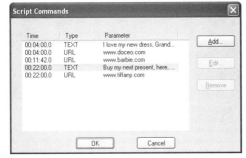

**Figure C.17** Here are all the script commands inserted in the file.

**8.** Do *one of the following*:

▲ If you selected a URL effect, enter the target URL in the Parameter box (**Figure C.15**).

▲ If you selected a text effect, enter the text in the Parameter box (**Figure C.16**).

**9.** Click OK.

**10.** Repeat Steps 4 through 9 until all script commands are inserted (**Figure C.17**).

**11.** Do *one of the following*:

▲ To save the changes to the *same* file, click Save and Index (Figure C.7). File Editor saves the file.

▲ To save the file as a *new* file, click Save As and Index. File Editor opens the Save As dialog box (Figure C.8).

**12.** Enter the target name and location and click Save.

## ✔ Tips

■ You can speed this process by browsing through the file in Windows Media Player beforehand and noting the desired time for all script commands. That way, you can skip Steps 4 and 5, and simply enter the script command time manually each time you open the Script Command Properties dialog box.

*continues on next page*

**WORKING WITH WINDOWS MEDIA FILE EDITOR**

- Note that for the URL scripts to work, the viewer must configure Windows Media Player to run script commands. You accomplish this on the Securities tab of Windows Media Player's Options dialog box (**Figure C.18**), which you open by choosing Tools > Options from Windows Media Player's main menu and then selecting the Security tab. If you view a lot of streaming media from the Web in WMV format, this could allow other video producers to open your browser to a desired start page while watching these videos, which is more an annoyance than a real security risk.

- To see text messages, the viewer must enable captions and subtitles (**Figure C.19**), accomplished by choosing Play > Captions and Subtitles > On If Available. Note the text message at the bottom of the screen, which appeared as directed at the 4:00 mark.

- A text message remains on the screen until replaced by another.

## To add or modify file attributes:

1. Click Start > Programs > Windows Media > Utilities > Windows Media File Editor.
   File Editor opens (Figure C.3).

2. Click File > Open.
   The Open dialog box appears (Figure C.4).

3. Navigate to the target file and click Open.
   File Editor loads the file.

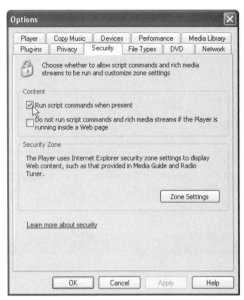

**Figure C.18** For either text or URL scripts to execute, your viewer must check the Run Script Commands When Present check box.

**Figure C.19** To view text messages, your viewer must have Captions and Subtitles On If Available selected.

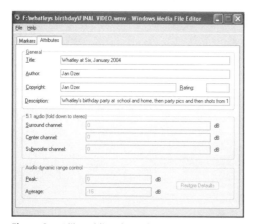

**Figure C.20** I like adding these descriptions to help me remember what's in each file.

**Figure C.21** In addition to viewing the file information from Windows Media Player as shown in Figure C.2, you can right-click the file in Windows Explorer and click the Summary tab.

**4.** In the upper-left corner, click the Attributes tab.

File Editor opens the Attributes tab (**Figure C.20**). Note that the audio information located below the General Attributes section is unrelated to production in Movie Maker so I won't discuss it.

**5.** Type the desired information.

**6.** Do *one of the following*:

▲ To save the changes to the *same* file, click Save and Index (Figure C.7). File Editor saves the file.

▲ To save the file as a *new* file, click Save As and Index. File Editor opens the Save As dialog box (Figure C.8).

**7.** Enter the target name and location and click Save.

## ✔ Tips

■ In my tests, File Editor didn't update the Attributes information when I saved to the *same* file, only when I saved to a *new* file. To check whether the information has been updated, load the file in Windows Media Player and choose File > Properties from Windows Media Player's main menu and then click the Content tab (Figure C.2). If you get the same results as I did, you'll have to create a new file (using the Save As command in Step 6) to change your attributes.

■ You can also view some of this information by right-clicking the file in Windows Explorer and clicking the Summary tab (**Figure C.21**).

# Encoding with Windows Media Encoder

When you produce Windows Media Video files professionally, Microsoft's Windows Media Encoder (WME) is the top of the mountain. Though most video editors can produce WMV files competently, no other program provides as much flexibility and control over the encoding parameters applied to a particular clip. It's also the least-expensive alternative for producing real-time streams for live events like concerts and sporting events.

My goals are a bit less ambitious; here, I encode a file in Windows Media Video version 7 format so I can post it to a Web site and be certain that viewers running Mac OS 8.1 or 9 can view the file. It's a two-step process: one step to set the basic encoding parameters, and the next to select the WMV 7 codec. Though the first step is reasonably straightforward, I'll ask you to put your blinders on for the second, because if you look around, you'll see parameters galore, far too many to explore here.

Note that to produce a file to encode with WME, you should follow the guidance provided in the sidebar "Rendering for Additional Production" in Chapter 16. The shorter course is to render from Movie Maker in DV-AVI format, which is the highest-quality format that Movie Maker can output.

**Figure C.22** Starting the file conversion wizard in Windows Media Encoder.

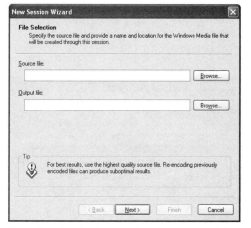

**Figure C.23** Here's where you insert the source file for encoding and choose the name and location for the encoded file.

**Figure C.24** Use this dialog box to browse for the source file.

## To select basic encoding parameters with WME:

1. Click Start > Programs > Windows Media > Windows Media Encoder.

   The New Session dialog box opens (**Figure C.22**).

2. Click Convert a File.

3. Click OK.

   The New Session wizard starts (**Figure C.23**).

4. Click Browse beside the Source File field.

   WME opens the Browse for Source File dialog box (**Figure C.24**).

5. Find the file and click Open.

   WME inserts the file in the Source File field (**Figure C.25**), automatically names the output file, and sets up to store the file in the same directory as the input file.

   *continues on next page*

**Figure C.25** WME will automatically name the file for you and place it in the same folder as the source file.

**6.** If necessary, click Browse beside the Output File field to rename or relocate the output file.

**7.** Click Next.

The New Session wizard opens the Content Distribution pane (**Figure C.26**).

**8.** Click Web Server (Progressive Download).

This will produce a file for posting to a Web site that isn't running the Windows Media server. For example, I use this option to create files for my company Web site, www.doceo.com, which is hosted by Earthlink. When producing files for a corporation running the Windows Media server, I would use the immediately preceding option.

**9.** Click Next.

The wizard opens the Encoding Options pane (**Figure C.27**).

**10.** Click the Video list box and choose the quality level you want (**Figure C.28**).

See the sidebar "Choosing Your Compression Settings" in Chapter 16 for guidance on setting all the encoding parameters in this exercise. Here, I'm choosing VHS quality to produce a 400-Kbps data rate, which is ideal for the broadband connections now enjoyed by both sets of grandparents.

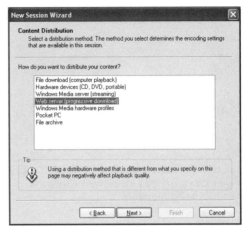

**Figure C.26** The categories are self-descriptive; I'm encoding for uploading to my Earthlink-hosted Web site.

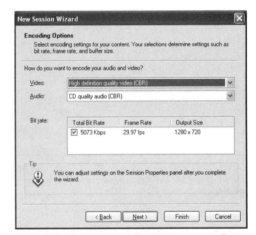

**Figure C.27** Here's the Encoding Options pane, offering a bit more detail than Movie Maker does.

**Figure C.28** I'll go with VHS quality because this preset can encode at 400 Kbps, which delivers good quality and doesn't take forever for the grandparents to download, now that both sets have broadband connections.

**Figure C.29** Let's go with CD-quality audio.

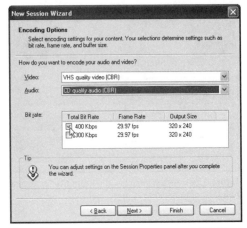

**Figure C.30** Now that I've chosen my preset, WME lets me choose the target bit rate.

**11.** Click the Audio list box and choose the target quality level (**Figure C.29**).

**12.** Select the target bit rate (**Figure C.30**).

**13.** Click Next.

The wizard opens the Display Information pane (**Figure C.31**).

**14.** If desired, complete the information; then click Next.

The wizard opens the Settings Review pane (**Figure C.32**).

*continues on next page*

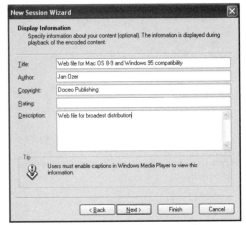

**Figure C.31** Insert your display information here.

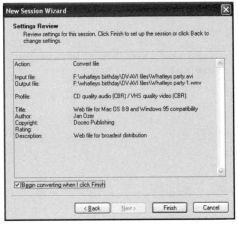

**Figure C.32** Last chance before you click Finish. Uncheck the Begin Converting When I Click Finish check box to further adjust the encoding parameters.

**15.** Do *one of the following*:

▲ To encode the file using the selected parameters, click Finish.

WME starts encoding the file, which will *not* play on Mac OS 8 or 9 computers.

▲ To enter WME and change the encoder to the WMV 7 encoder, uncheck the Begin Converting When I Click Finish check box in the lower-left corner of the Settings Review window (Figure C.32) and click Finish.

The Windows Media Encoder application opens (**Figure C.33**).

### To change to the Windows Media Video 7 codec:

**1.** Click the Properties button on the WME toolbar.

The Session Properties dialog box opens.

**2.** At the top of the Session Properties dialog box, click the Compression tab (**Figure C.34**).

**3.** Click the Edit button.

The Custom Encoding Settings dialog box opens.

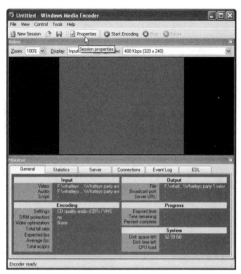

**Figure C.33** Here's WME; click the Properties button to edit the compression settings.

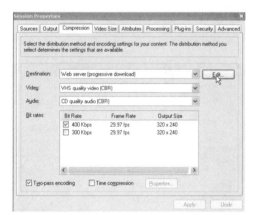

**Figure C.34** Click the Compression tab and then the Edit button.

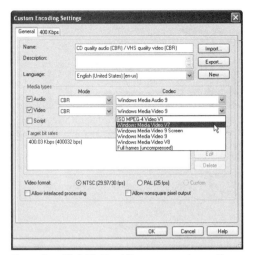

Figure C.35 All righty then! Now you can choose the Windows Media Video V7 codec, the whole purpose of this exercise.

Figure C.36 Codec updated; click here to begin encoding.

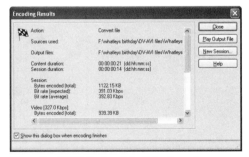

Figure C.37 WME displays this dialog box when encoding is complete—lots of good file details.

**4.** Click the Video Codec list box and choose the Windows Media Video V7 codec (**Figure C.35**).

According to the WME Help file, and confirmed directly by Microsoft, Windows Media Players for Mac OS 8 and 9 can play files encoded with Windows Media Audio 9. Accordingly, there is no need to change the audio codec, just the video codec.

**5.** Click OK to close the Custom Encoding Settings dialog box.

**6.** Click Apply (Figure C.34) to accept the new settings.

**7.** Click the Properties button on the WME toolbar.

WME closes the Session Properties dialog box.

**8.** Click the Start Encoding button on the WME toolbar (**Figure C.36**).

WME starts encoding the file. When encoding is complete, the Encoding Results dialog box appears (**Figure C.37**).

**9.** Do *one of the following*:

▲ Click Close to close the dialog box and return to WME.

▲ Click Play Output File to play the encoded file.

▲ Click New Session to start another wizard-driven encoding session.

## ✔ Tip

■ For more on encoding with Windows Media Encoder and other Series 9 tools, I recommend Nels Johnson's book, *Windows Media 9 Series by Example*.

# About Screen Capture with WME

The screen capture codec captures mouse movements, mouse clicks, the opening and closing of application windows, data entry, data deletion—basically, anything that's happening on the screen when you're capturing. The file produced is a video file, which when played back, shows actions very similar to the original onscreen actions.

During setup, you designate whether WME captures activity within the entire screen, a specified region in the screen, or a designated window. You'll produce the most-compact, highest-quality file when you capture small regions of your screen and minimize the amount of motion involved.

Opening and closing application windows typically doesn't degrade quality significantly, and neither does normal mouse motion and data entry. However, if you drag an application window around the screen or work with full-screen images at 1024x768 or higher resolution, you may have trouble producing good-quality results at low bit rates.

To maximize quality, Microsoft recommends reducing screen resolution to 800x600 and color depth to 16-bit when capturing full-screen images. These settings aren't necessary for the example presented here, which involves only a portion of the screen, but they're definitely the right ones for full-screen captures. For more on changing screen resolution, open the Windows XP Help and Support Center by clicking Start > Help and Support; then type `screen resolution` in the Search field and click the Start Search button (**Figure C.38**).

**Figure C.38** You may have to customize screen resolution to use the WME's screen capture facility. Read how by searching for the term screen resolution in Windows XP's Help and Support Center.

**Figure C.39** We're off to see the wizard again, this time for the screen capture.

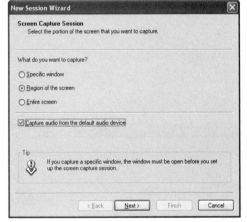

**Figure C.40** Here's where you choose which part of the screen to capture.

Note that while recording your screen animations, you can also record voice narration. This is a great feature, since even the most explicit screen capture can use some voice description. See "Recording Narration" in Chapter 12 for more information on setting up for and scripting your narrations.

Before starting, you should also have the application you'll be capturing open to the target screen, with any required files loaded and ready. Note that the screen capture process works most efficiently when only two applications are open—Windows Media Encoder and the target for the screen capture—so close all other programs.

In the example presented here, I'm creating a short video describing how to add titles in Movie Maker. If you want to view the file, it's posted at www.doceo.com/moviemaker.html.

## To perform a screen capture with WME:

1. Click Start > Programs > Windows Media > Windows Media Encoder.

   The New Session dialog box opens (**Figure C.39**).

2. Click Capture Screen.

3. Click OK.

   The New Session wizard starts, opening to the Screen Capture Session pane (**Figure C.40**).

   *continues on next page*

**4.** Click the target capture area.

**5.** If desired, select Capture Audio from the Default Audio Device.

**6.** Click Next.

**7.** Do *one of the following*:

▲ If you choose Specific Window in Step 4, you'll see the Window Selection pane (**Figure C.41**). Click the Window drop-down list, choose the target window, and click Next. Go to Step 10.

▲ If you choose Region of the Screen in Step 4, you'll see the Screen Region pane (**Figure C.42**). Go to Step 8.

▲ If you choose Entire Screen in Step 4, you'll see the Output File pane (**Figure C.43**). Go to Step 10.

**Figure C.41** If you elected to capture a window, click the Window drop-down list and select the target window.

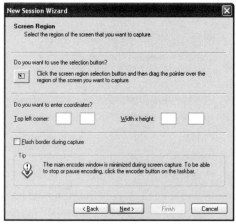

**Figure C.42** Two options for defining the screen region. You can drag the pointer over the screen area to be captured or enter the coordinates directly.

**Figure C.43** Insert your target file name here and browse to a new location if desired.

Region Selection box

**Figure C.44** I'm drawing a region around the relevant area of Movie Maker's Title Maker tool.

**Figure C.45** Once you drag the target area, WME enters the target coordinates, which you can now adjust. Or you can enter the target coordinates directly and skip the dragging.

**8.** To set the region for screen capture (Figure C.42) do *one of the following*:

▲ Click the screen region selection button, click Alt-Tab to move to the target application, and drag from the upper left of the target region to the bottom right (**Figure C.44**). You can repeat this process multiple times until you accurately define the target region.

WME enters the selected coordinates in the boxes in the middle of the screen (**Figure C.45**).

▲ Alternatively, you can enter the target coordinates and width and height directly in the respective boxes in the Screen Region pane (Figure C.45).

**9.** Click Next.

The wizard opens the Output File pane (Figure C.43).

**10.** Type the desired name, and if necessary, click the Browse button to set the location for the encoded file.

*continues on next page*

ABOUT SCREEN CAPTURE WITH WME

**11.** Click Next.

The wizard opens the Settings Selection pane (**Figure C.46**).

**12.** Select the target setting.

I typically use the High setting to maximize quality. In my experience, even at maximum quality, file sizes are very compact.

**13.** Click Next.

The wizard opens the Display Information pane (Figure C.31).

**14.** If desired, complete the information; then click Next.

The wizard opens the Settings Review pane (**Figure C.47**).

**15.** Leave the Begin Capturing Screens When I Click Finish box checked and click Finish.

WME disappears, leaving the target application displayed.

**16.** Start performing the desired mouse and keyboard actions while talking into the microphone. When the screen capture and narration is complete, click Alt-Tab, which brings WME back into the foreground and pauses the screen capture (**Figure C.48**).

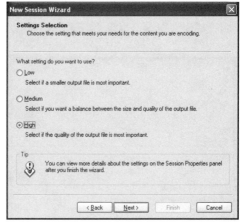

**Figure C.46** Select the encoding quality here. So long as you've limited screen size and motion, High quality should work just fine.

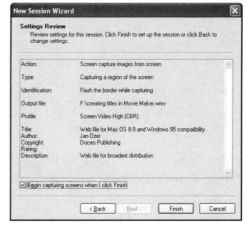

**Figure C.47** Okay, we're all ready to start. Click Finish to make WME disappear and then start clicking and talking.

**Figure C.48** WME records until you press Alt-Tab to bring it back to the foreground. Then you can click Start to add to the captured file or Stop to cease encoding.

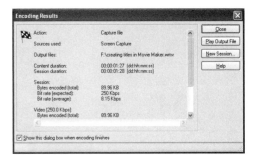

**Figure C.49** Once you stop, you'll see this familiar file, with detailed file information.

**17.** Do *one of the following*:

▲ To continue with your screen capture, click Start Encoding and then repeat Step 16.

▲ To stop the capture and save the screen capture file, click Stop. When you click Stop, WME displays the Encoding Results dialog box (**Figure C.49**).

**18.** Do *one of the following*:

▲ Click Close to close the dialog box and return to WME.

▲ Click Play Output File to play the encoded file.

▲ Click New Session to start another wizard-driven encoding session.

## ✔ Tip

■ When recording either a screen region or a screen window, WME gives you the option of flashing a box around the window or region during recording—select the Flash Border During Capture check box in the Window Selection pane (Figure C.41) or Screen Region pane (Figure C.42). I find this distracting, but if you perform lots of screen captures, you may want to try it.

# Index

INDEX

**INDEX**

INDEX